D0919667

# GAY
# MEN

# GAY MEN

## THE SOCIOLOGY OF MALE HOMOSEXUALITY

EDITED BY

### MARTIN P. LEVINE

Harper & Row, Publishers
New York, Hagerstown,
San Francisco, London

To Richard Buckley
for his encouragement and support

**Library of Congress Cataloging in Publication Data**

Main entry under title:

Gay men : the sociology of male homosexuality.
  Bibliography
  Includes index.
  1. Homosexuals, Male—United States—Addresses, essays, lectures. 2. Subculture—Addresses, essays, lectures. I. Levine, Martin P.
HQ76.2.U5G39     301.41′57     78–69628
ISBN 0–06–012586–1
ISBN 0–06–090695–2 pbk.

    80   81   82   83   10   9   8   7   6   5   4   3   2

FIRST EDITION

*Designed by Janice Stern*

# Contents

ResPur

# Introduction

The material gathered in this volume reflects sociology's current understanding of gay men. Organized around a minority group framework, it depicts their true place in the fabric of American society. To reach as wide an audience as possible, the material was chosen and edited for the nonprofessional community. Each selection describes a different facet of the gay experience. The authors are either nationally recognized experts on male homosexuality or prominent members of the gay community. Lesbians are excluded from this anthology because their experience differs radically from that of gay men, having more in common with the life-style of heterosexual women.[1] When reading the book, the reader should keep in mind how gay men's social situation parallels that of our racial and ethnic minorities.

The picture painted in this volume diverges sharply from the popular image of gay men. To most Americans, gay men are represented by several interrelated stereotypes: the hopeless neurotic, the moral degenerate, the nelly queen, the effete dandy. The first image presents gay men as mentally ill. Strong, domineering mothers and weak, passive fathers supposedly cause hatred for women, resulting in the "pathological" condition. Riddled with anxiety, paranoia, depression, and self-hatred, they are extremely unhappy, often suicidal. If they don't kill themselves, they lash back with vicious tongues. Owing to their neuroses, they are incapable of intimate relationships, leading lonely lives of compulsive promiscuity.

According to the moral degenerate stereotype, gay men are thoroughly and completely debauched. They are sex crazed, and orgasm is their only interest in life. They reputedly solicit indiscriminately, even preying upon young children and adolescent boys. So miserable are their depraved lives that they must seek comfort in alcohol or drugs.

The nelly queen notion depicts gays as men who look and act like women. Supposedly thin and hairless, they walk with swishing gaits, talk with lisping voices, and wear bras and skirts. Naturally, they all work in "feminine" professions—hairdressing, designing, decorating.

As effete dandies, gay men are viewed as exemplars of style and art. Sophisticated and trendy, they inhabit a world of gourmet cuisine, high fashion, and chic night spots. Witty and bright, they dominate artistic, intellectual, and literary salons. Their sensitive and creative souls bring about strong interest in ballet, opera, and theater.

What is most disheartening about these stereotypes is their inaccuracy. Nowhere is there a greater gap between popular thinking and scientific knowledge. Two decades of extensive research have proved them completely invalid. They bear about as much resemblance to gay men as Shylock or Sambo did to Jews or blacks. This book details the inaccuracy of these images.

**OPPRESSION**

The opening section shows how our society systematically frustrates gay men's growth and development. Americans are deeply prejudiced against homosexuality; this homophobia is the wellspring of gay oppression.[2] In the first article, Kinsey Institute researchers Levitt and Klassen record its prevalence as well as that of stereotypical beliefs among the public. One of their noteworthy findings is the profile of our nation's most homophobic segments. Other studies have shown this segment to be most likely to hate Jews and blacks and hold conservative views in regard to women's place and morality.[3]

Religion and psychiatry are homophobia's major underpinnings, actively formulating and propagandizing antigay sentiments. Based on literal interpretations of the Bible, Judeo-Christianity regards procreation as the only purpose of sexual relations.[4] Coitus in marriage thus is the only sanctioned form of sexual expression. All others, including homosexuality, are prohibited as heinous sins, to be punished through excommunication, denial of last rites, and even death. Although liberal elements within the church recently have articulated a more accepting position, such is the prevailing attitude.[5] Viewing gay men as morally corrupt, conservative denominations support much of the ongoing antigay offensive, consistently leading the fight against gay rights.

To psychiatry, homosexuality is not a sin but instead a mental illness which can be cured through therapy. In the second paper, Dr. Robert Gould traces the rise and fall of the mental illness doctrine. As he notes, Freud formulated its theoretical foundation, later expanded and modified by other clinicians. Gould shows how the doctrine fell into disfavor; when subsequent research proved its assumptions invalid in 1973 the American Psychiatric Association stripped homosexuality from psychiatry's official lexicon of mental disorders.

Religion and psychiatry's homophobia has caused gays untold suffering and harm. Our institutions picked up this attitude, incorporating it into many of their programs and practices, leading to wholesale discrimination, persecution, and disesteem. Families tend to disown their homosexual sons.[6] Gays are the target of contempt, jokes, and even violent attacks. The third paper details how the law criminalizes gay sexual behavior, resulting in police harassment. Richard Zoglin reveals how gays are often denied employment or advancement in the workplace. While Zoglin comments on business, the situation he describes is typical of the entire work world.[7] Sometimes the situation is even more dire. Employers have been known to fire gays when their sexual orientation is discovered.[8]

To avoid these harsh sanctions, most gay men tend to pass, hide their sexuality from the nongay world. Passing is no easy matter; it demands the construction of a heterosexual mask. Zoglin presents some of the ploys used in building straight fronts. The psychological costs of passing are high, e.g., the strain of pretending to be what you are not, the constant fear of being discovered.[9] Preferring not to pay the price, some gay men admit their orientation, frequently taking jobs in tolerant fields.[10]

Perhaps homophobia's most noxious effect is on gay self-concept. Accepting societal attitudes, many gay men regard their sexuality with a mixture of repugnance, shame, and guilt. Homosexuality makes them feel inferior and unhealthy. To change their orientation, some gays have entered therapy. Clinicians attempt to "cure" gays by helping them resolve supposed identification problems and fear of heterosexuality, while at the same time accounting for all their problems in life on the basis of homosexuality and pushing them into heterosexual relations.[11] But the psychiatric treatments just do not work; the probability of changing sexual orientation is extremely slight.[12] In the last selection, Michael Riordon recounts his experiences with aversion therapy, a procedure condemned by many clinicians as unethical, barbaric, and ineffectual.[13]

## CULTURE

Confronted with an oppressive reality, gays withdrew from the surrounding society into a subculture. The gay world, however, is not a safe refuge. Homophobia mars its contours, shaping much of what unfolds within it.

## Identity

At the core of the current definition of what constitutes a homosexual is gay identity, the knowledge that one is homosexual. In the past a simplistic position was taken: a man was gay if he responded sexually, either in fantasy or in behavior, to another man.[14] Research has proved this view invalid. Kinsey and his associates discovered that a large segment of the male population had some homosexual experience: Between adolescence and old age, 37 percent had relations with another man to the point of orgasm.[15] In addition, 13 percent had more homosexual than heterosexual experience between the ages of sixteen and fifty-five, and 4 percent were exclusively homosexual. Only 50 percent of their subjects reported that they were exclusively heterosexual, that they were never aroused by or had contact with another man. To show how men were capable of both heterosexual and homosexual response, Kinsey investigators devised the famous Kinsey continuum. Men were placed on it according to the degree to which they exhibited either response: predominantly heterosexual men at the low end of the scale, predominantly homosexual men at the high end.

From these data, Kinsey researchers concluded that homosexual desire or relation is not sufficient grounds for labeling a man homosexual. If it were, then 50 percent of the nation's males would be homosexual! To the Kinsey group, a man is homosexual if he is predominantly or exclusively homosexual in overt sexual activity and/or psychic response.

Subsequent research proved the situation to be more complicated. Limiting homosexuality to genital behavior and erotic response, Kinsey investigators ignored its subjective dimensions.[16] One important dimension disregarded was definition, construing same-sex relations as homosexual. There are numerous situations in which men have sex with each other and do not label the experience homosexual. Martin Hoffman's male prostitutes illustrate this point. These young men do not consider sex with clients homosexual because they assume the "male" position, inserter in fellatio. A second dimension is preference. Gay men prefer to have sexual and emotional relations with men. This is not true of all those who engage in genital homosexuality. Some prefer women as lovers and sex partners, yet have sex with men because it is easier to obtain. Such men comprise many of the participants in public rest room sex.[17]

Gay identity is another key dimension. Many men have relations with men but do not think of themselves as homosexuals. An example of such men are Brian Miller's "trade fathers." Regularly having same-sex contact, they are not gay-identified and regard themselves as heterosexuals. To many sociologists, gay identity is the crucial element because such an identity signifies that homosexuality is central to the way in which the person organizes his life—who his friends are, where he lives, what he does for a living.[18]

Homosexuality, then, is an intricate mesh of behaviors, emotions, and definitions. What is most important in this discussion is that men are homosexual in a number of different ways. All of these dimensions do not have to be present; any one or combination is sufficient to define a male homosexual.

The articles in this section explore in detail the dimension of gay identity. Barry M. Dank records the long and often painful process through which a man develops a homosexual identity, a process that accompanies socialization into the gay world. Homophobia explains many of the difficulties gay men experience in coming out. Internalizing negative societal attitudes, gays regard their own homosexual desires negatively and frequently repress them, suffering emotionally. Dank shows how entry into gay life enables the novice to acquire information that dispels negative feelings, leading to a healthy adjustment and a gay identity.

Humphreys' paper also deals with internalized homophobia. Gay liberation radically altered homophobia's impact on gay identity. Humphreys argues that consciousness raising, gay power, and coming out mitigate its effects by erasing negative feelings and replacing them with pride and feelings of self-worth. To Humphreys, closet culture's passing signifies not only the demise of identity problems but the transformation of gay culture into a rich and diverse cultural unit, one that contributes much to the larger society.[19]

## Scene

Scene details the round of places and activities that characterize gay life. The opening two articles explore the central gathering places, gay bars and baths, and shed light on gay men's sexual behavior. As the authors of both pieces note, gay sexuality differs sharply from the moral degenerate stereotype. Gay men do not find every man attractive, only those who are their "type." Nor do they come on to all who fit the image. Cruising enables gays to restrict their overtures to those who indicate interest in sexual contact. Since the mechanisms of gay cruising are known only to homosexuals, heterosexual men are rarely propositioned; they just do not cruise back.

Generally speaking, gay men are extremely sexually active, as each paper records. They tend to have more casual sexual partners than any other segment of the population.[20] Anonymous sex can be had in a variety of places: baths, back-room bars, public rest rooms, pornographic bookstores and movie theaters, and sections of parks.[21] Most gays avoid such sex, preferring instead to meet men at bars for a one-night stand.[22] Yet these brief encounters turn out to be more than just a quick orgasm. One-night stands are characterized by much sociability and some affection and intimacy, often leading to longer-lasting relations.[23] Numerous gays, however, eschew all impersonal encounters, limiting sexual relations to one partner or practicing celibacy.[24]

What makes gay men so sexually active? Rejecting past psychoanalytic explanations, most experts consider male gender role as the primary cause: men in our society are told it is masculine to have numerous sexual relations as well as sex divorced from emotional commitment; gays are socialized as men during most of their formative years; accordingly, their sexual behavior reflects obedience to masculinity's dictates. While heterosexual men are socialized in the same fashion, they are less sexually active owing to women's sexual socialization. Women are taught to have sex only in the context of an emotional relationship; this obviously restrains the number of sexual encounters heterosexual men have. With gays this restraint is missing, resulting in greater sexual activity.[25]

The male role also explains Sage's depiction of the new "macho" gay man. Nelly queen was never an accurate portrayal of gay men's appearance. Research consistently underscores this point. Kinsey researchers were instructed to guess on the basis of effeminacy whether or not individuals had a homosexual background prior to asking questions about it. They were able to guess only 15 percent of the homosexuals.[26] In another study, the investigators evaluated each man's appearance for signs of femininity, finding that only 16 percent manifested womanly attributes.[27] Sage points out that gays have increasingly masculinized their image in recent years. In contemporary gay culture, masculinity is "hot," an asset in the sexual marketplace. Accordingly, gays are going to great lengths to achieve a manly image: devoting long hours to rigorous body building; donning the garb of male folk heroes (cowboys, truck drivers, lumberjacks); and developing such manful attributes as a firm handshake, deep voice, and butch poise. A few carry it to an extreme, becoming musclebound, leather-clad caricatures of masculinity.[28]

The third paper profiles the new urban phenomenon of the gay ghetto. The advent of such ghettos lays to rest once and for all the assertion that gay culture is so impoverished that it is incapable of sustaining a community.[29] Martin Levine shows that gay ghettos are indeed fully developed communities, housing a plethora of gay residents, churches, and small businesses. In these neighborhoods gay doctors hang their shingles, and politicians, gay or not, openly court the gay vote. Within the ghetto are also found most of the establishments and cruising places of the local gay scene.

The last paper discusses "camp," a sensibility unique to gay men. To Vito Russo, camp is a language and a style as well as a way of coping with homophobia. As a language, camp is the dialect of gay people, a sign of membership.[30] To talk camp means to replace male names with those of females (David becomes Daisy), likewise with male pronouns (he turns into she). As Russo illustrates, camp in many ways is the culture of the gay scene.

## Life-Styles

"Life-Styles" recounts the multiplicity of ways in which men are gay. Most Americans believe that homosexuals constitute a singular breed, depicted by the stereotypes. The truth of the matter is that gay life-styles are a far cry from these images and vary to the same extent as those of heterosexuals.[31]

The opening paper discusses the life-style of gay couples. Contrary to the stereotype, gays are capable of and do indeed form all sorts of loving relationships.[32] As Lloyd and Eric's affair shows, the emotions surrounding such liaisons are identical to those in heterosexual relationships. What is especially intriguing about their affair is that they met in that bastion of impersonal sex, the baths. Lloyd and Eric's affair illustrates how the male role creates problems for gay couples. Most experts agree with Rex Reece's assertion that it is masculinity, not the homosexual's "diseased condition," that is responsible for gay couples' often noted instability.[33]

The next two articles profile the world of men who pass, the covert community. Comprised mainly of older men in respectable occupational or social positions, it includes a number of different life-styles. Carol A. B. Warren describes the life-style of men who are gay-identified and active in homosexual circles but who hide their sexual orientation from the nongay world.[34] For these men, participation in gay life is a leisure-time activity. By recording the role women play in this world, she shatters the notion that gay men hate women.

With the exception of "publicly gay" fathers, Miller's fathers also practice covert life-styles. The life-style of his "gay" fathers is similar to that described by Warren; his "homosexual" fathers differ mainly in the extent to which they participate in the gay world since their married life severely curtails it. "Trade" fathers are completely different, lacking a gay identity and entering gay life only for anonymous sex. "Publicly gay" fathers illustrate the other side of the coin, men who openly acknowledge their homosexuality, the overt community.[35]

The battle cry of the antigay offensive is that homosexuals molest children. In describing gay fathers' parenting, Miller proves it a false accusation. Far from molesting their children, gay men are warm and loving parents. Two other research reports reinforce Miller's point. A massive study done by the staff of the Institute for Sex Research found that gay men are not typical offenders. A child molester is much more likely to be a heterosexual man who has relations with little girls.[36] Another study reported similar findings: for every twelve incidents of child molesting in the United States, eleven are committed by heterosexual men against little girls.[37]

Elderly gays' life-style is depicted in the fourth paper, a life-style completely removed from the stereotype. As Jim Kelly notes, older gays are remarkably well adjusted. Few fit the image of the lonely derelict; most age in the company of a group of friends, a group that functions as a surrogate family. Yet older gays do encounter a special set of problems. Kelly shows how homophobia, not homosexuality, accounts for these problems.

In the fifth selection, John Victor Soares explores the world of black gays. As he points out, racism pervades gay life, forcing blacks into a separate scene. Soares discusses racism's impact on the lives of black gays as well as the round of activities that comprise the black gay scene.

Life in the gay underworld is portrayed in the last paper. Sequestered at the core of most cities, the underworld houses pornographic bookstores and movie theaters as well as bars and street corners frequented by male prostitutes and their clients. Martin Hoffman leads us through the nocturnal world of hustlers and johns.

## Movement

The closing section tells the story of the gay struggle against oppression. At various times and in various places gays have banded together to fight the forces that subjected them. From a radical perspective, the first article recounts the history of this struggle, tracing it across centuries and continents. Barry D. Adam argues that capitalist society created the social conditions that allowed for the development of a gay subculture and movement; this explains the emergence of such movements in late-nineteenth-century Europe. After outlining its progressive phases, Adam ponders the movement's future. Which direction will it take? Assimilationist or revolutionary?

Focusing on the American scene, the second paper explores some of the movement's constituent organizations, noting parallels to black political groups. As Yearwood and Weinberg record, blacks and gays share a similar social position. Both are discriminated against because the larger society disfavors their

distinguishing characteristic (race or sexual orientation), causing them to be economically and socially disadvantaged. In
addition, society regards them as pariahs, making them the butt
of hatred, ridicule, and violence, leading to all sorts of identity
problems. In reaction to this, gays and blacks formed distinct
subcultures as well as social movements devoted to changing
their subordinate status. To Yearwood and Weinberg and numerous other social scientists, these commonalities warrant the
labeling of gays as a minority group.[38]

Of all the movement organizations, college-based gay liberation groups undoubtedly had the greatest impact. During gay
liberation's earliest days, these were often the only centers of
movement activity.[39] Organized by courageous young gays on
campuses across the nation, gay liberation groups faced tremendous obstacles. In the third selection, Martin Rogers discusses
the typical problems these groups confronted.

The last paper profiles a newly emerged faction within the
movement: men's liberation. In reaction to the ever-increasing
masculinization of gay culture, groups have come together to
struggle against this trend. Through consciousness raising and
other means, some gays as well as heterosexual men are working
to free themselves from the male gender role. Jack Nichols
offers an overview of this struggle.

## CONCLUSION

Through a long and tedious process, our understanding of
homosexuality has undergone a radical about-face. Religion has
given way to psychiatry, only to be replaced with the behavioral
sciences. No longer a sin or sickness, homosexuality is a minority's alternative life-style.

For the most part, the American people are unaware of the
new perspective. Public opinion polls repeatedly record the
prevalence of the old image, providing much of the fuel for the
ongoing antigay offensive. Whenever gay rights is an issue, the
opposition chants that homosexuals molest children, homosexuals wear dresses, homosexuals are sinners. In Miami, St. Paul,
Wichita, and Eugene, convinced citizens voted to strip gay men

of basic civil rights, and in Oklahoma a law was passed barring gays from teaching in public schools. Similar measures are being debated in Arkansas and California.

Less than fifty years ago and on another continent, a different minority faced a similar situation. Playing upon the populace's stereotypical beliefs, the Nazis launched their infamous attacks on Jews. At first the assault was confined to civil liberties. Slowly each city and state deprived Jews of the right to vote, the right to own property, the right to education. Jews were then denied economic opportunity: fired from teaching posts, dismissed from the civil service, and removed from the bar. The German people supported these measures at the ballot box, voting for representatives or plebiscites favoring such actions. As the Nazi assault progressed, the measures increased in severity, ending in the monstrous final solution.

While the two situations are different, the similarities are enough to warrant concern. Contemporary attacks on gays bear a striking resemblance to early Nazi assaults on Jews.[40] Will these oppressive actions follow Nazi footsteps? Currently no one in the antigay camp is calling for genocide. But the holocaust symbolizes what can happen to a minority beset by forces of bigotry and ignorance. I hope that this book helps in the struggle against such forces. Within its pages lies gay men's true story— one that should help dispel the stereotypical nonsense surrounding homosexuality.

Martin P. Levine

**NOTES**

1. The social organization of the lesbian community is remarkably different from that of gay men, a difference most experts explain through the female gender role. Lesbians are typically feminine in much of their behavior, e.g., they court each other for long periods of time, sex is approved of only when it occurs within an emotional relationship, the community is organized around couples. This is in complete contrast to gay men's often noted promiscuity and single status. See Janet Saltzman Chafetz, *Masculine/Feminine or Human?: An Overview of the Sociology of Sex Roles* (Itasca, Ill.: F. E. Peacock Publishers, 1974); William Simon and John H. Gagnon, "The Lesbian: A Preliminary Overview," in John H. Gagnon and William Simon, eds., *Sexual Deviance* (New York: Harper & Row, 1967).

2. "Homophobia" is a clumsy word that is used in two different ways. Specifically, it refers to irrational fear or dread of homosexuality. It is also used in a more general way to mean antigay. See Gregory Lehne, "Homophobia Among Men," in Deborah S. David and Robert Brannon, eds., *The Forty-Nine Percent Majority: The Male Sex Role* (Reading, Mass.: Addison-Wesley, 1976); George Weinberg, *Society and the Healthy Homosexual* (Garden City, N.Y.: Anchor Books, 1973).

3. Patrick Irwin and Norman L. Thompson, "Acceptance of the Rights of Homosexuals: A Social Profile," *Journal of Homosexuality* 3 (Winter 1977): 107–21; A. P. MacDonald, Jr., "The Importance of Sex Role to Gay Liberation," *The Homosexual Counseling Journal* 1 (October 1974): 169–80; Kenneth L. Nyberg and Jon P. Alston, "Analysis of Public Attitudes Toward Homosexual Behavior," *Journal of Homosexuality* 2 (Winter 1976–77): 99–107.

4. Religious attitudes are discussed in detail in James B. Nelson, "Homosexuality and the Church," *Christianity and Crisis* 37 (April 4, 1977): 63–69; John J. McNeil, *The Church and the Homosexual* (New York: Pocket Books, 1976); Wainwright Churchill, *Homosexual Behavior Among Males: A Cross-Cultural and Cross-Species Investigation* (Englewood Cliffs, N.J.: Prentice-Hall, 1967).

5. A summary of this position occurs in J. Nelson, op. cit., and J. McNeil, op. cit.

6. Marcel T. Saghir and Eli Robins, *Male and Female Homosexuality: A Comprehensive Investigation* (Baltimore: Williams & Wilkins, 1973), pp. 170–73.

7. For an overview of gays in the workplace, see Jeffrey Escoffier, "Sexual Oppression and Economic Deprivation," *The Homosexual Counseling Journal* 2 (January 1975): 12.

8. Examples of this are found in Saghir and Robins, op. cit., pp. 173–74, and Jonathan Katz, *Gay American History: Lesbians and Gay Men in the U.S.A.* (New York: Thomas Y. Crowell, 1976).

9. For a discussion of passing, see Martin S. Weinberg and Colin J. Williams, *Male Homosexuals: Their Problems and Adaptations* (New York: Oxford University Press, 1974), pp. 177–96.

10. Job tracking refers to gay men's tendency to gravitate toward occupations that accept homosexuality, usually "feminine" jobs. Escoffier, op. cit., pp. 12–13.

11. For an overview of psychiatric treatment procedures, see Jerome P.

Frank, "Treatment of Homosexuals," *National Institute of Mental Health Task Force on Homosexuality: Final Report and Background Papers* (Washington, D.C.: U.S. Government Printing Office, 1972); Edwin Schur, *Crimes Without Victims* (Englewood Cliffs, N.J.: Prentice-Hall, 1965), pp. 104–7; C. A. Tripp, *The Homosexual Matrix* (New York: McGraw-Hill, 1975), pp. 243–67; G. Weinberg, op. cit., pp. 41–68.

12. J. Frank, op. cit.; E. Schur, op. cit.; G. Weinberg, op. cit.

13. Gerald C. Davidson, "Homosexuality, The Ethical Challenge," *Journal of Homosexuality* 2 (Spring 1977): 175–204; Charles Silverstein, "Homosexuality and the Ethics of Behavioral Intervention," *Journal of Homosexuality* 2 (Spring 1977): 205–11.

14. For a more detailed discussion of this psychoanalytical position see Judd Marmor, "Introduction," in Judd Marmor, ed., *Sexual Inversion: The Multiple Roots of Homosexuality* (New York: Basic Books, 1965), pp. 1–26; Walter B. Pomeroy, "Homosexuality," in Ralph W. Weltge (ed.), *The Same Sex: An Appraisal of Homosexuality* (Philadelphia: Pilgrim Press, 1969).

15. Alfred C. Kinsey, W. B. Pomeroy, C. E. Martin, *Sexual Behavior in the Human Male* (Philadelphia: W. B. Saunders, 1948), pp. 610–66.

16. This discussion draws heavily from Erich Goode and Richard Troiden, "Male Homosexuality," in Erich Goode and Richard Troiden, eds., *Sexual Deviance and Sexual Deviants* (New York: William Morrow, 1974), pp. 149–60.

17. Laud Humphreys, *Tearoom Trade: Impersonal Sex in Public Places* (Chicago: Aldine, 1970), pp. 111–17.

18. Goode and Troiden, op. cit., p. 152; Kenneth Plummer, *Sexual Stigma: An Interactionist Account* (London: Routledge and Kegan Paul, 1975), pp. 134–52.

19. The discotheque, camp, and butch fashion are but a fraction of what gays have contributed to American culture. See Maureen Orth, "Get Up and Boogie!," *Newsweek*, vol. 88, November 8, 1965, pp. 94–98; Susan Sontag, *Against Interpretation* (New York: Delta Books, 1964), pp. 275–92; Scott St. Clair, "Fashion's New Game: Follow the Gay Leader," *The Advocate*, 186 (March 26, 1976): 18–19.

20. Saghir and Robins, op. cit., pp. 53–77; Alan P. Bell and Martin S. Weinberg, *Homosexualities: A Study of Diversity Among Men and Women* (New York: Simon & Schuster, 1978), p. 92.

21. For a discussion of impersonal homosexual encounters in public places, see Edward William Delph, *The Silent Community: Public Homosexual Encounters* (Beverly Hills, Calif.: Sage Publications, 1978).

22. Bell and Weinberg, op. cit., pp. 75–78.

23. Ibid., p. 80.

24. Ibid., pp. 129–34.

25. Ibid., pp. 72, 101; Saltzman Chafetz, op. cit., pp. 189–90.

26. Tripp, op. cit., p. 99.

27. Saghir and Robins, op. cit., pp. 106–8.

28. This look is usually associated with the fringes of the gay community, those who practice sadomasochism.

29. William Simon and John H. Gagnon, "Homosexuality: The Formulation of a Sociological Perspective," in R. Weltge, op. cit., p. 22.

30. For a discussion of gay language, see David Sonenschein, "The Homosexual's Language," *The Journal of Sex Research* 5 (November 1969): 281–91.

31. This is discussed in Bell and Weinberg, op. cit., pp. 217–31.

32. A more complete examination of gay dyads is found in Saghir and Robins, op. cit., pp. 56–61, 72–77; Bell and Weinberg, op. cit., pp. 219–23.

33. Dank and Hoffman emphasize homophobia as the cause of instability: internalizing homophobia, gay men feel guilty and ashamed of their sexual desires; feeling this way, they cannot build intimate relationships because they unconsciously devalue their partner for having what they consider depraved sex with them. See Barry M. Dank, "The Homosexual" in Goode and Troiden, op. cit., p. 188; Martin Hoffman, *The Gay World: Male Homosexuality and the Social Creation of Evil* (New York: Bantam Books, 1968), pp. 174–75.

34. For a more detailed analysis of the covert community, see Carol A. B. Warren, *Identity and Community in the Gay World* (New York: Wiley, 1974).

35. Other aspects of the overt community are detailed in Laud Humphreys, *Out of the Closets: The Sociology of Homosexual Liberation* (Englewood Cliffs, N.J.: Prentice-Hall, 1972); Esther Newton, *Mother Camp: Female Impersonators in America* (Englewood Cliffs, N.J.: Prentice-Hall, 1972).

36. M. Hoffman, op. cit., pp. 90–92.

37. Vincent DeFrancis, *Protecting the Child Victim of Sex Offenders* (Denver: The American Humane Association Children's Division, 1976).

38. See Helen Mayer Hacker, "Homosexuals: Deviant or Minority Group?," in Edward Sagarin, ed., *The Other Minorities* (Waltham, Mass.: Ginn and Company, 1971); L. Humphreys, 1972, op. cit.; Franklin E. Kameny, "Homosexuals as a Minority Group," in E. Sagarin, op. cit.; Saghir and Robins, op. cit.; Weinberg and Williams, op. cit.

39. Sal J. Licata, "The Emerging Gay Presence: Part III 1969 and After the Stonewall Generation," *The Advocate* 247 (August 9, 1978): 17.

40. This point is developed in Barry M. Dank, "Social Construction and Destruction of the Homosexual" (Paper presented at the Twenty-eighth Annual Meeting of the Society for the Study of Social Problems, San Francisco, September 1–4, 1978).

# PART I

# Oppression

# Public Attitudes Toward Homosexuality

Part of the 1970 National Survey
by the Institute for Sex Research

EUGENE E. LEVITT AND
ALBERT D. KLASSEN, JR.

This paper is a partial report of the findings of a four-year investigation supported by the National Institute of Mental Health. One purpose has been to assess the prevalence and interrelatedness of attitudes and perceptions concerned with homosexuality, and to determine their relationship to demographic and behavioral characteristics of the American public.

The findings are based on interviews with a nationwide probability sample of 3,018 American adults during 1970. This sample represented with reasonable accuracy the noninstitutionalized adult population of the United States according to the full range of variables usually considered to be fundamental in describing a population.

We obtained more than six hundred bits of information from each of our respondents in a two-hour interview. We present here a portion of our findings depicting the public's perceptions of, and attitudes toward, homosexuality.

## SEXUAL BEHAVIOR

Attitudes in the sexual sphere were assessed in a number of ways. A major series of questions sought to tap moral attitudes toward various sexual behaviors, including homosexual acts,

*Journal of Homosexuality* 1 (1974): 29–43. Reprinted by permission of the Haworth Press and the authors.

under various circumstances. The responses are summarized in Table 1.

It is apparent that sex between same-sexed persons, regardless of their relationship, is regarded as wrong by a considerably greater number of the respondents than premarital heterosexual intercourse, a not at all surprising finding. An interesting discovery is in the contrast of attitudes toward sex under affectional as compared with nonaffectional circumstances. The data leave little doubt that Americans still cherish the concept of love as a basis for sexual behavior. The average difference between approval of acts with and without affection was just under 15 percent. It was more than 15 percent in every instance *except homosexuality,* for which it was only 7.5 percent. One might infer that the public has difficulty in recognizing that love can exist between persons of the same sex.

More is learned about moral attitudes regarding homosexual sex by comparing them with opinions concerning extramarital sexual intercourse. The moral repugnance toward extramarital sex is so high in the adult population, with 72 percent saying it is always wrong, that it ranks almost as high as society's repugnance for the homosexual act without affection. In fact, combining the "always" and "almost always wrong" responses, it ranks higher in prevalence of repugnance than sex with a person of the same sex regardless of whether affection is involved. (In two pretests, extramarital sexual behavior was differentiated as to gender and affection, but these distinctions yielded only insignificant differences in moral judgments.) This seems to suggest that the moral indignation engendered when institutional vows and responsibilities embodied in marriage are betrayed or threatened—jeopardizing such societal values as fidelity and family cohesion stability—corresponds in strength to the indignation toward sexual activity considered by many to be "unnatural" and "perverted."*

---

* To fill out this perspective on sexual morality judgments, it is necessary to consider data on masturbation at the least repugnant extreme and child-adult sexual involvement at the most repugnant extreme. Pretest data revealed about 92 percent expressing strong negative evaluations representing the incest taboo and offensiveness of child molesting (always wrong). Masturbation, now considered totally harmless by virtually all professionals, was still considered always wrong by 26 percent of our sample of 3,018.

## TABLE 1

### Moral Attitudes (Presented in Percentages)

| | What is your opinion of sex acts between two persons of the same sex when they: | | What is your opinion if a married person has sexual intercourse with someone other than the marriage partner? | If a teenager (boy/girl) 16–19 has sexual intercourse with a (girl/boy) without love? | If an unmarried adult (man/woman) has sexual intercourse with a (woman/man) when they love each other? |
|---|---|---|---|---|---|
| | have no special affection for each other? | love each other? | | | |
| Always wrong | 77.7 | 70.2 | 72.2 | 51.7 | 31.5 |
| Almost always wrong | 8.4 | 8.4 | 14.3 | 19.4 | 14.0 |
| Wrong only sometimes | 6.3 | 7.2 | 10.7 | 19.6 | 22.2 |
| Not wrong at all | 5.6 | 11.4 | 2.1 | 5.0 | 28.7 |
| Don't know | 1.6 | 2.2 | 0.4 | 4.0 | 3.5 |
| No answer | 0.1 | 0.3 | 0.1 | 0.1 | — |
| Total percent | 99.7 | 99.7 | 99.8 | 99.8 | 99.9 |
| Total sample | 3018 | 3018 | 3018 | 3018 | 3018 |

## FEELINGS OF DISTRUST AND REPUGNANCE

The public's bias against homosexuals extends beyond mere moral disapproval. The data of Table 2 indicate the extent to which the public would bar the homosexual from employment in certain significant professions and occupations. Substantial majorities agree that homosexual men should be allowed to work in the arts and in artistic occupations, but almost equally large majorities believe that they should not be permitted to engage in professions of influence and authority. Three-quarters would deny to a homosexual the right to be a minister, a schoolteacher, or a judge, and two-thirds would bar the homosexual from medical practice and government service. An evident conclusion is that the public distrusts the homosexual in positions of public responsibility, particularly when this explicitly involves moral leadership.

Twenty-seven items sought to explore dimensions of opinion and perception surrounding this distrust of homosexuals. Perhaps the most obvious and fundamental considerations are those involving fear and offensiveness. Table 3 presents those items tapping such feelings of threat.

Nearly three-quarters of the adult population believe that there is at least some truth to two different notions about homosexuals seeking to become involved with children. In fact, about 45 percent *strongly* agree that for this reason it is dangerous to have homosexuals as teachers or youth leaders, while 35 percent agree strongly with the proposition that frustrated homosexuals seek out children for sexual purposes.

Nearly 60 percent believe that more than half of all homosexuals are high security risks in government jobs. (Most of these, or 43 percent of the sample, hold this to be true of all or nearly all homosexuals. Whether they suppose homosexual activity is a more serious basis of risk than heterosexual activity cannot be answered with these data.) Almost two out of five feel that more than half of the homosexual population tend to corrupt their co-workers (about 23 percent believe that nearly all do). More than one out of six still suppose it to be true of more than half of the

## TABLE 2

### Occupational Attitudes (Presented in Percentages)

Homosexual men should or should not be allowed to work in the following professions:

| | Court judge (7)* | Schoolteacher (8) | Minister (9) | Medical doctor (3) | Government official (5) | Beautician (2) | Artist (1) | Musician (6) | Florist (4) |
|---|---|---|---|---|---|---|---|---|---|
| Allowed | 22.8 | 23.1 | 23.4 | 32.3 | 32.6 | 71.7 | 84.5 | 85.2 | 86.8 |
| Not allowed | 77.2 | 76.9 | 76.6 | 67.7 | 67.4 | 28.3 | 15.5 | 14.8 | 13.2 |
| Total responding | 2957 | 2974 | 2970 | 2961 | 2954 | 2969 | 2960 | 2974 | 2972 |
| No answer | 61 | 44 | 48 | 57 | 64 | 49 | 58 | 44 | 46 |
| Total sample | 3018 | 3018 | 3018 | 3018 | 3018 | 3018 | 3018 | 3018 | 3018 |

*Parenthetic numbers in each column heading indicate the order in which inquiry was made in the interview.

## TABLE 3

Opinions of Homosexuals as Dangerous, Homosexuality as Threatening, Offensive (Presented in Percentages)

| | Homosexuals are dangerous as teachers or youth leaders because they try to get sexually involved with children | Homosexuals try to play sexually with children if they cannot get an adult partner | Homosexuals are a high security risk for government jobs* | Homosexuals tend to corrupt their fellow workers sexually* | If homosexual men can't find men for partners, they try to force their attentions on women* | Homosexuality is a social corruption that can cause the downfall of a civilization | Homosexuality in itself is no problem, but what people make of it can be a serious problem | To what extent do you think homosexuality is obscene and vulgar?† |
|---|---|---|---|---|---|---|---|---|
| Strongly agree | 44.7 | 35.1 | 43.1 | 22.8 | 6.9 | 25.0 | 27.3 | 65.2 |
| Somewhat agree | 28.8 | 36.0 | 15.8 | 15.6 | 10.9 | 23.8 | 27.8 | 18.6 |
| Somewhat disagree | 11.9 | 9.9 | 12.0 | 19.0 | 22.2 | 18.8 | 16.9 | 7.4 |
| Strongly disagree | 9.5 | 8.5 | 20.8 | 35.0 | 45.4 | 24.6 | 23.0 | 7.5 |
| Don't know | 3.9 | 9.8 | 7.2 | 7.0 | 13.7 | 7.2 | 3.8 | — |
| No answer | 0.8 | 0.6 | 0.8 | 0.6 | 0.5 | 0.7 | 0.8 | 1.0 |
| Total percent | 99.6 | 99.9 | 99.7 | 100.0 | 99.7 | 100.1 | 99.6 | 99.7 |
| Total sample | 3018 | 3018 | 3018 | 3018 | 3018 | 3018 | 3018 | 3018 |

*These three items provided responses concerning how many homosexuals are like this: "All or almost all?" "More than half?" "Less than half?" "Hardly any or none?" "Don't know," and a "No answer" category.
†This item provided five response categories: "Very much?" "Somewhat?" "Very little?" "Not at all?" and "No answer."

homosexual population that they will victimize women when they fail to find male partners; there are even 7 percent who believe this to be true of nearly all homosexuals.

When translated into implications for society at large, nearly 50 percent agree (half of these strongly) that homosexuality, as a corruption of society, can cause a civilization's downfall. On the other hand, there are 55 percent at least somewhat in agreement (and half of these strongly) that homosexuality is no problem in and of itself, though serious problems can be made of it. Finally, nearly two-thirds of our adult population find homosexuality "very much" obscene and vulgar to them.

Given these indications of perceived danger and offensiveness, it should not be surprising that a majority of the adult population tend to see homosexuals as different "from the rest of us." (See Table 4.) Nearly 70 percent agree that they "act like the opposite sex" (22 percent concur strongly), and nearly 60 percent agree (22 percent strongly) that homosexuals have unusually strong sex drives. Fifty-six percent espouse the notion (16 percent feel strongly) that homosexuals fear the opposite sex. There are still almost three out of eight who believe, and one of every eight who feels strongly, that they can recognize a homosexual by how he looks. Finally, though a number of theoretical and clinical perspectives more or less support the notion that "there is an element of homosexuality in everyone," only 30 percent accept that at all, and less than 10 percent are sure of it, in the adult population at large.

## RIGHTS OF HOMOSEXUALS

This prevalence of fears, and the tendency of the general population to set the homosexual apart as "something else," something different, raise questions about what rights this society is prepared to grant homosexuals. The data in Table 5 give additional evidence of their offensiveness, in the public's overwhelming objection to homosexuals' dancing with each other in public places—55 percent strongly object, and nearly three-quarters have at least some objection. Nearly one-half (46 percent) do not agree that homosexuals should be allowed to

## TABLE 4
Opinions Setting Homosexuals Apart from Heterosexuals (Presented in Percentages)

| | Homosexuals act like the opposite sex | Homosexuals have unusually strong sex drives | Homosexuals are afraid of the opposite sex | It is easy to tell homosexuals by how they look | There is an element of homosexuality in everyone |
|---|---|---|---|---|---|
| Strongly agree | 22.1 | 22.4 | 15.9 | 11.8 | 9.5 |
| Somewhat agree | 46.7 | 36.1 | 39.8 | 25.0 | 29.9 |
| Somewhat disagree | 15.7 | 14.7 | 22.2 | 24.7 | 16.2 |
| Strongly disagree | 6.7 | 6.5 | 10.9 | 30.0 | 34.0 |
| Don't know | 7.6 | 19.4 | 10.7 | 7.8 | 9.7 |
| No answer | 0.9 | 0.6 | 0.5 | 0.7 | 0.7 |
| Total percent | 99.7 | 99.7 | 100.0 | 100.0 | 100.0 |
| Total sample | 3018 | 3018 | 3018 | 3018 | 3018 |

## TABLE 5
### Opinions on Rights of Homosexuals (Presented in Percentages)

| | Homosexuals should be allowed to dance with each other in public places | Homosexuals should be allowed to organize groups for social and recreational purposes | Bars serving homosexuals should be permitted | Homosexuals should be allowed to organize groups to deal with their social problems | Homosexuals should *not* be allowed to be members of churches or synagogues | What consenting adult homosexuals do in private is no one else's business |
|---|---|---|---|---|---|---|
| Strongly agree | 7.3 | 17.5 | 19.4 | 41.0 | 8.9 | 38.1 |
| Somewhat agree | 15.1 | 29.3 | 31.0 | 33.2 | 7.9 | 29.9 |
| Somewhat disagree | 18.0 | 15.7 | 15.8 | 8.3 | 20.2 | 14.0 |
| Strongly disagree | 54.9 | 30.6 | 27.3 | 12.2 | 58.2 | 14.1 |
| Don't know | 3.7 | 5.8 | 5.8 | 4.1 | 3.6 | 3.4 |
| No answer | 0.7 | 0.8 | 0.5 | 0.8 | 0.9 | 0.5 |
| Total percent | 99.7 | 99.7 | 99.8 | 99.6 | 99.7 | 100.0 |
| Total sample | 3018 | 3018 | 3018 | 3018 | 3018 | 3018 |

organize for social and recreational purposes (31 percent object strongly), and 43 percent would not permit bars serving homosexuals (27 percent feel this strongly).

There is a substantial majority, however, 74 perçent, that will grant homosexuals the right to organize to deal with their social problems (presumably short of flagrant public activism, though our question did not tap this), and nearly 80 percent disagree with the notion of excluding homosexuals from membership in churches and synagogues. Two assumptions may be implied here: Homosexuals will not flaunt their offensive sexual preferences there, and they might be exposed to the more acceptable moral influences ascribed to the religious segment of the population.

Finally, privacy remains sacred for many, even if in the interests of the homosexual: Nearly 70 percent at least cautiously assert, and 38 percent feel strongly, that "what consenting adult homosexuals do in private is no one else's business."

## CAUSES AND CURES OF HOMOSEXUALITY

One might expect that if a perspective of moral repugnance toward homosexual individuals is prevalent in our society—and indeed, as we have seen earlier, approximately three-quarters of the adult population consider homosexual activity to be immoral always in any case—then that would be predictive of a voluntaristic view concerning the origins of "causes" and the "cures" of homosexuality. But this is not the case (Table 6).

About 62 percent say that for at least half the homosexual population it is a sickness that can be cured; nearly 40 percent believe this true of the entire homosexual population. This, of course, represents population lag behind the profession of psychiatry—the American Psychiatric Association in December 1973 found homosexuality per se no longer to be classifiable as a pathology. Only 40 percent believe that more than half of all homosexuals could "stop being homosexuals if they want to," and hardly more than half of those (23 percent) feel this is true of all homosexuals. About one-quarter of the population think at least half of the homosexual males could be turned into hetero-

## TABLE 6

Homosexuality: Opinions Concerning Causation and Cure (Presented in Percentages)

| FOR HOW MANY HOMOSEXUALS IS EACH STATEMENT TRUE? | "Cures" | | | | "Causes" | | | |
|---|---|---|---|---|---|---|---|---|
| | Homosexuality is a sickness that can be cured | Homosexuals can stop being homosexuals if they want to | Homosexual men can be turned into heterosexuals by women who have enough sexual skills | Homosexual women can be turned into heterosexuals by men who have enough sexual skills | Young homosexuals become that way because of older homosexuals | Homosexuals are born that way | People become homosexuals because they are not attractive to the opposite sex | People become homosexuals because of how their parents raised them |
| All or almost all | 37.9 | 23.0 | 8.8 | 13.7 | 18.7 | 16.7 | 11.5 | 13.6 |
| More than half | 24.0 | 17.4 | 16.4 | 20.4 | 23.8 | 13.6 | 17.8 | 24.9 |
| Less than half | 16.5 | 20.8 | 26.1 | 22.4 | 21.6 | 18.0 | 22.8 | 24.1 |
| Hardly any or none | 12.9 | 29.2 | 31.2 | 26.2 | 26.4 | 43.9 | 39.6 | 31.2 |
| Don't know | 7.8 | 8.6 | 16.5 | 16.3 | 8.7 | 7.4 | 7.2 | 5.4 |
| No answer | 0.9 | 0.7 | 0.9 | 0.7 | 0.5 | 0.5 | 0.6 | 0.8 |
| Total percent | 100.0 | 99.7 | 99.9 | 99.7 | 99.7 | 100.1 | 99.5 | 100.0 |
| Total sample | 3018 | 3018 | 3018 | 3018 | 3018 | 3018 | 3018 | 3018 |

sexuals by sexually skilled women, but about one-third believe at least half of the homosexual females could be swung over to heterosexuals by sexually skilled men, an interesting and perhaps telltale difference reflecting beliefs about which sex is most influential in sexual matters.

Of the opinions probed concerning origins—or "causes"—of homosexuality, only two propositions would seem open to construing a voluntarism theory of cause, yet even these contain strains of causal determinism. Of the four causal notions probed, the most popular proposition is that "young homosexuals become that way because of older homosexuals." (Noted earlier were the widespread fears that homosexuals will molest children.) About 42 percent of the general population believe this to be the origin of more than half of the homosexual population, and 19 percent believe it to apply to all homosexuals.

A second potentially voluntaristic notion sees homosexuality as the result of failure to attract the opposite sex (a sort of "homosexual is better than nothing" choice implied here). But less than 30 percent see this as true for more than half the homosexual population; less than one out of eight would apply it to all homosexuals.

Granted, there are other propositions of voluntaristic cause that could have been posed and were not, but now consider the substantial support for two quite deterministic—and apparently mutually exclusive—causal propositions. Thirty percent say at least half of all homosexuals are simply "born that way" (one of every six says this explains all homosexuality). But then nearly 40 percent suppose that more than half of the homosexuals are products of "how their parents raised them," with more than one-eighth claiming this explanation for all homosexuality. True, it may seem surprising that so few espouse a view of parental upbringing as the causal nexus, when it surely represents an array of most popular theories among professionals. But, aside from possibilities of incongruous and illogical contradictory responses on the part of many members of our sample, our data would suggest that there remains a widespread possibility that the United States adult population will not ultimately choose to hold individuals morally responsible for having homosexual preferences. They may yet recognize that preference does not necessarily imply choice, a proposition that currently concerns many persons who find themselves to have homosexual preferences.*

## LEGAL CONTROLS OF SEXUAL BEHAVIOR

Another approach to attitude measurement was to assess the respondents' willingness to support legal sanctions against various forms of sexual behavior. We found that 59 percent of our respondents believe that there should be a law against sex acts between persons of the same sex, more than twice as many as espouse a law against heterosexual intercourse between unmarried adults, though not so different from the 52 percent desiring legal sanction against extramarital sex.

The severity of the penalty advocated by those opting for legal controls seems to be unrelated to the proportion desiring such control. Thus, more than 8 percent (14 percent of those desiring a law) believe that a person convicted of a homosexual act should be sentenced to at least a year in prison, and 6 percent (nearly 12 percent of those who want a law) chose this penalty for adultery. But only 4 percent (about 6.5 percent of those seeking a law) would be so punitive with a prostitute or her client in a first conviction, though the call for a law against prostitution evoked even more "ayes" (63 percent) than homosexuality.

## HOMOSEXPHOBIA

Finally, we administered to our sample five items that were selected to provide data that we would scale in Thurstone fashion to yield a single attitude score for each respondent. The basic findings for this set of items are shown in Table 7 in the

---

* Admittedly, this treatment of 27 items of data may raise as many questions as it answers, perhaps most basically in the matter of to what extent many of the attitudes and perceptions are interrelated, thus constituting potentially complex stereotypic-cognitive-perceptual structures. This will be explored and reported after subsequent analyses of the data.

## TABLE 7

Thurstone Scale Items for Homosexphobia Scale (Presented in Percentages)

| | I won't associate with these people if I can help it (1.0)* | I think some of our best citizens come from this group (9.2) | I suppose they are all right, but I've never liked them (3.6) | I think they should be regarded as any other group (6.8) | I have no particular love or hate for this group (5.4) |
|---|---|---|---|---|---|
| Very true | 58.9 | 11.4 | 33.1 | 20.7 | 40.5 |
| Somewhat true | 22.0 | 24.8 | 31.2 | 25.5 | 35.6 |
| Somewhat untrue | 9.3 | 24.9 | 17.0 | 22.4 | 12.1 |
| Very untrue | 9.0 | 34.7 | 15.2 | 29.9 | 10.3 |
| Don't know | — | — | — | — | — |
| No answer | 0.7 | 4.3 | 3.1 | 1.5 | 1.6 |
| Total percent | 99.9 | 100.1 | 99.9 | 100.0 | 100.1 |
| Total sample | 3018 | 3018 | 3018 | 3018 | 3018 |

*Homosexphobia Scale values in parentheses.

order in which they were asked. The distribution of the national sample used in the present study is given for this scale in Table 8.

We call the dimension measured by this scale *homosexphobia*. Individuals in our sample who were high on homosexphobia (i.e., had low scale scores) tended to be rural, white persons who were raised in the rural Midwest or South. Such persons were more likely to claim a current religion, with a slight tendency to be a fundamentalist Protestant. The homosexphobic tended also to deny the possibility of ever enjoying homosexual behavior, and to deny ever having feared becoming a homosexual. The homosexphobic is less likely to have had any childhood sexual experience, especially homosexual experience, and had more guilt about the latter when it did occur. Finally, the homosexphobic tended to be relatively more conservative and less lenient about accepting sex and sexual behavior in general.

Such variables as age, sex, educational level, marital status, occupation, and reported general enjoyment of sex were unrelated to homosexphobia scores.

Some of the data in Table 7 merit individual consideration, beyond their role in the homosexphobia scale. *Three of every four* respondents express "no particular love or hate" for homosexuals, a praiseworthy neutrality. Yet, *less than half* believe that homosexuals "should be regarded as any other group," and *more than 80 percent* prefer not to associate with them. The operation of denial is evident in these conflicting feelings.

A substantial majority (81 percent) of our respondents view their attitudes toward homosexuality as consistent over time. A much smaller number (16 percent) report that they were less approving at one time, but very few admit that they have ever been *more* approving.

Twenty-seven percent of our respondents had at one time or another been subjected to a sex education course, approximately equally divided between regular courses and some sort of ad hoc teaching. This might have been an opportunity to learn something about homosexuality, but was it?

More than 60 percent of those who had sex education reported that they had been taught nothing at all about homosexuality.

## TABLE 8

### Distribution of Sample on Homosexphobia Scale*

| Scale Midpoints | 1 (Most Prejudiced) | 2 | 3 | 4 | 5 | 6 | 7 | 8 | 9 (Most Accepting) | Total Percent | Percent Base | No Answer | Total Sample |
|---|---|---|---|---|---|---|---|---|---|---|---|---|---|
| Percent | 4.9 | 10.9 | 28.8 | 16.9 | 20.6 | 16.2 | 0.8 | 0.8 | 0.2 | 100.1 | 2982 | 36 | 3018 |

*Technical details on the development and application of this scale may be requested of the authors.

Among those who had been taught something about homosexuality, two-thirds were told that it was always wrong, and only 1.5 percent were advised that it was not wrong at all. Evidently, sex education, at least as it has been structured in the past, was hardly likely to have presented a veridical picture of homosexuality.

A postscript to the public's illiberal position on homosexuality is found in reactions to the laws in Illinois and Connecticut which do *not* forbid sex acts between persons of the same sex, if they are consenting adults, and if the acts are done in complete privacy. Sixty percent of our respondents disapproved of such a law, in spite of the fact noted earlier that 68 percent agree—at least cautiously if not strongly—that "what consenting adult homosexuals do in private is no one else's business."

# What We Don't Know About Homosexuality

## ROBERT E. GOULD

As psychiatrists or as laymen, we are still afraid of what we don't know—even about our own sexuality. We need only think of the revelations of Kinsey and Masters and Johnson to realize how few important studies of sexual behavior have ever been undertaken. And on the subject of homosexuality, despite its presence in virtually all cultures past and present, our lack of knowledge is extraordinary. Little wonder, then, that over the years we have taken for granted a number of sexual "facts" that now turn out to be the basis for heated controversy.

Take, for example, the "fact" that homosexuality is a form of mental illness. Until December 15, 1973, psychiatry never wavered from the judgment that homosexual* behavior resulted from a pathological sidetrack in the psychosexual development of a normal human being. But that day the American Psychiatric Association's thirteen-member board of trustees voted unanimously to remove homosexuality from the category of mental illness. The significance of this act will reverberate in the homosexual and psychiatric worlds—and in the heterosexual world as well—for years to come. The new official definition uses the term "sexual orientation disturbance" for "individuals who are either disturbed by, in conflict with, or wish to change, their sexual orientation." The trustees hastened to add that "the diagnostic category is distinguished from homosexuality, which by itself does not necessarily constitute a psychiatric disorder."

*The New York Times,* February 24, 1974. © 1974 by The New York Times Company. Reprinted by permission of the publisher.

* There are several ways to define "homosexual," but the safest is still the simplest: A homosexual is any individual whose sexual object choice is someone of the same sex.

Like many historic statements, the A.P.A.'s ringing pronouncement turned out to need further clarification. Robert L. Spitzer, a Columbia University psychiatrist and spokesman for the nomenclature committee responsible for the text of the resolution, when questioned about the term "sexual orientation disturbance," hedged: "We're not saying that homosexuality is either 'normal' or 'abnormal' . . . but that homosexuality per se is not a psychiatric disorder."

Within the profession there are already rumblings of discontent. A number of critics are charging that psychiatry bowed to the political pressures of the gay liberation movement, and too quickly abandoned a valid concept of psychiatric disorder, for the sake of being "with it." Opponents of the change have easily obtained the required two hundred signatures on a petition to force a referendum on the board of trustees' decision.

But to the gay activists who lobbied for the decision, psychiatry is a prime source of persecution. Ronald Gold, publicity director of the National Gay Task Force, recently summarized the homosexuals' view. "The diagnosis of homosexuality as a 'disorder,' " he charged, "is a contributing factor to the pathology of those homosexuals who do become mentally ill. . . . Nothing is more likely to make you sick than being constantly told that you are sick. . . . We believe that this socially imposed self-image, currently certified by the psychiatric profession, is reinforced by efforts to 'cure' our sexual orientation."

Another leading spokesman for the gay movement is Charles Silverstein, a homosexual psychologist and director of the Institute for Human Identity in New York City. This group treats homosexuals with emotional problems. Dr. Silverstein maintains that "environmental stresses" on gay people, stemming from religious, legal, and psychiatric sources, add up to oppression. As for psychiatry, he says: "Unfortunately, we continue to believe the myth that therapy is politically neutral. It is not. Any method of behavior change has political implications. This is just as true of techniques of behavior modification as the political uses of psychiatric commitments, and the politics of medieval inquisitors." Dr. Silverstein charges that when treatment is directed only toward the victim of environmental stress (the homosexual), and not toward the cause of the stress (social institutions), the net effect of the treatment is political—"to strengthen the status quo."

So the issue is drawn, and the questions it implies are real. What role has politics—past and present—played in psychiatry? Was the previous basis for the mental illness theory purely scientific—or did the politics of oppression influence scientific theory, as the homosexuals now charge?

Modern theory of the nature of homosexuality started with Sigmund Freud, whose own lack of clarity on the topic served as a model for the psychiatric profession for more than half a century. Despite his voluminous writings and many references to sex, Freud never presented a full theory on the nature of homosexuality. He said different things at different times without bothering to tidy up either the loose ends or the contradictory implications.

Freud's libido theory was founded on his belief that a child's instinctual sex drive had to be tamed and channeled successfully through the Oedipal phase in order to achieve healthy, mature sexuality. The Oedipal phase, which occurs between ages six and eight, involves the boy's desire for his mother as his first love object, and the need to compete with his father in an intense sexual rivalry for his mother's love. This phase, in Freud's view, ends when the boy conquers his lust for his mother, fearing that if he doesn't, his father will punish him (by castration). The Oedipal conflict is successfully resolved when the boy identifies with his father and decides to find a woman like his mother when he grows up. Freud theorized that failure to resolve the Oedipal conflict could take many forms, which then would become the basis for a wide variety of personality disorders, including homosexuality.

In explaining the influence of childhood experiences, Freud spoke of an "inverted Oedipal complex," which prevents the small boy from following the usual Oedipal progression. In such cases, the boy hates his mother for preferring his father to himself and finally rejects her in favor of his father, who thus becomes the boy's first homosexual love object. Freud believed that all humans were constitutionally bisexual, and that if a boy had a strong female component (a more "feminine" and "passive" nature), he might fail to work his way through the Oedipal conflict, and thus might become homosexual.

Narcissism, in Freud's view, may also play an important role in homosexual development. By using the mechanism of "projection," a boy may seek, in relations with other boys, an idealized image of himself. He then loves other boys as he would have wanted his mother or father to love him. Freud felt this could happen especially if the boy started with an intense attachment to his mother, and if his father was an absent or detached figure. In general, a fear of women due to unconscious castration anxiety, or fear of punishment by other males for desiring a woman sexually, all stem from a poor resolution of the Oedipal phase of development. . . .

Since Freud viewed homosexuality as essentially caused by constitutional factors, and also as a perversion, he saw little hope for "curing" the condition through therapy. He believed that perversion was the antithesis of neurosis. The distinction is important because a perversion meant that the person "acted out" his sexual drives and therefore was untreatable. Freudian psychoanalysis was designed to treat the neuroses, in which sexual drives were inhibited or repressed. Most analysts today view homosexuality in terms of a neurosis or character disorder; they therefore consider it treatable.

This briefly summarized version of a brilliant theorist's complicated vision was dutifully absorbed in the thinking and practice of many of his disciples, but Freud's largely unproved and undocumented assumptions made it inevitable that later psychiatrists would add to, subtract from, and modify the great man's ideas.

Among the leading modern authorities on homosexuality, the following subscribe to the "mental illness" theory, based, more or less, on Freud:

• The late Edmund Bergler, a noted Vienna-born psychiatrist who declared that all homosexuality represented serious pathology. Bergler claimed that he found the following traits in all homosexuals: depression and guilt feelings, extreme jealousy and an irrational belief that homosexual drives are universal. Bergler viewed homosexuality as a regression to the earliest level of psychic development—the oral stage. As Bergler saw it, the male homosexual chooses the penis as a substitute for his mother's breast. Bergler also stated flatly: "There are no happy homosexuals."

• Irving Bieber, of New York City, who conducted the best-known United States study of homosexuals in 1962. Bieber and nine associates connected with New York Medical College compiled data on 106 homosexual patients (compared to a control group of 100 nonhomosexual patients) and found several distinct patterns in the family backgrounds of the homosexual group. The most common pattern, they reported, involved an overprotective, close-binding mother and a detached, absent, or brutal father. Bieber concluded, on the basis of his studies, that if there is a warm, affectionate, good relationship between father and son, homosexuality cannot occur.

• Charles Socarides, another New York City psychiatrist who has treated many male homosexuals in private practice, claims that fear of "engulfment" by the dominant mother is the key factor preventing the boy from becoming independent and progressing to heterosexuality. Socarides believes that the boy's failure to separate from his mother, which points him toward homosexuality, occurs in the pre-Oedipal phase (between ages two and five).

Both Socarides and Bieber have spent years in clinical research on homosexuality and are well known among psychiatrists—and also among homosexuals—for their theories. They have both told me, and have stated publicly, that homosexuals consider them public enemies Nos. 1 and 2 (their respective positions change from year to year), because of their firmly held beliefs that homosexuals are severely stunted in their psychosexual development, and that, if possible, they should undergo therapy to "cure" their condition.

• Lawrence Hatterer of Cornell University agrees with Bieber and Socarides that homosexuality is a "curable" disorder. But in his studies of hundreds of male homosexual patients, Hatterer found many other causes of male homosexuality besides family influences. Diverging also from Freud and many of Freud's followers, Hatterer postulates a "hypersexualized consciousness," apart from Oedipal and castration complexes, through which the homosexual views every aspect of his life in sexual terms. Hatterer speaks of "trigger" mechanisms that cause homoerotic responses. These "triggers" include environmental stimuli such as homosexual friends or milieus, imagery of past homosexual contacts or dreams during or preceding masturbation. Hatterer also believes that the homosexual, through his sexual contacts, is searching for the maleness that he feels he lacks. By possessing the "idealized male" erotically, in Hatterer's view, the homosexual identifies with or incorporates this virile ideal into his own self-image.

• Lionel Ovesey of the Columbia psychoanalytic school sees homosexuality as an "adaptation" to a sexual inhibition or fear of normal heterosexual functioning. To such an inhibited person, the "choice" of homosexuality seems safer and allows him to cope with his anxiety.

In broadening the concept of homosexuality, Ovesey coined the term "pseudohomosexual" to describe individuals in whom the predominating dynamics of homosexual behavior were not inherently sexual, but had to do with power and dependency.

• Clara Thompson, who was director of the William A. White Institute of Psychiatry in New York City until her death in 1958, also viewed homosexuality as a symptom of various underlying nonsexual problems such as fear of adult responsibility, a need to defy authority, an attempt to cope with hatred for or extreme competitiveness with members of one's own sex, or a child's awareness that his (or her) parents would have preferred a child of the opposite sex.

Aligned against these influential "illness" theorists is a relatively new group of researchers who believe that homosexuality can be a normal variant in the total spectrum of sexual behavior. Leading members of this group include:

• Judd Marmor, a Los Angeles psychiatrist and former vice-president of the A.P.A., who has long been an advocate of the move to reconsider homosexuality and to stop calling it a disorder. Marmor discounts the disturbed-family theory on the ground that many nonhomosexuals had similar childhoods, yet grew up "straight" and, conversely, that many homosexuals come from families that do not conform at all to the classic homosexual-producing "type."

Marmor also defends homosexuality as falling within the biological norm for mammals, and cites the work of comparative psychologist Frank Beach, whose studies indicate that bisexuality occurs "naturally" in many mammalian species besides man. . . .

Finally, Marmor charges that a happy, socially well-adjusted homosexual cannot be called "pathological" solely on the ground that his or her sex life differs from the socially accepted norm.

• The Wolfenden group. In the welter of recent studies suggesting that homosexuality is not per se related to sickness, an important early piece of research has tended to be neglected by psychiatrists in the United States. Prepared in 1957 by the British Committee on Homosexual Offenses and Prostitution, under the chairmanship of Sir John Wolfenden, the study dealt with a large number of homosexuals over an extended period of time. Although the report is best known for urging repeal of British laws against homosexual acts between consenting adults, its findings also revealed that homosexuals generally are well-adjusted individuals. . . .

• Evelyn Hooker, a California psychologist who also gave a series of comparative psychological tests to a group of nonpatient heterosexuals and nonpatient homosexuals. She also reported that the two groups, based on results of the tests, were virtually indistinguishable psychologically.

Freud guessed that, ultimately, the causes of homosexuality (and of almost all disorders) would be found in biology. In one of his last revisions of his *Three Essays on the Theory of Sexuality* (1920), he expressed the hope that hormones might someday provide the ultimate answer to the riddle of homosexuality. Prophetically, the only new findings of the last two years are being offered by theorists who claim to have found significant hormonal differences between hetero- and homosexuals.

There is a small but growing body of research indicating that hormonal imbalances may be involved in the explanation for at least some homosexuality. In a study reported from the Masters and Johnson sex research institute (1971), researchers found that young men who were predominantly or exclusively homosexual had lower levels of the male hormone testosterone than those of young heterosexual men. A Los Angeles endocrinologist, Sidney Margolese, analyzed seventeen ketosteroids in the urine of forty-four active male homosexuals and thirty-six male heterosexuals. He found clear-cut endocrine differences that matched, 90 percent of the time, with the sexual orientation of the individual. . . .

Although these findings are interesting, and even provocative, there are many questions still to be answered about the role of hormones in homosexuality. For one thing, these findings have not been confirmed in other laboratories, and in some cases, they have actually been refuted. Also, the cause-and-effect relationship still needs to be examined. Might homosexual behavior actually produce changes in hormonal level, rather than be the result of hormonal imbalance? Attempts to "cure" homosexuals by administering testosterone did not change the direction of their sex drive, but merely increased it. Finally, even if hormones do play an important role in causing homosexuality, the investigators cannot yet tell how important. There have been no analytic studies of individual cases where hormonal imbalance occurs, nor is there as yet any indication of how common such imbalance may be among the homosexual population as a whole. . . .

Many of these theories . . . have been based on narrow and skewed studies. Yet despite their inconclusiveness, they have been generally accepted, and have remained unchallenged for far too long. The theories do not explain homosexuality or prove that it is a mental illness.

The only point that the "illness" theorists agree upon is that homosexuality is a disorder "in function." Beyond this, there are widely divergent views about when and how the "dysfunction" occurs, and what causes it. Freud said the problem develops in the Oedipal stage; Bergler and Socarides say it is pre-Oedipal, and Bieber says the timing is irrelevant—only the pattern of family interaction is important. But what pattern? Again, the "illness" theorists disagree.

Virtually every kind of parent-child relationship has been implicated by one authority or another in the fostering of homosexuality. Some point to the mother who is seductive, close-binding, and "engulfing." Others blame a mother who is too aloof or "castrating" to the boy or to her husband.

When such differing—if not conflicting—claims are made to "explain" the homosexual, and when the claims are based on studies of psychiatric patients rather than the general population, one must question the "illness" theory itself. After all, as Judd Marmor and others point out, many families that seem to fit the classic homosexual-producing model produce "straight" children, and many other, totally different families produce homosexual children. What are we to make of this paradox, if not a skeptical view of all the explanations?

Another question gay activists justifiably raise—and psychiatrists fail to answer satisfactorily—is how psychiatrists, who see only a small number of "disturbed" homosexuals, can reach conclusions about all homosexuals, when the vast majority do not come in for treatment, and when many appear to be living well-adjusted, constructive lives.

Bieber, Socarides, Hatterer, Ovesey and others dating back to Freud may have seen an aggregate total of several thousand homosexual patients, but none of them have ever done control studies comparing their homosexual patients with nonpatient homosexuals or comparing nonpatient heterosexuals with nonpatient homosexuals.

Until the theorists who view homosexuality as pathological do undertake comparative studies with "healthy" (nonpatient) homosexuals, this serious charge cannot be dismissed, either by the profession or by the public. The few studies that *have* compared nonpatient homosexuals and nonpatient heterosexuals have not borne out the theory that homosexuals are sick or even different, except for their sexual preferences.

If the body of psychiatric theory does not prove that homosexuality is an illness, neither does it refute another possibility—that homosexuality exists to a certain degree in all people, and that it is repressed by cultural forces in favor of heterosexuality.

That strong cultural taboos against homosexuality exist in our society is beyond question. American society is based on the nuclear family, which offers an exclusively heterosexual model. And up to now our culture has tended to exaggerate and polarize maleness and femaleness, making it difficult for men and women to relate to each other in any way except sexually. Men are afraid to be in touch with the soft, passive, emotional "feminine" side of their own nature. In order for a man to play the strong, silent, "macho" role prescribed by our cultural rules, he is forced to repress these "feminine" characteristics, and to develop homophobic responses to deny this part of himself. Women, likewise, have been forced to bury traits traditionally thought to be "unfeminine"—strength, assertiveness, ambition, and even sexual initiative—thus denying the inborn "masculine" side of their nature. . . .

And yet despite these taboos, it is significant that so many youngsters experiment homosexually during the preadolescent and adolescent period. Homosexual incidents are so common that most psychiatrists consider them within the range of "normal" for that stage of development. In preadolescence it is common for boys and girls to develop "chums"—best friends of the same sex. It is also natural to experiment sexually with those one feels closest to and most comfortable with. Yet most youngsters proceed through the "dating" period in adolescence and, more or less successfully, navigate the stormy waters of sexual initiation, finally arriving on the socially approved shores of exclusive heterosexuality.

This is not necessarily the case in other societies. In a comprehensive and well-known study of other cultures, anthropologist Clellan Ford and psychologist Frank Beach found that in forty-nine of seventy-six societies homosexual activities were considered both normal and socially acceptable. And historians have confirmed that in ancient Greece homosexuality was sanctioned, institutionalized, and openly practiced by large numbers of individuals.

The question we need to ask is: Does becoming exclusively heterosexual represent genuine advancement to a more mature level of sexual functioning as we give up "adolescent" experimenting? Or can it mean that if heterosexual functioning is rewarded, expected, and approved, whereas homosexual activity is violently disapproved of on virtually every level of society, most individuals learn to repress the homosexual components of their nature in favor of the heterosexual? If they can achieve even moderate pleasure from heterosexual activity, isn't it logical to assume that they will choose this "approved" sexuality and deny their other urges?

This is not to deny that some homosexuality is indeed "sick" or "disturbed" behavior. But I believe there are three distinct "types" of homosexuals:

First, there are those who are disturbed and whose homosexuality reflects that disturbance symptomatically. An intense fear or hatred of the opposite sex would indeed constitute disorder, manifested in homosexual behavior.

But intense fear or hatred of the other sex can also be expressed in many kinds of heterosexual activity. Sex can be used to dominate, humiliate, or manipulate another person. Sick needs such as sadomasochism may be acted out heterosexually. In such cases it is not the gender of the sexual partner that makes the activity a disorder, but rather the dynamics and motivation involved in the relationship. If the relationship is based on destructive needs, the chances are that sex will be used destructively.

Second, there are disturbed individuals for whom the homosexuality is not related to the psychiatric problem. Since many psychiatrists tend to connect the homosexuality with emotional disorder as a matter of course, even in situations where this would not be appropriate, the therapy in such cases is likely to be misapplied, or even harmful to the patient.

Finally, there are those homosexuals who are not psychiatric patients, and who live comfortable, happy, and productive lives, often committed to long-lasting, intimate and constructive one-to-one relationships. This "low-profile" homosexual group is obviously largely unknown to psychiatrists, many of whom state categorically (and wrongly) that homosexuals are incapable of attaining such a stable life-style.

As more homosexuals in this silent minority decide to "come out," the general public (and some professionals) may be forced to realize that homosexuals can be as well—or as poorly—adjusted as many "normal" heterosexuals.

Some people fear that once psychiatrists take a more relaxed stand on homosexuality, society as a whole will follow their lead and there will be an epidemic of rampant homosexuality. But those who are so worried tend to be the same ones who believe in the illness theory. And one might ask why they are so worried, if homosexuality is indeed a serious disorder stemming from particular destructive family patterns, and if it reflects a serious warp in psychosexual development. For if these diagnoses are sound, then merely saying homosexuality is not a mental illness could hardly cause a mass flight from healthy heterosexuality.

On the other hand, the worriers are probably right in predicting an increase in overt homosexuality (and bisexuality). There may very well be more of it around, but I think much of it will be healthier—less polarized and less fraught with anxiety—than it is now. . . .

My first professional contact with men and women who were both bisexual and reasonably healthy involved a group of hippies in communes on the Lower East Side of New York City in 1967 and 1968. (There were, of course, hippies who showed all kinds of mental disturbance, but I am speaking now of the small number that I interviewed who were not mentally ill, and who formed close erotic attachments to partners of either the same or opposite sex.)

The hippies' revolt against conventionality and sexual hypocrisy, and their credo of "loving anything that moves," loving in an oceanic sense, transcending the barriers of maleness and femaleness, made it easier for them to engage in bisexual behavior than it was for their peers who grew up adopting, without question, the more conventional sexual mores of their parents. Neither group is necessarily "right" and the other "wrong"; the important point is that there are significant cultural reasons for some youngsters today to differ so markedly in their sexual attitudes from their parents' generation.

I recently spent a weekend at a Middle Western college for a men's conference on the problems of male sexuality and male-female relations. Apart from the formal talks and workshops, I had a number of rap sessions with male students and found several who maintained that they functioned bisexually—they would spend several months to a year in heterosexual activity and a like time engaging in predominantly (although not exclusively) homosexual behavior. These men (aged eighteen to twenty-one) have masturbated fantasying erotic activity with both men and women (although none reported fantasying both simultaneously).

Psychiatry has not, up to now, been hospitable to the notion of true bisexuality, usually maintaining that anyone who describes bisexual activity is basically homosexual, with heterosexual behavior superimposed.

It seems to me, from my studies of these hippie and college groups, and from recent conversations with several psychiatrists working in universities, that in such individuals the term bisexual applies—with no connotation of a predominant homosexual disposition or pathology. These young people appeared reasonably normal and well adjusted, in the limited clinical interviews I had with them. I should add that neither I nor my colleagues who shared my findings saw such students twenty or even ten years ago when we went to college.

Freud said we are all born bisexual, and young children are "polymorphously sexually perverse"—their sexual drives strike out in all directions. He believed that if the innate, constitutional proportion of maleness (or femaleness) is right, we will make the appropriate (opposite) sexual object choice through the "civilizing" process of what the nuclear family teaches us.

Based on what we have observed in children and adolescents, our knowledge (although sketchy) of animals and other cultures past and present, the studies done comparing nonpatient groups of homo- and heterosexuals, and, finally, my own recent observations of changing sexual patterns among young adults, I have come to believe that if there were no social restrictions on sexual object choice, most humans would be functioning bisexuals. Accidental, personal experiences might predispose an individual to lean more in one direction than another without pathology or disorder being involved. Indeed, if all the taboos were lifted, pathology might very well consist of exclusive interest in one sex, regardless of which sex one chooses.

Those who insist that only heterosexuality is normal often argue that nature decreed it that way in order to insure the propagation of the species. Sexual desires between male and female and the perfect fit of the male and female sexual organs all seem to "prove" that nature had only heterosexual mating in mind for humans as for all animals.

The idea that sex was designed for propagation is a theological argument, but not a scientific one. If it were valid scientifically it would mean that no sex act was "natural" unless it was performed solely for the purpose of procreating. The fact that the penis and the vagina "fit" for sexual intercourse and unite to produce a baby hardly invalidates other sexual activities as normal and natural. If nature designed human sex only for procreation, it would have limited sexual desires to the female fertile period—as in lower animals. To speak of the "fit" of penis and vagina as proof of nature's intention for their exclusive union is pure teleological reasoning—imposing a meaning or purpose upon a simple natural phenomenon.

Animal behavior studies have also been used, and more often misused, to draw inferences about what is "natural" for sexuality in humans. Depending upon one's point of view, it is easy to find animal studies that will suggest homosexuality as either "normal" or "abnormal." But from his well-known studies of animal behavior, Dr. Frank Beach concludes that mating behavior of lower animals has nothing to do with sexual behavior in humans. The concept of normality, he maintains, is "species-limited." And so behavior deemed normal or abnormal in other animals is simply not applicable to humans, although it may suggest ideas for studies in people. Beach and virtually all anthropologists note that the higher one goes in the mammalian scale, the less important is the role played by hormonal and instinctual ("natural") drives, compared with the influence of social and cultural conditioning.

It is my guess that the "sexual revolution," which has mainly had to do with reducing hypocrisy and sexuality and relaxing the "double standard" for the sexual behavior of men and women, has only just begun. Understanding homosexuality will be part of this revolution, and we still have a very long way to go. In this light, in fact, we can make the final point:

So long as we don't know very much about the functioning and nature of homosexuality, we cannot know much more about heterosexuality. For they are inextricably bound together in the complex fabric of human sexuality.

The problem recalls Freud's agonized question about his failure to understand women—"What does a woman want?"— which should have been followed with an equally agonized question about his understanding of men. Since the interrelationship of men and women is so interwoven, Freud, of all scientists, must have known that it was impossible to understand one and not the other.

There remains an urgent need for the study of sexuality, hetero- and well as homo-, female as well as male. For without understanding all of it, we can never truly understand any of it.

# Statutory Oppression: An Overview of Legalized Homophobia

## MEREDITH GOULD

"There must be a realm of private morality and immorality which is, in brief and crude terms, not the law's business."
Section 61, *The Wolfenden Report*.

The statutory language of sex laws and the methods of their enforcement reveal a serious contradiction in American life between traditionally cherished ideals of individual freedom and a crucial separation of church and state on the one hand, and an ethical stance sanctifying restrictive sexual standards on the other. In the twentieth century, the United States remains one of the few countries in the world where the state actively defines, regulates, and punishes adult citizens for any and all noncoital activity. The conflict between a Puritan heritage of repressed sexuality and an equally strong heritage of civil libertarianism is all the more distressing because it is rarely resolved; instead it submerges, becoming the subtle tension of hypocrisy. Historically, resolution usually occurs at the expense of individual freedom, and always forbodes severe consequences for the lives of sexual minorities.[1]

The state takes its cue from the Judeo-Christian ethic, a moral code originating in the religious texts of Judaism and Christianity. The Scriptures are a powerful body of myth, legend, and divine law which have significantly shaped the ideology of Western civilization. The portion of the code regulating sexuality is firmly entrenched in the assumption, and indeed prescription, that sexual intercourse is for procreation; only through reproduction can sexual activity of any sort be condoned. Consequently, masturbation, cunnilingus, fellatio, and anal intercourse are fundamentally heretical, threatening the natural order established by a stern, moralistic God. Anything other than penis-vagina coitus is condemned as sinful and morally rank according to the Christian church. When church and state doctrine merged into one system of law, as they did by the fourth century A.D., "unnatural" sexuality simultaneously became a crime against both God and the state. Heresy and treason became immutably united, and the torture, mutilation, and burning of women and men as suspected homosexuals was used more or less consistently and effectively after the early Christian emperor Constantius declared homosexuality a capital crime. The progressive shift to secular law that occurred as early as the twelfth century did not alter what had already become a cultural value supported by the then developing medical sciences and, much later, psychiatry.[2]

During the late 1940s, the famous Kinsey Institute studies captured public attention, compelling Americans to recognize that human sexuality involves a wide range of activity, as well as myriad and complex feelings and attitudes about such behavior.[3] Despite ample historical and crosscultural evidence about the nature and prevalence of homosexuality, public attitudes are still dominated by stereotypes that are simply untrue. American culture is sex negative; all sexuality is viewed with repugnance. American society is also sexist; behavioral expectations are in many ways codified into sex-specific rules for gender and sexual behavior: Men must be "masculine," women "feminine," and everyone heterosexual. Individuals or groups defying strict cultural notions of what men or women ought to do or be are distrusted and feared in a society guided by rigid definitions of masculinity and femininity. Homosexuals are not in fact uniformly "effeminate," "flighty," or "promiscuous" men, but are often defined as such since American society is ill equipped to deal with human variation.[4] The result is vehement homophobia, an irrational fear of homosexuality, which is further sanctioned, and therefore perpetuated, by an administration of justice tainted by covert religiosity.

Most people live the majority of their life without confronting the law or dealing with the courts. Certainly most people do not consider "sex laws" an oppressive influence in their daily lives; few in fact know what the term "sodomy" means. Even those persons arrested for sodomy often fail to understand the range and possible impact of these laws until they are already caught in the maze of statutory oppression. Yet these laws exhibit remarkable durability despite their demonstrated unenforceability. Laws regulating sexuality can, in theory, be applied to the majority of sexually active adults. As one would expect, sexual activity between "consenting adults" in "private" is rarely examined or even questioned, let alone regulated—provided those adults are heterosexual. If anything, the rapid growth of popular "sex manuals" since the late 1960s, explicitly encouraging heterosexual experimentation and emphasizing sexual technique, suggests an American public increasingly conscious of and concerned with sexual freedom and expression. The libertarian impulse is abandoned outright when the issue is that of regulating sexual expression between same sex partners. Sex laws today are invoked only against certain people—homosexuals.

Homosexuals, like heterosexuals, comprise a heterogeneous population. They are members of diverse classes, religions, and racial and ethnic groups, and embrace a variety of life-styles. Gays no more organize the entirety of their lives around sexual conduct than do heterosexuals. Yet because the predominant sexual practices of homosexuals are considered "perversions" by law, growing up gay also means growing painfully aware of laws carrying such severe penalties as life imprisonment or "rehabilitative" incarceration in state hospitals. The legal abuse of lesbians overlaps to a great extent the abuse due to the social invisibility of women in general, making it difficult to ascertain which legal nonstatus is more inhibitive. Homosexual men, in contrast, routinely encounter blatant and humiliating invasions of privacy and freedom which lesbians have been spared—such is the bitter irony of a sexist society. While the legal plight of other sexual minorities is by no means inconsequential, the following overview examines specifically the horrifying predicament of gay men. These laws have the power, if enforced, to alter the lives of over eight million homosexuals in the United States.

## STATUTORY LANGUAGE: A VAGUE TRAP

The enduring presence and influence of organized religion is a major block to the legal reform of sex statutes, which are distinguished from the rest of the body of law by their moral tone, ambiguity, and extraordinary definitional range. It is not unusual to find laws that clearly demonstrate the influence of the Judeo-Christian ethic. One blatant example is the anachronistic language of a North Carolina statue that reads, in its original version:

Any person who shall commit the abominable and detestable crime against nature, not to be named among Christians, with either mankind or beast, shall be adjudged guilty of a felony, and shall suffer death without the benefit of clergy.[5]

The Model Penal Code drafted by the American Law Institute in 1955 advocates the decriminalization of consensual sodomy between adults, a recommendation consistent with those proposed by the National Association for Mental Health, the Task Force on Homosexuality of the National Institute of Mental Health, and the National Commission on Reform of Federal Criminal Laws in the United States, the Wolfenden Committee in Great Britain, and the International Congress on Criminal Law. Strong sociological and psychological evidence also favoring decriminalization has not effectively influenced legal reform in the United States.[6]

Since individual states have the constitutional right to establish their own statutes, an overview of sex laws is virtually impossible; legal definitions vary almost as much as the behavior they attempt to restrict. Most states, however, refer to "sodomy," "crimes against nature," "unnatural intercourse," and "buggery" separately and in a variety of elaborate combinations without making explicit the sexual behavior being regulated. Consequently, in the absence of clear descriptions of the sexual act(s), sodomy statutes become catch-alls for any and all behavior the court includes. In a legal system based on case law, courts can and do make interpretative judgments. The law as written exists merely as a guideline, its applicability determined by the arduous process of adjudication and appeal. Courtroom decisions, even when pronounced by a jury, may be modified through sentencing, or substantively reinterpreted by opinions and dissents issued by the bench. Even the humanity of appeal can be reduced by a powerful judiciary, which is in turn significantly influenced by the surrounding social climate. While there are anomalies in any system, judicial opinion seldom strays from public opinion. Public sentiment concerning sexuality is clearly negative. Nevertheless, the obscure, almost medieval language of the "sodomy" laws has occasionally been found unacceptable and in direct opposition to an important legal canon which asserts that the law must be understandable to those who heed it as well as those who are called upon to enforce it. While seemingly a reasonable ground for declaring these laws unconstitutional, the "void for vagueness" doctrine has not been applied successfully in sodomy cases.[7] During the early 1970s several lower courts challenged these wordings as "fatally vague" and as such unconstitutional. The Supreme Court in turn found such statutes to be clear, precise, and unambiguous—an impasse that remains unresolved.[8]

The push for clarity should not be misconstrued as a move toward liberalization. States that have rewritten these laws generally define sodomy as ". . . carnal copulation in any opening of the body except sexual parts, with another human being, or . . . with a beast. . . ."[9] Twenty states have adopted the same or similar wordings in an effort to clarify what is still considered perverted sexuality. Furthermore, lest the statutory sentiment be misinterpreted, Arizona, Arkansas, and Oklahoma rewrote their laws to specify the criminalization of homosexuality.

Penalties also vary. Sodomy may be considered anything from a felony carrying long, even indeterminate sentences and fines to a misdemeanor. In California, for example, persons arrested for a range of activity including any sex-related crime are required to register with the police as "sex offenders."[10] In lieu of imprisonment, courts may require mandatory therapy under "sexual psychopath" laws, even though homosexuality was officially removed from psychopathologic status by the American Psychiatric Association in 1973.[11]

In the final analysis, these laws can be removed from the books only by legislative action. Illinois was the first state to decriminalize consensual sodomy in 1961. Since then only fifteen others have done so.[12] Attempts to overhaul oppressive statutory sex provisions through either judicial or legislative action have routinely failed, and continue to fail. The law remains fundamentally unaltered, a vague and effective trap.

## ENFORCEMENT AND THE CREATION OF EVIDENCE

Sexual intimacy is generally considered an especially private area of behavior, making it difficult to imagine how people are actually arrested and prosecuted for such activity. Because most sexual behavior is indeed private, it stands to reason that if people do not behave sexually in public, then enforcement officials must somehow gain access to the private realm where it does take place. Here the officially sanctioned abuse of the fundamental rights of personal freedom, privacy, and association is shockingly visible. Are homosexual men actively pursued and prosecuted? The answer is a frustratingly ambiguous "yes and no."

The police employ a variety of techniques and go to what seem farcical extremes to apprehend and arrest homosexuals. The major methods include observation, entrapment, and decoys. All are common procedures and are used both separately and in conjunction with one another.

Direct observation is perhaps the easiest method to rationalize since the key argument for decriminalization advanced by gay liberationists and civil libertarians emphasizes private, consensual sodomy. Police apprehension of persons engaging in public sexual activity seems morally justifiable, as well as consistent with an image of police as public servants and protectors. Consequently, police regularly patrol common "cruising" areas hoping to stumble upon public sexual activity. Most felony arrests, however, result from observational techniques that extend to bizarre limits, far beyond routine patrol.[13] It is not unusual for observational arrests to be obtained by any of the following methods: peering into parked cars; filming sexual interactions through one-way mirrors installed in public restrooms; wiring park benches and public toilets for subsequent tape recordings; learning and using foot-tapping codes created by the homosexual community for its own protection; drilling holes into bathroom stalls to watch and photograph otherwise private acts; counting the number of feet in closed stalls; or noting any other "suspicious" activity such as kissing or touching—an outrageous and offensive list by any objective measure.[14] Police may actively collude with a community to facilitate homosexual arrest. One particularly flamboyant example of this occurred in 1969 when a vigilante citizen group organized and patrolled a local park with police consent. Because the park was a reputed cruising area, they destroyed a substantial number of trees and shrubs, finally razing the park with power saws while the police looked on; no one was arrested for creating *this* public disturbance.[15]

Observational evidence is extremely problematic. When police conceal themselves for hours in rest-room attics to photograph other men using the facilities, they observe and record everyone. This blatant disregard for privacy is consistently rationalized by a court policy of "balancing." Community protection is balanced against an obvious abridgment of personal freedom. In many jurisdictions where evidence obtained from enclosed stalls is inadmissible, police simply remove the stall doors, thereby eliminating any accusation of an illegal search. Spying is also subject to perverse legal distinctions. Previously drilled peepholes which the police "find" and use are weighted differently from those drilled specifically by the police to gather evidence.

Most misdemeanor arrests are made by police decoys actively engaging in entrapment. Decoys are plainclothes officers trained to understand and imitate the style and conduct of the gay community. They are usually assigned to patrol known gay areas, or to frequent bars and parks to entice unwitting men, inviting their oral solicitation. Since oral solicitation involves interaction, entrapment is suspiciously akin to provocation on the part of police. Its later admissibility in fact depends upon the police officer's ability to convince the court that "intent to commit the crime originated in the mind of the defendant [not] the officer."[16] Furthermore, since inducement is illegal when an "innocent" is lured into criminal activity, men in and around so-called homosexual hangouts are presumed to have a preexistent intent to solicit.

Despite the questionable methods used to obtain evidence and despite the fact that courts often declare it all inadmissible, there is little indication that police intend to alter their approach to law enforcement. Depending on the immediate community, cases may be thrown out, heard, or transferred to another court altogether. So far the United States Supreme Court has avoided ruling on the constitutional issues involved simply by refusing to hear cases of any significance to the homosexual community. If surveillance procedures were more closely scrutinized, sodomy laws would be practically unenforceable.

Even when gay men fail to be lured into illegal activity, they are subject to relentless harassment; the possibility of arrest remains an omnipresent threat. Under a variety of public order statutes, gays can be arrested for chatting on a street corner, sitting on a building stoop, or strolling in a public park. These statutes refer to behavior generally considered a public nuisance—loitering, solicitation, disorderly conduct, and vagrancy. Although these particular laws do not deal specifically with sexuality, they are vague enough to include sexual behavior, and are used selectively against homosexuals. In the often imprecise language of the law, citations for "outrageous conduct" or "lewd and lascivious behavior" may be levied against gay individuals or groups.

Like any other social entity, gay people congregate in order to meet one another. Heterosexuals have a singles' bar culture; gays as well have a bar culture. The reasons for congregating appear to be sexually related only because this society clearly lacks a socially acceptable way or place for gay people to socialize. It makes little difference to the casual observer, or the law, that some people gather for social reasons and others for sexual ones; in the case of the gay community, social contact is assumed to be sexual conduct. The reasoning proceeds something like this: Sexual intimacy is assumed to be a logical, healthy outcome of close interpersonal involvement. In order to fulfill this romantic ideal, same-sex couples must engage in sexual practices that are, by law, criminal. Accordingly, any place homosexuals gather is assumed to harbor, if not promote, criminal activity. One may, in fact, be a "virgin" homosexual and have no intention whatsoever of changing that status. Yet an admission of homosexuality is simultaneously an admission of intent; that intent is criminal. Court decisions on related issues effectively illustrate the double-bind nature of this presumption of inherent criminality. In 1970, Los Angeles Police Chief Edward M. Davis, a longtime foe of the homosexual community, denied a parade permit to a coalition of thirty-four homosexual and sexual freedom groups from Los Angeles County and the San Francisco Bay area. At the hearing he reasoned, "We would be ill-advised to discommode the people to have a burglars', or robbers', parade or a homosexuals' parade from a legal standpoint."[17] Earlier that same year, the Gay Activists Alliance in New York City was denied a certificate of incorporation by the secretary of state. Although the decision was later unanimously reversed by the Appellate Division of the New York Supreme Court, the original ruling denied their petition because ". . . they [the G.A.A.] are professing a present or future intent to disobey a penal statute of the State of New York. . . ."[18] As recently as 1976, gay student groups applying for recognition on state campuses faced long court battles about their intent to promote criminal activity. When they do appear, seemingly positive court decisions are gutted of their import for future decriminalization by focusing solely on first amendment rights.[19]

In many communities, gay bars are frequently raided or have their liquor licenses revoked when decoys fail to provoke other misdemeanors. Building and fire inspectors may issue citations for inconsequential, or even nonexistent, building violations. This all adds up to more than petty harassment because once someone is arrested that arrest has serious consequences even if the case never goes to trial. An arrest record, in reality, differs little from a prison record. The net effect is that criminal and victim become one.[20]

## VICTIMIZATION

Victimization does not end with the prosecution of a person for sexual acts. In fact, as social scientists and observers of the gay scene note, the rate of victimization for homosexuals increases because they are homosexual, with or without the intervention of law enforcement agencies.[21] The problem is quite complex. Police try to enforce unenforceable laws by questionable means. At the same time, the police are often compelled to protect the lives and safety of victimized homosexuals who, because of their criminal status, are understandably reluctant to appeal to police; it's a vicious and unfortunate cycle.

Their virtual lack of legal status makes homosexuals an easy mark in a homophobic society. It is not uncommon for teenagers to consider "queer bashing" an evening's entertainment for which there is little formal reprobation. Juvenile delinquents prowl gay neighborhoods and social spots to assault gay men, often brutally and sometimes fatally. A clear connection does exist between sexual assault and murder regardless of sexual orientation. Nevertheless, dismembered corpses and mutilated or missing genitalia provide police a grotesque clue that the homicide was motivated primarily by a hatred and fear of homosexuality.[22] In 1976, a young gay man was beaten to death in Arizona by four teenage boys one Saturday night. In this particular case, the judge failed to pass sentence for their subsequent murder conviction because the teenagers lacked previous violations and were "good students, worthwhile citizens, no danger to the safety of the community, all living at home and active in organizations."[23] In cities such as New York City, gay men have organized vigilante groups to protect themselves and their neighborhoods from assault, in rare instances with the support of local police. However, even this "solution" places homosexuals in jeopardy since the public usually deplores any attempt at undermining police power. Moreover, police tactics themselves may have tragic and no less brutal consequences. During a 1970 raid on the Snake Pit, a Greenwich Village after-hours bar, 167 men were arrested for disturbing the peace. One of them was Diego Vinales, a young Argentinean immigrant in the country on a visa. Understandably fearful of arrest, Vinales attempted escape by jumping from a precinct window. He was impaled on the fourteen-inch spikes of a picket fence surrounding the station. Vinales remained in critical condition for over a week, and was hospitalized for over three months after surgeons and city firefighters removed the spike with an electric saw. From an eyewitness report at the time:

The remarks the cops made after this happened were unbelievable. One cop said to a fireman, "You don't have to hurry, he's dead, and if he's not, he's not going to live long." . . . Then the other kids started crying. They saw what was happening and they were shaken. But the remarks kept coming from the cops. They probably thought they were justified. Diego was a faggot, they said. They used the word so many times, it was unbelievable. . . . [24]

It is highly unlikely that a man who actively or covertly pursues homosexual activity will escape arrest directly or tangentially related to his homosexuality. Even if he is fortunate enough to do so, the crippling fear of anticipation is no less debilitating than an arrest record.

Victimization need not be as blatant as arrest. Homosexuals are painfully aware of subtle, constant oppression. In a society where identity is strongly linked with employment, job discrimination against homosexuals is a heavy penalty indeed. Instead of prosecuting by statute, the courts persecute by removing openly homosexual employees from their occupations. The only constancy in court action regarding employment discrimination against homosexuals is its inconsistency. Courts at all levels have rendered decisions in every conceivable direction, deciding homosexual acts prior to employment are both sufficient and insufficient for dismissal; openly acknowledged homosexuality does, and does not, violate national security.

Occupational licensing, always essential to membership in the professions, is an increasingly important mechanism of control in

other fields as well. It is used to determine who shall or shall not
enter a field, influencing the lives of over seven million people.
Again the rationale for restricting gays from occupational licensing is vaguely worded, based on false stereotypes, and varies
widely in enforcement. Basically it is assumed that homosexuality involves some sort of moral decay, and if the person has an
arrest or criminal conviction for sodomy, he is adjudicated unfit
for licensing.[25]

Homosexuals are assumed to be especially vulnerable to
blackmail and are consequently refused jobs that require any
type of security clearance. While there is some evidence to
support this susceptibility, there is no documented relationship
between homosexuality and the disclosure of classified information under threatened exposure.[26]

Victimization need not be visible as public brutality. One
important case, *Norton* v. *Macy*, evolved from the arrest of a
government employee for a traffic violation. Two Morals Squad
officers observed Norton, as he was driving his car, pull over to
the curb to pick up a man, drive once around the area, only to
leave him off at the starting point. The officers subsequently
followed and arrested both men for traffic violations. While the
summons were being issued, both were questioned extensively
about their sexual histories. Meanwhile, the head of the Morals
Squad telephoned the Chief of Security of NASA, the agency at
which Norton was employed, inviting him to monitor the interview. After the traffic summons was issued, Norton was invited
down to NASA, where he was subsequently interrogated by the
Chief of Security and an associate until after six o'clock in the
morning. Although he denied being homosexual, Norton was
subsequently fired from NASA for the occasional homosexual
activity he admitted to during the early morning interrogation.
The court later ordered him reinstated, ruling that "possible"
embarrassment to the civil service for off-the-job conduct was
insufficient and arbitrary grounds for dismissal. The case is an
excellent example of how seemingly minor infractions may lead
to extreme consequences in other areas of an individual's life.[27]

For men in American society, the armed forces is one major
means of socialization into adulthood. Open or suspected homo-

sexuality is unequivocable grounds for dishonorable discharge.[28] The person, regardless of his service record, loses all veteran benefits. Perhaps the most famous and publicized case was that of Sergeant Leonard Matlovich. A Vietnam veteran and in every way an exemplary member of the Air Force, Matlovich challenged the dishonorable discharge of gay military personnel in 1975; he lost.

The problem for homosexuals in the military is twofold. For many, the skills acquired during military service feature heavily in future occupational employment and mobility. When homosexuals are restricted from military service, a significant population of men are denied access to important skills. Secondly, since most employers hold military service in high regard, the stigma of a dishonorable discharge represents a serious impediment to future employment altogether. The abolition of the draft and the establishment of a "volunteer" army has not eased the latitude of life-style for men in the military.

Homophobia is insidious, reaching into every aspect of an individual's public and private biography. While women and unmarried persons suffer similar legal discrimination, they are not viewed as inherently criminal. Homosexuals often cannot simply counteract legal abuse when and where it occurs, but must fight a battle for legal status and civil rights simultaneously. While heterosexuals enjoy many rights and privileges by virtue of marriage, homosexuals in similar long-term relationships forfeit legal and financial protection such as community property rights, inheritance, tax breaks, and insurance premium reductions. Protection may be contracted for, but it is unlikely the courts will find these agreements any more binding than the antenuptial agreements for heterosexuals which they usually regard as unenforceable.

In the realm of family law, child custody cases to date have concerned themselves with the legal problems of lesbian mothers. Since men are generally considered unfit child rearers to begin with, and as a rule do not win custody, the likelihood of a homosexual father retaining his children is inconceivable.

Welfare, food stamps, social security, and other governmental programs do not ostensibly discriminate against homosexuals.

Guidelines, however, cannot and do not control against disparate treatment by caseworkers. Similarly, while gays may not be denied housing or public accommodation in states with all-inclusive human rights ordinances, there is nothing that prevents individual landlords, restaurateurs, or private employers from discriminating against homosexuals. Almost every single right and opportunity granted United States citizens is abrogated by homosexuality. Homosexuals are sentenced by society to a lifetime of endless and assorted legal problems.

## IN CONCLUSION

The prospects for legal change are not reassuring to those concerned with human liberation. A review of cases affecting the lives of sexual minorities reveals a disturbing inertia in the courts. If change is forthcoming, it will be through legislative, not judicial, action. During the early 1970s, gay liberation had a momentous impact on the status of discriminatory laws and procedures. Using both anger and reason, these groups did educate the public and catalyze legislative change in the form of all-inclusive human rights ordinances and the decriminalization of sodomy in several states. This trend has not continued.

In the three years since the bicentennial celebration of American freedom, ordinances protecting gay people have been systematically repealed across the United States. Forces working for more stringent laws against homosexuals are unabashedly related to religious orthodoxy and interwoven with legal misconceptions. Repeal campaigns are well financed, not infrequently violent, and religiously rooted in fundamentalist sects, and prey upon the legal and sociological ignorance of the populace to advance civil repression. Because the general public remains for the most part unaware of, or at best indifferent to, the future status of human rights ordinances and the nature of homosexuality, campaigns that appeal to a deeply ingrained ethical ideology of sexual repression are effective. Homosexuality remains a facet of human sexual behavior and sentiment unalterable by ridicule, imprisonment, or other gross forms of punishment. Again it becomes the task of the oppressed to struggle against passivity, self-hate, and fear, fighting instead for personal freedom. Clearly a choice between repression and liberation is no choice at all.

## NOTES

1. Walter Barnett, *Sexual Freedom and the Constitution* (Albuquerque: University of New Mexico Press, 1973); H. L. A. Hart, *Law, Liberty and Morality* (Stanford: Stanford University Press, 1963); Charles Lister, "The Right to Control the Use of One's Body," in Norman Dorsen, ed., *The Rights of Americans* (New York: Random House, 1970), pp. 348–65.

2. Wainwright Churchill, *Homosexual Behavior Among Males: A Cross-Cultural and Cross-Species Investigation* (Englewood Cliffs, N.J.: Prentice-Hall, 1967).

3. Alfred C. Kinsey, W. B. Pomeroy, C. E. Martin, *Sexual Behavior in the Human Male* (Philadelphia: W. B. Saunders, 1948).

4. E. Levitt and A. Klassen, "Public Attitudes Toward Homosexuality: Part of the 1970 National Survey by the Institute for Sex Research," *Journal of Homosexuality* 1 (Fall 1974): 29–43.

5. The North Carolinan statute was revised in 1965 to read: "Crimes against nature. If any person shall commit the crime against nature with mankind or beast, he shall be guilty of a felony" (Section 14–177 N.C. Criminal Code).

6. For example, the Kinsey Institute studies cited above and the Hooker studies. Evelyn Hooker, "The Adjustment of the Male Overt Homosexual, *Journal of Projective Techniques,* vol. 21 (1957), 18–31, and "Preliminary Analysis of Group Behavior of Homosexuals," *Journal of Psychology* 42 (1956): 217–25.

7. Barnett, op. cit., pp. 21–51.

8. See, for example, *Stone* v. *Wainright* 478 F.2d 390 (1973) (reversed).

9. Iowa Code §701.1 (1962).

10. California Welfare and Institutions Code §5501 (a.); §5500–5522.

11. See for example California Civil Procedure §1871.

12. California, Colorado, Connecticut, Hawaii, Indiana, Iowa, Maine, New Hampshire, New Mexico, North Dakota, Ohio, Oregon, South Dakota, Washington, West Virginia.

13. "The Consenting Adult Homosexual and the Law: An Empirical Study of Enforcement and Administration in Los Angeles County," *UCLA Law Review* 13 (March 1966): 643–832.

14. These practices are discussed in detail in Laud Humphreys, *Tearoom Trade: Impersonal Sex in Public Places* (Chicago: Aldine, 1970); Churchill, op. cit., pp. 226–31; *UCLA,* op. cit.

15. Donn Teal, *The Gay Militants* (New York: Stein and Day, 1971), pp. 26–27.

16. *UCLA,* op. cit., p. 701.

17. Quoted in Barnett, op. cit., p. 9.

18. *Gay Activists Alliance* v. *Lomenzo,* 66 Misc. 2d 456, 320 NY Supp. 2d 994 (1971); *Owles* v. *Lomenzo,* 38 App. Div. 2d 981 NY Supp. 2d 181 (1972).

19. See, for example, *Gay Students Organization* v. *Bonner,* 509 F.2d 652 (1974); *Gay Alliance of Students* v. *Matthews,* U.S. District Court for the Eastern District of Virginia (1975); and *University of New Hampshire* v. *April,* New Hampshire Sup. Ct. (1975), reported in *Journal of Homosexuality* 1 (1976): 329–30.

20. Edwin Schur, *Crimes Without Victims* (Englewood Cliffs, N.J.: Prentice-Hall, 1965), p. 68.

21. Edward Sagarin and Donal E. J. MacNamara, "The Homosexual as a Crime Victim," *International Journal of Criminology and Penology* 3 (1975): 13–25; Laud Humphreys, *Out of the Closets: The Sociology of Homosexual Liberation* (Englewood Cliffs, N.J.: Prentice-Hall, 1972).

22. Sagarin and MacNamara, op. cit.

23. *The Advocate,* November 17, 1976, p. 9, and June 30, 1976, p. 10.

24. Teal, op. cit., pp. 117–18.

25. E. Carrington Boggan, Marilyn G. Haft, Charles Lister, John P. Rupp, *The Rights of Gay People* (New York: Avon Books, 1975), pp. 33–42.

26. "Government-Created Employment Disabilities of the Homosexual," *Harvard Law Review* 82 (1969): 1738–51.

27. *Norton* v. *Macy* 417 F.2d 1161 (1969).

28. Humphreys, op. cit., pp. 34–39; Colin J. Williams and Martin S. Weinberg, *Homosexuals and the Military: A Study of Less Than Honorable Discharge* (New York: Harper & Row, 1971).

# The Homosexual Executive

## RICHARD ZOGLIN

### WHAT IT'S LIKE TO BE GAY
### IN A PIN-STRIPED WORLD

Something peculiar is going on at the New York bank where an account officer whom we'll call Robert has worked for ten years. He has been trying since last November to get transferred out of government services, the division he has been in for seven years. First he was told that he would be moved to a staff position. Three months later he was told that he would *not* be moved to a staff position, but that interviews would be arranged for him with various department heads to see what could be done. Since then he has heard nothing.

"I'm beginning to feel that I don't fit the mold," Robert says. "I'm not moving up as fast as I should be." More specifically, he is concerned that something about his personal life has become known that he has been trying to keep hidden: He is a homosexual.

Homosexuality in business is still largely an unmentioned and unexplored problem. Companies themselves do not officially recognize its existence. Personnel directors insist that the sexual proclivities of employees are irrelevant and never questioned. To complicate the matter, homosexuals in business—unlike other minorities—are largely invisible. Only a few of them exhibit any stereotyped "gay" behavior. And most of them wish to remain indistinguishable from their heterosexual colleagues; often no one in the company, except perhaps one or two close associates, is aware that they are homosexual.

Yet during the past few years, as the issue of homosexual rights—the last oppressed minority to speak up—has become more prominent, the homosexual executive has begun to surface. Gay activists are encouraging their closeted brothers in business to come out into the open—both for their own good and for the good of the cause. Some are beginning to reveal themselves, although the movement thus far has been slow and tentative.

Getting hard facts and statistics on homosexuals in business is a difficult task. Even the most liberated gay executive—one whose homosexuality is common knowledge in the company—is very cautious about discussing the subject with an outsider. Getting information on the large-scale incidence of homosexuality in business is almost impossible. Since no data are kept on the subject, all we can do is rely on the more or less educated guesses of homosexual executives themselves.

However, from a number of interviews conducted with gay executives across the country—most of whom stipulated that neither their names nor the names of their companies be published—some general observations can be made:

• Homosexuals constitute a significant minority of the business community. By the best estimates available, fully 10 percent of all businessmen and women in the United States are homosexual.

• Homosexuals are found in every part of the country and in every field. Certain more "creative" fields such as advertising and publishing have traditionally had a higher incidence of homosexuality, but even the most conservative segments of the business community—insurance, banking, the utilities—have their share.

• Homosexuals are present at every level in business—from clerical jobs to the executive suite. For example, the chairman of the board of a major oil company and the president of a large consumer products firm are homosexual.

The estimate that 10 percent of all executives are homosexual is based on the widely mentioned figure of 10 percent for the population as a whole. (Kinsey found that 10 percent of the population is predominantly homosexual, and his is still the most authoritative estimate.) However, some observers contend that the incidence of homosexuality in business is not that high. In a survey of 5,600 executives by Dr. Harry J. Johnson, only 4.4

percent revealed that they were homosexual. (His survey, it should be noted, is weighted heavily toward executives over thirty-five.) Some homosexuals themselves, based on their own experience in business, would cut the 10 percent figure in half.

On the other hand, some gay executives regard 10 percent as an underestimate. David Goodstein, a gay San Francisco stockbroker who spent many years in Wall Street dealing with large banks, claims that homosexuals constitute 20 percent of all executives in banking—traditionally considered a conservative field. "If all the gays in banking went on strike," Goodstein contends, "all the banks would have to close down." A gay lending officer for a large San Francisco bank tends to confirm Goodstein's estimate. Of some 150 people whom he knows personally in his department, he says that 15 "for sure" are gay. That is 10 percent, but he estimates the actual figure may be closer to 15 or 20 percent.

Such figures, of course, are irrelevant to the individual homosexual executive. His situation is an individual one, and he must devise his own strategy for coping with it on a day-to-day basis. He is faced with several questions: How can I balance my desire to "be what I am" with the possibility that what I am is not what the company wants? How far should I go in attempting to conceal my homosexuality? What would happen if it became known? Whom, if anyone, is it safe to tell?

The stance taken by the homosexual executive usually falls into one of three categories. First, there are the gay executives who have "come out"; their homosexuality is generally known in their company, and they make no attempt to hide it. Although their number is growing, this is undoubtedly the smallest group.

Second is the large, invisible group of homosexual executives who fully lead a double life. To their associates they present a normal heterosexual front; many actually are married and have children. The deceptions they go through to hide their secret may be elaborate and pervasive. Since, by their very nature, these hidden homosexuals are the ones who are the most difficult to find (they are least likely, for example, to have anything to do with a gay organization), it is hard to estimate how numerous they are.

The third group, however, may be the largest of all. These executives steer a middle course between complete openness and outright deception. They have not yet accepted the messianic urgings of their activist brothers to throw off their shackles and proudly reveal their homosexuality. But neither do they fit the stereotype of the frightened, inwardly tormented homosexual, perpetuating elaborate deceptions to avoid discovery.

"I don't try to hide it, but I don't advertise it either," says the homosexual personnel director of a New York area service company, and he speaks for a large number of gay executives. It is a private matter, they insist, that simply has no place in the office. "It doesn't affect the way I do my job, so there's no reason for the company to know," says an executive in the public relations department of a large utility. "Why do they have to know about anybody's private sexual habits? Should a married guy tell the company how he performs with his wife?"

For the most part, these executives seem to be at peace with themselves and don't find their situation too much of a problem. Their homosexuality is simply irrelevant, and as long as the subject doesn't come up, there is no difficulty. Yet there is the sense of attempting to solve a difficult problem by simply avoiding it. Most of these gay executives say that their homosexuality is not known in the company; when pressed, however, they admit it may be suspected. The tacit understanding—on both sides—appears to be that the subject is best ignored.

Typically, in his day-to-day dealings with fellow employees, the gay executive tries to avoid the subject of his private life. "Discretion is the game I play," says a San Francisco executive. "I insulate my private life from the business. I don't socially mix on any kind of intimate basis with the people I work with." Too much intimacy with fellow employees, clearly, could be dangerous.

However, few executives can avoid the subject of their private life completely, and when it comes up, gay businessmen must decide how far they will go to cover up their homosexuality. The director of data processing for a paper manufacturing company says that his associates know that he is going steady—"they just assume it's with a girl. When I talk about what I did over the weekend I tell the truth—I just change the personal pronoun.

"I will often be eating lunch with one of the vice-presidents or the controller or somebody," he continues, "and the talk will get to sex—as it always does. I will play along. For example, when we comment on girls, they all know what 'my type' is." He has devised a nice rationalization to help him live with his deception: "I probably would sleep with a woman if I got the chance, and there are certain kinds of women who appeal to me more than others—so I'm really not lying when I talk about my type."

A gay executive for a Fort Worth, Texas, utility recalls similar experiences. "When I first came here I would make up stories about what I did over the weekend, drop the names of girls, and so on," he says. "But after a couple of years I stopped that. I have decided that I don't want to live a lie any more than I have to.

"If people ask me about girls, I just say that I don't date much, or I joke that I'm too old to get around anymore [he is thirty]. When I go to office parties I'll often go alone; occasionally I have taken a female, but she is always either a lesbian or a close friend who knows I'm gay."

As this executive has become more active in the gay movement, he has made less of an effort to cover up his homosexuality. Last year he marched in a Gay Pride parade in Dallas and was caught by the TV cameras ("luckily I was so small, I doubt anybody saw me"); his name has appeared as a writer in a local gay newspaper (he has since begun to use a pseudonym for his writing); he has even used the company Xerox machine for copying movement literature—and once accidentally left some of it lying out.

This may sound like courting disaster, but it is indicative of an attitude being adopted by an increasing number of gay executives—a posture that might be termed "liberated laissez-faire." They have decided to try to live their lives as naturally as possible, to make only minimal attempts to cover up their homosexuality—and to let events run their course.

These gay executives have usually revealed their homosexuality to their close associates. When they do so, they often discover that their colleagues are far more understanding than they expected. Typically, a gay executive begins to get potentially embarrassing questions from an associate, and finally sits his colleague down "for a little talk"; he reveals his homosexuality in a straightforward manner, and the reaction is nearly always sympathetic.

The treasurer of a national hotel chain received an anonymous phone call saying, "Your assistant treasurer is a fag." The gay assistant treasurer recalls how his boss came to him disturbed and cautiously said he wanted to ask a question. "Before he finished, I said, 'Yes, I'm a homosexual. Now what else important do you want to ask me?' " The treasurer was somewhat taken aback by his casualness, but he was relieved—and their working relationship has not been affected.

A lot depends on how the gay executive views his own homosexuality—and how he conducts his life. The assistant treasurer has revealed his homosexuality to most of his immediate superiors, and has emphasized that he is discreet about his private life. "I have told them that I have a lover; I wouldn't have homosexual encounters with anyone in the company; I don't go cruising the bars. These are the standards I live by."

His observations illustrate a pervasive double standard where homosexuality is involved. In order to be accepted, the gay executive must be more discreet about his private life than his heterosexual counterpart. Heterosexual affairs within a company are tolerated, for example, while homosexual affairs are not. "I recognize the double standard," says the assistant treasurer, "but I am willing to operate within it."

The gay executive who comes out usually experiences a combination of relief and elation at the reaction of his coworkers. A senior executive for a national retailer recently was "revealed" when he let himself be interviewed on a TV news show last year (for a story concerning some local homosexual murders). "I was scared to come to work the following Monday," he recalls. "But the reaction was fantastic. People came up to me and said, 'I saw you on TV.' One guy hastily added, 'I was watching with my fiancée'—just to make sure I knew he was straight. My immediate boss never said a word to me. The store manager just sent me a note saying, 'I'm glad you finally decided to come out of the closet—but did you have to do it on TV?' " His working situation has not been impaired, he says. In fact, the only bad reaction came, not from his straight associates, but from other gays—who started avoiding him, afraid they might be suspected.

Clearly, despite the reassurances of their uncloseted colleagues, most gay executives retain a vague fear that letting their homosexuality be known will damage their career. Few expect that they would actually be fired. But discrimination can take more subtle forms—such as passing over the gay employee for raises or promotions. Most gay executives feel that their advancement would be slowed down or halted completely were their homosexuality discovered. An assistant director of advertising and public relations expects to move into the top slot soon, but is certain he wouldn't get it if his homosexuality were known. A bank lending officer feels he would be moved to a non-public-contact position that would be a dead end.

There may be justification for this fear. The hotel chain assistant treasurer was being considered for the position of treasurer earlier this year. The outgoing treasurer (who had learned of his assistant's homosexuality) felt obliged to inform the vice-president of finance, "I think there's one thing you ought to consider: He is a homosexual." When this got back to the assistant treasurer, he had a frank talk with the vice-president, in which he admitted his homosexuality and insisted that it should not be considered a factor. The vice-president agreed. However, in the end the job went to someone from the outside.

The assistant treasurer blames a bigoted attitude at the top levels of his company for the decision. But, as in most instances of possible discrimination against homosexuals, this one is hard to prove. The executive admits that he had been with the company a short time and that his inexperience may have counted against him; he expects to get the position the next time it becomes available. Still, his homosexuality may have been a factor in the decision—possibly the crucial factor.

Aside from actual discrimination, gay executives often express a fear of the effect disclosure of their homosexuality might have on the attitudes of their co-workers and superiors. "In my job, I am constantly involved in convincing other people of my ideas," says the director of data processing quoted earlier. "It's a very delicate thing. People have to respect you. Without the personal respect I have built up, my work would be hindered. I'd be snickered at behind my back. I would be the local fag."

Credibility with superiors is the crucial thing. The gay personnel director contends that knowledge of his homosexuality "would hamper my ability to hire people. Just like when a Jew is personnel director, people assume that he will try to hire other Jews into the company. If it were known that I am gay, every time I'd recommend someone, they'd say, 'Oh, God, here he comes with another queer.' "

There may indeed be a conscious or subconscious prejudice that homosexuals are simply not suited for the hard-driving corporate world. It is a prejudice, in fact, that is shared by some homosexuals themselves. "The typical gay person's life revolves around sex much more than the straight person's," says the gay data processing director—who considers himself an exception to the general rule. "To most homosexuals, business is a bore. They get their enjoyment from other areas—whether it is the arts, decorating, or whatever. Gays don't, in general, have the drive, the initiative, the *balls,* to make it to the top positions."

Such a viewpoint is anathema to gay activists intent on breaking down the stereotypes. "You have to grasp that gays are just like other employees—and in some cases better," says David Goodstein. "They don't have families that take up their time or wives that tell them what to do."

Goodstein argues that the best way to attack prejudice is for the homosexual to reveal himself without fear. "If you treat it as something fearful and shocking, it makes people think there's something wrong with it. But if you come right out and tell your supervisor that you are a homosexual in a way that isn't hostile and aggressive, you give him space to deal with his prejudice."

Most gay executives who have come out would agree. Yet it only takes one bigoted person in a high position to cause trouble for the gay executive—and business is not free of such people.

Officially, no company will admit to any discrimination

against or special treatment of homosexuals. They profess to take no notice of it—although there is the story of the New York employment agency that used to key certain résumés with the initials *h.c.f.*—standing for "high-class fairy."

Where discrimination does occur, it usually is due to the company's concern over its "public image": fear of what the public might think if an admitted homosexual were in a prominent position. A spokesman for Northwestern Bell Telephone last year stated that his company would not hire known homosexuals, because to do so "would tend to have an adverse effect on how our company is regarded by other employees and the general public." After much protest by Minnesota homosexual organizations, the policy was rescinded, and parent corporation American Telephone & Telegraph now says that "individual sexual preference per se is not a criterion either for becoming an employee or remaining an employee of AT&T or its subsidiaries."

David Goodstein moved from New York to California to take a job as head of a division in a bank's holding company. After learning of his homosexuality, however, "they decided that a gay person couldn't be in such a prominent position," says Goodstein. "They offered me some job in the back room where I wouldn't be so visible, but where they could still, as they put it, use my brain."

Companies themselves may be able to accept homosexual employees, but they are less certain of the broad-mindedness of their customers and the general public. The dominant attitude appears to be: "We don't mind having a homosexual work for us—just so no one else finds out about it."

Similarly, business appears to be less afraid of homosexuals than it is of overt homosexual *behavior*. An official of AT&T's personnel department states: "When we have had problems, it has been where the overt behavior has been such that it has disrupted the work force. [For such behavior]which impairs the efficiency or reduces the productivity of the work group, we take whatever action is necessary"—ranging from a warning to outright dismissal. Even the gay personnel director quoted earlier says that he would not hire a "flamboyant, swish-type homosexual. The kind that's always flitting around the office with painted fingernails and hair teased in all directions can create a problem—just as you wouldn't want a person who smoked dope in the office because of the disruptive effect he would have."

The fear, again, appears to be that homosexuality should not be too visible: It's all right as long as we can't see it. This kind of attitude may indicate more of a latent prejudice against homosexuality than most people are willing to admit.

Still, the situation for homosexuals in business is slowly improving. Ten years ago it would have been difficult to find even one executive willing to make his homosexuality known. Gay activists are continually trying to get more gay executives to come out and show that they are no different from anyone else. The activists must contend, however, with a much more conservative attitude on the part of the rank and file of homosexuals in business: an understandable reluctance to risk their positions and careers for the sake of the "movement." To be sure, the road to unconditional acceptance of homosexuals by the nation's corporations will be a long one. But the journey has begun.

# Capital Punishment:
# Notes of a Willing Victim

## MICHAEL RIORDON

. . . . . . . . . . . . . . . . . . . . . . . . . . . . . . . . . . . . . . . . . . . . . . . . . . . . . .

Dr. Gray smiled. With his eyes resting on Martin, he opened a folder in the exact center of his desk. It held several sheets of white paper covered in neat script. The desk was black with stainless-steel edges; except for the folder, and a black marble penholder, it was empty. Behind the doctor a dark blue silky panel rose the height of the room—he seemed to sit in a night sky, flanked by floor-to-ceiling books. For two weeks a Picasso lithograph hung there, then it disappeared. Things came and went like that, as the room was composed for different effects. This week a large urn crouched in one corner. Behind the patient's tall, blue-flowered chair, the room was vague, in semidarkness. There may have been more books, or a rambling potted plant. And the equipment. It would have to be somewhere in the room, but out of sight, not to spoil the tranquil setting. The doctor lived in some other part of the old house.

The doctor's voice floated from him, hardly moving the air—it had no edges, no sharp points. Colleagues envied it.

"How are you today, Martin?"

"Fine, thank you. And you?"

A slight laugh, not quite condescending. "I'm all right, thanks." He folded his fine, long hands. (He washed them before and after each patient.) His eyes, without flickering noticeably, absorbed Martin's taut seasick grip on the arms of his chair, his wide-planted feet braced for an assault, his dull hair flattened. The patient's face was slightly flushed, from the cold outside or

*The Body Politic,* no. 17 (January/February 1975), pp. 14–21. Reprinted by permission of the publisher and author.

from strain. The eyes wandered up and down the blue panel, across the books, to the floor. Martin licked his lips.

"Have they been able to fix your suspension?"

"Yes. Finally, I hope."

"You've had a lot of trouble with that car—the garage has it more than you do!"

"I wouldn't say that—"

"I'm exaggerating, as usual. Isn't that a nervous habit?"

"It could be."

A little silence. A moment's grace. Martin looked to the window, nothing to see but white overlapping slats. A savage tune jerked in his head, just one phrase repeating, obscuring thought. He let it. His stomach congealed, rolling, and swelled up to constrict his lungs. How could Dr. Gray help noticing the heaving of his chest? He governed it into long even breaths, shouted inside himself for control, and looked straight into the doctor's eyes. They held for a moment; nothing passed; Martin relaxed his focus. The cool, lazy face blurred in its night sky. His first year in practice. Thirty-five years old, thirty? How long did they study to do this? Below the face, fingers unlaced, white cuffs moved on the desk, the black pen jotted something.

"I wish I could see your notes."

"They aren't very interesting, just reminders."

"Even so." Just reminders . . . father dead . . . textbook stuff, pages of it, twenty-four years' worth. And a note somewhere, "curable."

"Well, Martin—" He left it hanging.

"Yes, I can't sit here making small talk at forty dollars an hour." A laugh, withdrawn as soon as sounded.

"That's right."

Dr. Gray leaned, opened a drawer, pulled out two small black boxes, then a slide projector. He connected them, and switched on the projector, throwing a white rectangle on the wall at Martin's right. Martin labored to say something, something funny. Short lines tumbled about, he practiced an offhand tone.

"World premiere."

Dr. Gray smiled, and rose. "Will you roll up your pant leg, please?"

"Which one?"

"It doesn't matter." Dangling from his hand, a thin wire with insulation scraped off the end. It ran to the black box. Martin rolled his left pant leg, and moved his chair to face the lighted wall. Dr. Gray handed him the wire—he accepted it gingerly.

"It isn't live yet."

And a tiny piece of tape. "To the calf would be best." Martin taped the wire to his calf. He touched cold sweat on the inside of his knee. Dr. Gray might explain the process again and swallow the rest of the time. A tiny strand of wire pricked him. He rubbed, to flatten it. One of the black boxes, with a foot pedal, lay near his right foot. He tapped it experimentally. The projector whirred and clicked, threw black on the wall, then white again.

"Good." Dr. Gray sat on the edge of the desk. "We're set. Do you understand what we're going to be doing?"

"Yes." Get on with it. If it isn't this appointment, it will be the next.

"The current should be strong enough to hurt. I'll have to rely on your judgment. Are you ready?"

"Yes." No. No, no, NO! for Christ's sake, *why??*

"Press the switch then, the pedal."

Martin tapped his foot—black, then white again. "Nothing—" an angry stab in the calf; the muscle twitched, he jumped. A buzz accompanied the shock.

"How's that?"

"Lovely."

A cordial laugh from the doctor. "Seriously."

"It hurts."

"Is it enough?"

"No." Homosexual.

Dr. Gray turned a dial on the black box beside him. "Press again."

"Press on, MacDuff." He pressed. A red-hot pin. No, a whack with a rubber belt. No, different from anything else—a tickle insanely heightened. Put a finger in a light socket. The leg bounced. Dr. Gray watched Martin's forehead shine.

"That's fairly strong, Martin."

"It can be higher." His voice lay flat, as if he were reading something technical, a will, nothing to do with him. The cure: three times a week, fifty minutes or so, before work. Six months, a year or two. "It depends very much on the strength of your will to change." The shock with the buzz. A cry stifled in Martin's throat, he controlled his voice: "That's enough. Think of your hydro bill." He leaned to rub his calf. He could easily pinch the tape a little so it wouldn't touch. He could jump every time he heard the buzz, and look pained. He straightened. He had heard the word "faggot" for the first time only a week ago, at the office, in a joke. He laughed no more and no less than anyone else. Dr. Gray had returned to his chair behind the desk, taken a tray of slides from the drawer and wiggled it into place atop the projector. He noticed that Martin's beige sweater was stained at the armpits.

"Are you absolutely sure you want to do this, Martin?" The patient's face turned to stare at him through the white projector beam. With the guillotine halfway down, he asks the victim if he wants to reconsider! "Of course I want to do it."

"What do you expect of it?"

"Everything." Dr. Gray disappeared beyond the cold light. Only his eyes glowed, and the glint of a tie pin. "We're not miracle workers. The impetus *must* come from you. I'll help as much as I can."

A week before his twenty-fourth birthday, Martin left home. His story: an especially good job had been offered him, he must go, it wasn't so far, 350 miles, he would return for visits as often as he could. He rented a car, filled it with his records and record player, some winter clothes, and left in a February rain. He made first contact with Dr. Gray at night, from a downtown phone booth, moved into a basement apartment, worked in an insurance company, pasting together pamphlets. "Worried about Retirement Years? Let our—" To be cured. Fixed.

"Press the switch, Martin."

The first slide fell into place, a red and white blur. The doctor focused. A young man with curly hair sat naked on a red blanket. His legs were spread, he leaned back on his arms. He looked slightly sideways at the camera. A flame in Martin's calf, and the wasp's buzzing. It went on. He cried over the noise, "How do I stop it??" "Press the switch!" He stamped on the pedal, the young man vanished. Another appeared, this one thickly muscled, an assembly of slabs. Veins stood out in a "V" in his forehead. Martin stared at a tattoo on one of his arms, some sort of bird. The shock came, he hit the pedal. Slide, short delay, shock, zzzz, pedal, slide, short delay, shock, zzzz—each time he was quicker with the pedal.

The item in *Time* had said aversion therapy was used on the obese, on alcoholics, on smokers, on homosexuals. "With some success." (There were those who disapproved of it.) Descended from Pavlov and his dogs, the principle of stimulus-response has been refined into giving electric shocks or nauseating drugs to make people dislike what they had been perverse enough to like—food, liquor, men, or women. At best, he knew, you only get the gist from *Time,* but that was enough, and the phrase "with some success" flashed like a neon sign.

A woman jumped onto the screen. Her legs, spread wide, dangled off the edge of a chesterfield. She cupped her heavy breasts with her hands, and smiled at the camera with violent red lips. No shock came. Martin glanced at Dr. Gray.

"A reward?" The doctor smiled. Martin looked again at the woman. His eyes kept sliding into the gap between her legs, then darting away to her feet, or the pattern on the sofa.

"It's an ugly photograph."

"That's what it looks like, Martin."

"That's what I'm supposed to try and get into . . ."

"I admit she isn't a girl you'd want to take home to Mother."

"If I press the switch, I'll have another shock, right?"

"Not necessarily. It could be another woman."

"If it's another man—"

"Even then it isn't certain. I've used a random pattern of shocks."

"Why?"

"It seems to work better." Seems. In their first interview, Dr. Gray asked Martin, "Have you had any homosexual experiences?" "No." "Do you want to have?" "No!" "All right. I think I can help you."

"But when I get one without a shock, I don't want to keep going."

"Of course you don't, that's the point of the exercise, isn't it? If you enjoyed it—"

"That's what I was afraid you'd say." Martin pressed on the switch very softly. It yielded under his foot, returning a slight pressure, then giving way. Another naked man flashed onto the screen. His back was turned to the camera, he looked over his shoulder with languid eyes, his lips parted. The photo was crooked; someone had photographed it from a magazine. No shock. Did he make his living from that, standing for photographs? How wonderful, thought Martin, to be so unashamed. He pressed the switch, softly again, as if the machine might react kindly. A man flexing his muscles looked as if he'd been inflated then polished to a mirror surface, very slippery. Zzzz, into Martin's leg—he stamped on the switch. Another man sprawled on a fur rug. Almost immediately, Martin hit the pedal—the slide changed without a shock. He pressed the switch four times in rapid succession, the projector rattled, four images popped on and off the screen. Two men, a woman, a man. He stopped. "Wait, that was a woman—can I go back?" "We can never go back," the doctor intoned. Zzzz. Martin switched. Another male, shirtless, in blue jeans, leaning against a fence post. Martin tensed for the shock, then relaxed. The man had a rope coiled in one hand. The top button of his jeans was open.

"Where did you get these?"

"Magazines, mostly."

"I threw mine out."

"Good for you." He'd stolen them from corner stores, never hitting the same place twice, pretending to read *Mechanics Illustrated* or *The New Yorker,* watching the cashier and the other customers, slipping *Mr. America* or *Strength and Health* inside his jacket, praying it wouldn't fall out or show at the opening, walking out slowly, fighting the urge to run, blushing, finally locking the thing safely in the bottom drawer of his desk at home. But he shredded them all, silent, tolerant friends become enemies, and flushed them down the toilet.

A little silence. Martin closed his eyes. A faint negative

image, a ghost in a black field, leaning on a fence post. What was the rope for? He passed his hand over his forehead, wiped the damp hand on his trousers. Queer. Unnatural. His head ached, dully, it felt as if it were rotting inside, as if it might collapse.

"I can avoid shocks by staying on one slide or by switching before it comes. Your answer to that is: It all depends on your will to change."

"True." That limpid voice, designed to calm lunatics. Martin wondered if he used it on friends, at parties, to the gas station attendant.

"If I'm not—if these pictures don't affect me—I mean if they don't—"

"Excite you? Do they not?"

"I don't know if I can tell."

"It isn't difficult, Martin. How do you feel about him, for example?"

Martin looked at the man on the screen. He waited for a reaction to form, but nothing did, at least nothing lasted long enough to put into words. A little snowstorm of fragments, but no whole thoughts. What does "excited" feel like? Stupid question, an erection comes. Then he wasn't excited. Was the coiled stomach excitement or something else, fear?

"Embarrassed, more than anything else."

"What embarrasses you?"

"Well, just sitting here looking at somebody like that."

"Be more specific. Somebody like what?"

"He's so obviously—he's so blatant."

"Blatantly sexual?"

"I don't know. It's hard to analyze—really all I can think about is the shock coming."

"You don't need to think or analyze to be aroused, it takes a more direct route."

"Mine is disconnected, I think."

"I doubt it." Dr. Gray glanced at his watch. "Are you going to continue?"

"Oh," said Martin.

A man in a shower. Water bounced off his chest.

"I wish I looked like that." Martin spoke just above a whisper, inaudible over the hum of the projector. The shock came, he started, banged on the pedal angrily. Another man. All of them were muscular, some grotesquely bulging, dinosaurs bound for extinction, some more graceful. "Maybe it isn't attraction—" Zzzz. The spot on his leg burned. What voltage was it? It would be proper to know, to have an accurate gauge of how bad it was. Ripley's *Believe It or Not.* The worst shock the human body can endure. "Maybe I'm not excited at all—" The shock cut into "excited"; he shouted "at all." He crashed on the switch, and said loud and fast, "What if it's envy?"

Dr. Gray leaned forward. "Be careful of that switch. I'm sorry, what did you say?" No shock. Martin slumped a little in his chair. His forearms ached from gripping the arms of the chair, as they did at the dentist's. "Isn't it possible I only want to *be* like that, to be that person?" He pointed at the man on the screen, who was imitating the discus thrower.

"It's possible, yes."

"Shouldn't I be lifting weights or something like that instead of sitting in this electric chair?"

"What do you think?"

"I? *I* don't know."

"In what respect do you want to be like him?"

"Not him specifically—any of them—well, some of them. I'd like to have dark hair like that, muscles like that, everything. He's very easy and sure of himself."

"How can you tell that from a photo?"

"Look at him. It isn't hard to tell. But he's probably an idiot."

"What about the genitals?"

"The—what about them?—I didn't notice." His voice trailed away. He picked at a wrinkle in the upholstered arm of the chair.

"Look."

"I'm looking." He was looking at the man's face, at a shock of black hair that curled down over his forehead, above the left eye—no, the right. The face is the mirror of the soul. Why look at genitals? Why were they covered, and faces not? Why did they all have names from dead languages—penis, clitoris, labia—and the sort of euphemisms used in toilet matters—"down there," "personal parts," "third leg"? With good reason. Martin cringed when he heard "cock" or "prick," "cunt," "hard-on," even "pubic hair." These things were better hidden. He pressed the switch. Dr. Gray leaned back in his chair. Zzzz. Martin struck both chair arms with his open hands, and winced. He stamped on the pedal. No shock on this one.

"I think that's enough for today, Martin."

"The hour isn't up yet, is it?"

"I think you've had enough. How do you feel?"

"I don't know."

"I didn't ask you what you knew, Martin, I asked you what you felt."

"I'm glad it's over, is that good enough?"

"It's something. You can take off the contact."

Martin leaned, pulled the tape and wire away from a tiny red spot on his calf. He rubbed it. His stomach muscles were knotted.

"Do you want some cream on that—is it burned?"

"It's all right." He rolled down the trouser leg, put the pedal box and wire on the desk, and turned his chair toward the desk.

"Well, Martin, what are you going to do this weekend?"

"Aggress."

Dr. Gray smiled. "I mean more specifically—are you going out?"

"I suppose I should."

"That's right. I don't want you to sit at home waiting for something to happen, as you put it. You know what I've told you about reinforcement. Without it we're just playing games here."

"I wish I didn't have to do any of this."

"What would you like to do?"

"Read a book, or sit in the dark. Eat. Go to movies."

"They're all things you do alone, aren't they?"

"That's interesting, isn't it?"

The doctor looked at his watch, and rose. "I'm afraid we've run out of time, Martin."

"I've met someone, a girl."

A mutual friend invited Martin and Lois to see Fellini's *8½* at a small, smoky cinema, full of people who call such movies "films." The friend told both: "I'm bringing along someone you might find interesting." Both said they didn't want to go, but were persuaded. To Martin, she seemed almost invisible in a black coat and cracked vinyl boots, her long heavy black hair tied at the back with an elastic band. But looking at her sideways, surreptitiously, he caught a little crooked smile at some parts of the movie. Afterwards, over tea, he harangued her about the sad state of movies; he said no one understood the "language of film." She considered him plain and arrogant, an odd combination. They agreed to go out to a concert together, the following week.

By spring they met two or three times a week. Martin wrote home about her, "She's different, very intelligent, frighteningly honest and very beautiful." It amazed him that on one day she could look radiant and aristocratic, and make him laugh, and on the next be wan and lifeless, dry as dust. They were driving home in strained silence after a concert. (Martin had bought a secondhand English sports car similar to Dr. Gray's, then, considering it a foolish investment, had it painted a funereal black.) Finally she burst out: "I've known you three months! Why haven't you ever tried to touch me?"

"It isn't that I haven't wanted to—" In the following hours he talked to her in the car, at the curb, over cocoa in her apartment. "You must have noticed how horribly shy I am." Beginning with the psychiatrist (but omitting the reason for the aversion therapy; why alarm her with something that would soon be cured . . .), he described his childhood and youth, part memory, part myth, part fancy. "I need you, Lois." She listened intently, shook her head, smiled tenderly, touched his hand. Very late he said, "I'm not sure I dare use the word, I don't really know what it means, but I think I may love you." She replied, quietly and clearly, "You are my sunshine, Martin." They kissed, chastely, and he went home. She waved from the open window until he had turned the corner. I should have stayed, he thought, any other man would have stayed. He smelled her hair on his hands. "Take the lead," Dr. Gray said, "Most of your troubles come from being passive. Nothing will happen unless you make it happen."

Late in the summer, a steamy night, they had eaten at his

apartment and listened to *Tristan and Isolde*. The subway was
closed, and she would stay over. While Martin tidied the
kitchen, she brushed her teeth, humming the Liebestod, and
changed into one of his shirts. He lit a candle beside the bed. She
smiled, as usual a little off center. On her upper lip he saw a
faint sweat shine. He blew out the candle, stripped to his
undershorts and lay down beside her. His first thought was, what
shall I say? Her fingers curled into his, warmer than his. He
touched her leg, which was cool and pleasant, and moved his
hand under the shirt into moist, wiry hair. He withdrew it.
Thank God the room was dark, he blushed furiously. In fact,
couldn't she feel his face burning? Sweat stung his eyes. Her
hand slid from his, would she fall asleep?—a moment later he
felt it under the waistband of his undershorts. He held his
breath. Her fingers ghosted over his hair and touched his penis.
My cock, he thought with distaste. She lifted it and closed her
hand around it. It felt tiny, detached, removed from him an
enormous distance, beyond recall—even worse, it was less than
air, without sensation, dead. He wished he were somewhere else.
He saw the pattern of a sofa, feet, toes pointed, legs in a V, veins
in a V, black hair matted, nipples, brown circles, a coil of rope,
tongue licking lips, a ghost in a field, swimming, sliding out of
reach. "Wait." He pulled off his undershorts and threw them on
the floor. He unbuttoned her shirt and leaned over her until his
lips touched her breast, a gentle rise. He found its point, nubbled
it with his lips. Is this what they do? She made a soft sound
*mmm*. What in God's name next? His fingers moved over her
stomach, slippery, back and forth as if patrolling the border of
her pubic hair—it tickled the edge of his hand. She must be
wondering what's the holdup, she must. He felt like a child
running down a steep hill—the faster you go, the harder to keep
your balance, the more precarious your balance, the faster you
have to go to keep it, the crash was inevitable. What was she
thinking? Dr. Gray—don't get into that, he thought, just do it—
*now!* He rolled onto her, she gasped from his weight. "Oh, I'm
sorry!" "No, no, it's all right." She held him there. His elbows
burned on the sheets. Let me go, let me go, cried in his head—he

awoke one night years before uncovered, erect, spilling over from a lost, heated dream, to see his grandmother in the doorway, pulling his mother closer to look. Now he felt sick and helpless, appalled by his sweating body and hers, by their stickiness and smell. He rolled off her, and pressed his hands to his eyes. The doctor said it would be easier and better each time.

"Did you have an erection?" "No." "Nothing?" "No." "Were you repelled?" "Yes—I was afraid." "Of what?" "That I'd make a fool of myself, that she'd be—" "What?" "Angry. Disappointed." "Was she?" "She said she wasn't. I don't believe her." "Why would she lie?" "Not to hurt my feelings." "Can't you give yourself the benefit of the doubt? Did you enjoy touching her?" "No. Yes—at the beginning—I didn't mind the breasts. But the other, no." "What's 'the other'?" "Below—the vagina." "Did that upset you?" "It was hot and sticky—I didn't expect that, I mean, I didn't know what to expect." "Isn't it about time you found out?" "I guess so, but how?" "Martin, you aren't in kindergarten anymore—*think*. There are books, you can ask. How do other people learn? When you want to find out about anything else, you don't ask how, I'm sure. Right here there are two shelves of books on this subject—you can borrow any of them, any time. This ignorance of yours, willful ignorance, isn't acceptable anymore, it really isn't." He leaned forward as he spoke, his eyebrows flicked, and he spoke a shade faster than usual. To Martin it seemed a towering rage. He colored and stared over the doctor's shoulder at a shelf of black books with gold lettering. The distance between diagrams, even photographs, and that steamy clump was infinite. Still, to know what was there, to remove some of the horror . . . "Do you have any idea how many men and women are just as afraid as you are, of failing or disappointing?" Martin shrugged. Small comfort. "Look how far you've come—you couldn't even get into bed with her a year ago." There's always tomorrow. Tomorrow. Another date, supper, a movie, a concert, drawing to a close, spoiled by nervous thoughts, coffee afterwards, pay the bill, walk hand in hand, so far so good, get into the car, red lights change to green, kiss, take the lead, take the goddamn lead, caress, don't stop, it's progressive, why isn't that bastard doctor here now, lay back the sheets, you know what's expected of you. I'm sorry, I'm sorry. Next time.

Fighting sleep, she forgave him and soothed him. He devoured her sympathy. Then he listened until her breathing was slow and even, slid his arm from under her and moved quietly to the couch in the other room. He lay awake, his right hand cupped protectively over his inert sex. Outside, some men were fighting, drunk; Martin was too tired to look. With sleep enclosing him, he thought: She must leave me, one way or another. What else can I do? Or I'll get better. Trust Dr. Gray.

In the morning, neither mentioned the night.

He tore the wire from his calf, pulling away some hairs, and shook his head: "I'm sorry." Dr. Gray's serene voice drifted from behind the desk. "Is it too strong? Perhaps we should turn it down." (The week before, Martin had said he was used to the shocks, it didn't hurt anymore. For the third time they increased the current. The second year of therapy was beginning.)

"No, it's stupid, but I can't do it today. It makes me sick."

"All right." (Coldly—he's angry, thought Martin.) "We still have forty minutes—do you want to talk, or call it a day?" He turned off the projector.

"Talk." . . .

"You have to *work* at therapy, Martin, it doesn't just happen. I have the feeling you're looking for magic a lot of the time—it doesn't exist. Therapy is hard work—by *both* of us."

Of course it was work, going there was work, taking the shocks was work, stamping on the bloody pedal, thinking of things to say—all work. But why shouldn't there be some magic as well—at least a small breakthrough now and then, one of those dawning moments when you burst out: "Yes, yes, that's it, why didn't I think of that before, it's so obvious!!" And you leave the office feeling light, strong, even exalted. Surely that spark must come from the doctor; if the patient could do it himself he wouldn't be there. He'd be swimming through his life with bold, powerful strokes, instead of drowning in it. Just a touch of magic now and then, was it asking too much? They used one tray of eighty slides; he had looked into every corner of every picture, at every eye, neck, bulge, vein, hair, and lip—he still avoided the genitals—and the shocks smeared together into a dull, continuous pain. It was almost welcome when the machine (and the shock) jammed, or when a shock came on a female slide, by mistake. Dr. Gray jumped up, chuckling. "My, my, that won't do!" he would say. Then the routine would continue. . . .

"Do you think I've made any progress?"

"Do *you?*" Questions always answered with questions. Martin shrugged. "Your relationship with Lois is a sign of progress, wouldn't you say?"

"Yes." . . .

"Martin, I'd like you to pay more attention to your appearance. I don't mean you have to go out and buy a lot of things—just take care of the basics, combing your hair, keeping your clothes clean and pressed—you know?"

"I want to be judged on what I am, not how I look."

"Yes, I know, but things are hard enough for you—why add to them? And, like it or not, people—most people—judge you by your appearance."

"I'm not interested in those people."

"Come on, Martin—'those people'? None of us is in a position to dismiss the world like that—you need them more than they need you, let's face it. In any case, our appearance generally expresses how we feel about ourselves. Need I say more?" One evening at a theater, Martin came alongside Dr. Gray in separate lines at the coatcheck. The doctor wore a ruffled shirt with mother-of-pearl studs, black formal tie, a burgundy dinner jacket with satin lapels, black trousers with a burgundy stripe, black patent leather shoes. Martin, in a sweater and brown corduroys, gaped but said nothing. Apparently Dr. Gray didn't see him; he picked up two coats, and went to join some other people.

He's saying dress up and you'll feel good and the world will love you, Martin thought. Isn't it the other way around? Why does he want to impose his standards on me? Why does he pick at me? There must be something more important to talk about than clothes. He should be making me stronger. Is this the basis of human power—keeping vital parts of other people locked away so they can't reach them—they may not even know they've lost them, or that they.ever *had* them, but they have to rely on you for certain life functions?

"Lois likes my hair, she says any woman would love to have it. They're welcome to it."

"How would you like to see yourself? What would you change?"

"Where do I start? Dark hair, good and thick, that doesn't go to hell in the slightest breath of air—masculine hair. This is my mother's hair." He tugged at it. "I'd rather be bald. No, I wouldn't."

"What else would you change?"

"I'd like to look strong—I'd like to walk down the street and have people notice me."

"Men?"

"Everybody. I'm almost invisible, I look at other people, they don't look at me."

"You'd have to wear better clothes, wouldn't you—brighter at least?"

"I'd wear jeans and a white T-shirt."

Dr. Gray smiled, or his lips curled at the corners. "Did you know that's practically a uniform for a lot of homosexuals?"

In one session, Martin asked the doctor what he thought of him, how he appeared to other people, what he must change in his behavior. After a moment he replied, "Sometimes I find you precious." He explained that he meant aloof or affected, more than effeminate. Martin flushed. "I don't understand. How can I change that?" Answer him back. He has no right to say things like that. He's not a judge, he's a doctor. Physician, heal thyself. He with his perfect nails and scents and honeyed voice. Fool, don't argue with him, you asked him a question, he's trying to help, he knows something, he's not the first to say precious, aloof, affected—effeminate. It joined in his memory with other evidence against himself. At the same time, in an inaccessible, unspeaking part of his mind, he began to sense in the man across the desk (in his eyes? or his voice? his words?) an enemy....

Martin, sitting two steps above, watched Lois huddle against the banister, her back curved, her arms wrapped around her legs.

Rocking slightly, she reached and covered her head with both arms. Martin thought of touching her arms. Martin thought of touching her hand. Instead he rose. "I'll start supper. Do you want a glass of sherry first?" She shook her head.

He gulped down a glass of sherry, cheap scorching stuff. And splashed some into the liver and onions. A little liquor wouldn't hurt the atmosphere. There was wine, but Lois would drink one glass, more made her sick. Beyond the window, roof silhouettes sharpened under frail lemon clouds. One tall building downtown was splashed with gold, but fading. For Martin the supreme moment of a summer day came when the light died—it seemed to reaffirm some primeval magic. He blundered about the kitchen, refusing to put on the lights, finally sitting to watch black overtake the room. Instead of sweet sadness in the moment, he felt an edge of disaster.

The liver and onions were overdone, the potatoes hard, the salad bitter. Lois drank her glass of wine in silence, Martin finished the bottle, saying it wasn't good enough to recork. He played the stereo to fill the empty space between them, then chattered loudly and nervously above the music, and got a headache. Finally Lois raised her eyes. Her face glowed in the candlelight, with an angry rush in the cheeks.

"You didn't want me up there on the weekend, did you?"

"What do you mean, I—"

She cut him off. "You didn't. It wouldn't have taken much persuasion—one word and I would have gone."

"You said it would be boring!"

"So did you."

"Yes, but to get out of the city . . . it *was* boring, you would have hated it. We ate too much, drank too much, played cards until we were all sick of it, but no one would admit it, and we talked about—what?—strikes, the cost of living—nothing. You would have hated every minute. I did. God knows why I went."

"Because I wasn't there."

"What?? Where do you get that from? I asked you and you said you didn't want to go—what was I supposed to do, drag you? Now you say you *did* want to go, what the hell is going on?"

"I didn't want to go, I wanted to spend the weekend with you, wherever. But you—(her voice rose and quivered)—you don't like me, Martin."

"What are you saying?? I like you more than anyone else in the world. You're the most fascinating—"

"I don't want to hear that. I've been very stupid for a long time." She left the table to stand at the window. Her face was cruelly lit by a streetlamp. "I never thought about it until this weekend. First I thought you'd fooled me deliberately, I began to see how I could easily hate you, then that seemed not to make sense, it was innocent, part of deceiving yourself, then I thought, no, it's me, he didn't do anything, but that doesn't work either. I don't know. You made me feel worthless this weekend, zero, minus. Not again."

Behind her, Martin felt panicky. He fidgeted, picked at the candle drippings. He swallowed. His voice came out thick and dry. "Most of the time I'm filled with guilt about you." The beginning of their act.

"Thank you, but it doesn't do much for us, does it?"

"I always end up thinking I should be trying to make—to screw you, it's a terrible pressure, every second."

" 'Should', 'pressure'—I'm not a torture chamber!"

"Aren't you frustrated?"

"Yes."

"You need someone to give you sex."

"Why not from a dispenser in Woolworth's? Don't tell me what I need, Martin. On the other hand why shouldn't you—I don't know what I need." So far, both of them recognized the drift of their conversation. It recurred from time to time, without resolution. Like two sticks propped together, they supported each other by inertia and gravity. If one moved suddenly . . .

Lois turned from the window, slumped in a deep old chair, almost invisible in the outer reach of candlelight. Martin lay on the floor, on his back, with his eyes closed.

"Lois, aren't you tired of me?"

No reply.

"You're a—you could do better."

Silence.

"I don't give you anything. Do I?"

Silence. She wasn't playing.

"I drag you down." He reached out and touched her ankle. "You used to hum little snatches of things mixed up, Beethoven and Edith Piaf, something from a movie, a bit of the Messiah— you'd stop and ask me what it was. You don't do it anymore. I'm dragging you down."

She shifted in her chair, causing her foot to withdraw. He crossed his hands on his chest. "Pater et filius et spiritus sanctus, amen. What if I'm a homosexual?" His big gun. She always answered that she didn't believe it.

("Dr. Gray, can you tell from observing me or from what I've told you whether or not I'm a homosexual? Am I?" "Martin, you know I can't answer that. Are you attracted to men? That's the only criterion." "You won't believe this, but I honestly don't know." "You're right, I don't believe it. What do you feel when you look at a man—do you look at men? Which ones? What do you feel when you do? What does it do to you? These are the questions you must ask yourself." Martin's mouth was dry. "I look at men who are well built. Who have what I call a kind of masculine grace, an easiness about them that says they know they're strong, they look good, they can handle anything—it's a physical . . . 'grace' is the only word I can think of. When I see a man like that, I have a tremendous feeling of envy, or of my own inadequacy—I usually do a thousand exercises, nothing happens, of course, I know he was either born like that or started when he was twelve, but . . . I don't know, do you call that attraction?" "Do you get an erection?" "No. But I don't when I look at a woman either." "What *do* you feel when you look at a woman, a good-looking one?" "Some are nice to look at, others—do I feel anything?—couldn't you just open some little trapdoor in my head and check the wires, I have no idea what I feel about anything." "What are your fantasies?" "I haven't any, at least I'm not aware of any." "None?" He shook his head. "That is unusual. Do you daydream?" "I see myself strong and capable, standing up to people, overcoming them." "Physically?" "Sometimes, yes." "Who are these people?" "Someone who's insulted me or got the better of me in some way—a parking lot attendant said I hadn't paid—I had." "What did you do?" "I paid again, it was less trouble than arguing." "Then you fantasized about him." "Yes. He tried to hit me and I had to fight him." "It's that passive thing again, isn't it?" "Yes, but that doesn't make me a homosexual." It occurred to Martin, for an instant then gone, that the doctor may have narrowly missed an essential question, that he'd veered off onto a blind path when he was very close to—what?—but it was gone. "Of course it doesn't. You want to sit back and have me say you're this or that, that you're a homosexual, you are not a homosexual. I won't do it, Martin, the decision is yours, or rather the determination." Decision, like what color socks to wear. . . . "Can you at least define what I should feel?" "Certainly not! I'm not your mother. Look, this isn't getting us anywhere. Why not proceed on the assumption that therapy is working, that you're adjusting satisfactorily to a heterosexual relationship?")

"What if."

Martin opened his eyes, startled. What was she doing?

"What would you do?"

"I wouldn't do anything. What would *you* do?"

"But how would you feel about me? Would you hate me?"

"No. I don't know how I'd feel. It seems to me you're asking the wrong questions."

The questions were the same as always. Why were her answers different? Something was breaking, or had broken. "Would you stay with me?"

"Why—in what capacity? Martin, if you are, you are—if you are, you won't want me, will you."


One Tuesday, Dr. Gray said: "I think we've gone as far as we can with this." Martin was terrified. Was it a failure, all those shocks for nothing? Was he incurable? "You're at a point of equilibrium, so to speak. The best thing for you now is continuing reinforcement of what we've accomplished so far. We'll go on meeting, but the shocks end this week. Does that please you?"

No more shocks. Next Tuesday he could eat breakfast, he could go directly to work in the morning, he wouldn't worry on the subway whether people could see his eyelid flickering, or that they'd guess somehow where he'd been. (After each shock session, it felt as if his face were flying apart.) Still, it was a little frightening, or at least unsettling—a unit in his routine suddenly dissolved, just like that.

"We can resume at any time, of course, but I hope it won't be necessary."

Like so many other things, therapy slipped away from Martin less by decision than by the lack of it. They met twice a week, once a week, every two weeks, once a month. Their conversation vaporized, like that of distant acquaintances with nothing to share, unable to avoid each other's eyes on the street, who stop, exchange words, smile, look past each other, hurry on.

Their last hour together was at eight on a Thursday evening. Before Dr. Gray came in, Martin looked into the dark recess behind his chair. It was empty. He walked out onto the sundeck. Summer's last humid waves and the city's hum rose from the street. Fat red geraniums sagged and spilled their petals; green scum coated the birdbath. "Shall we sit out here?" Dr. Gray's silky entrances no longer surprised Martin. They chatted briefly about the upcoming elections.

"I've sensed for some time that you might be competing with me, that you were resisting therapy, even once or twice that you might be trying to reverse our roles! Have you been aware of anything like that?"

"No." He'd thought frequently that he could talk circles around the other man. "Why would I want to compete with you?"

"I'm not sure you're completely candid with me, and I think it may be due to competitiveness. Perhaps you need an older therapist, or a woman. A female therapist might be very good for you. I know several, if at any time you'd like me to. . . ." Martin felt warmth rising in his cheeks, a blush coming. So he wasn't getting out after all. Another therapist. Start from scratch, spill your stuff to another face, I see, that's interesting, what do *you* think it means, therapy is work, we can help you if, I'm sorry our time is up. Another fool, so easy to throw: Reverse yourself again and again, send up clouds of confusion and they'd be enchanted—they'd think something was happening. Tell them anything you like with the right tone of doubt and they'd spring to the opposite conclusion. Give them signals to read, look away in mid-sentence, laugh nervously, dismiss your thought just before its climax ("I begin to wonder if I didn't really prefer—but it doesn't make sense, it's crazy." The doctor would lean forward: "Will you please finish your sentences? Stop censoring!"), make circles on circles, blur . . . for three years, finishing tonight. Why assume the doctor had been fooled? He hadn't been there at all.

"Well, Martin. . . ." He was trying to end it.

He stared at the doctor's face, a wintry lake barren and unforgiving. . . . Dr. Gray. His legs crossed, his hands folded in his lap, his head tilted to one side. Three years of mean, confusing whispers. No transformation, no cure, no promise of growth, no revelations, no increase in strength—bleakly, helplessly, no change. In the past year, like a decaying estate, Martin had closed his windows, from which he could see only streets boiling with angry, dangerous mobs, and then whole rooms of himself, imperceptibly. He floated in his melancholy person, waiting for dark, secure in the silence. Lois, perpetually hurt, rained forgiveness on him as long as she could. A few others waited patiently while he stared through them and rushed from them. A telephone ring terrified him; if he imagined a friendly voice from the other end, he didn't answer. Some days he saw in the mirror an enemy to be destroyed, on others a joke; on some he saw nothing. To live, he gathered himself about himself, reserved his strength, and waited.

Dr. Gray's buttery voice curled down the stairs after him: "Martin—keep in touch."

*(And:*

*Much as I would like to, I can't abandon Martin. I thought used lives could be thrown off like old clothes, but they carry with them too many layers of skin. My aversion therapy blurs a little, after three or four years of turbulence and change. In this case the willing victim escaped his capital punishment, I think. I hope. Finally, last year, 1974, Year 1, I came out publicly, blushing, amazed to discover human senses and feelings. The hard part, coming out in private—letting go—well, I'm still afraid to touch electric things and people. But then who isn't?*

*For you, Dr. Gray [Dr. Jameson], I wish another way of living than cannibalism.*

*Michael Riordon*
*February 1975.)*

# PART II
# Culture

Identity

# Coming Out in the Gay World

## BARRY M. DANK

There is almost no sociological literature on "becoming" homosexual. There is a vast literature on the etiology of homosexuality—that is, the family background of homosexuals*—but little is known concerning how the actor learns that he is a homosexual, how he decides that he is a homosexual. In terms of identity and behavior, this paper is concerned with the transition to a homosexual identity, not in the learning of homosexual behavior per se, or the antecedent or situational conditions that may permit an actor to engage in a homosexual act. One may engage in a homosexual act and think of oneself as being homosexual, heterosexual, or bisexual. One may engage in a heterosexual act and think of oneself as being heterosexual, homosexual, or bisexual, or one may engage in no sexual acts and still have a sexual identity of heterosexual, homosexual, or bisexual. This study is directed toward determining what conditions permit a person to say, "I am a homosexual."†

---

* See Bergler, 1951; Bieber et al., 1965; Freud, 1962; Gebhard et al., 1965; Hooker, 1969; Krich, 1954; Ovesey, 1969; Ruitenbeek, 1963; Schofield, 1965; West, 1959; Westwood, 1960.

† It should also be pointed out that from the subjective viewpoint of the actor, it becomes problematic exactly at which point a "homosexual" act should be viewed as such. A male actor may have a sexual contact with another male, but fantasize during the sexual act either that the other male is a female or that he himself is a female; in either case he may view the act as being heterosexual. Or a male actor may have a sexual contact with a female, but fantasize the female as being a male or himself as being a female; in such a case he might view the act as being homosexual (Stoller, 1968).

---

*Psychiatry* 34 (1971):180–97. Copyright © 1971 by The William Alanson White Psychiatric Foundation, Inc. Reprinted by special permission of the publisher and author.

## RESEARCH METHOD

This report is part of a study that had been ongoing for over two years in a large metropolitan area in the United States. The analysis is based on data obtained from lengthy interviews with fifty-five self-admitted homosexuals, on observations of and conversations with hundreds of homosexuals, and on the results of a one-page questionnaire distributed to three hundred self-admitted homosexuals attending a meeting of a homophile organization. The statistical data are based on the 182 questionnaires that were returned.

The four- to five-hour interviews with the fifty-five self-admitted homosexuals were generally conducted in the subject's home, and in the context of a "participant-observation" study in which the researcher as researcher became integrated into friendship networks of homosexuals. The researcher was introduced to this group by a homosexual student who presented him correctly as being a heterosexual who was interested in doing a study of homosexuals as they exist in the "outside world." He was able to gain the trust of the most prestigious person in the group, which enabled him, on the whole, to gain the trust of the rest of the group. The guidelines employed in the study were based on those outlined by Polsky (1967) for participant-observation studies.

There is no way of determining whether the sample groups studied here, or any similar sample, would be representative of the homosexual population. Thus it remains problematic whether the findings of this study can be applied to the homosexual population in general or to other samples of homosexuals.* Since age is a critical variable in this study, the questionnaire sample was used in the hope that the replies to a questionnaire would

---

* In addition, it should be pointed out that the sample employed may be skewed in an unknown direction since the questionnaire response rate was approximately 60 percent. In the interview sample, the researcher received excellent cooperation from both those who viewed themselves as being psychologically well adjusted and those who did not; those more reluctant to participate tended to occupy high socioeconomic positions.

### TABLE 1
#### Age Characteristics of Sample

| Age | Age Distribution | | Age of First Sexual Desire Toward Same Sex | | Age at Which Decision Was Made That Respondent Was Homosexual | |
|---|---|---|---|---|---|---|
| | N | (%) | N | (%) | N | (%) |
| 0–4 | 0 | (0) | 1 | (0.5) | 0 | (0) |
| 5–9 | 0 | (0) | 28 | (15) | 1 | (0.5) |
| 10–14 | 0 | (0) | 83 | (46) | 27 | (15) |
| 15–19 | 13 | (7) | 54 | (29) | 79 | (44) |
| 20–24 | 36 | (20) | 14 | (8) | 52 | (29) |
| 25–29 | 39 | (22) | 1 | (0.5) | 11 | (6) |
| 30–34 | 28 | (16) | 1 | (0.5) | 4 | (2) |
| 35–39 | 21 | (12) | 0 | (0) | 3 | (2) |
| 40–44 | 18 | (10) | 0 | (0) | 1 | (0.5) |
| 45–49 | 6 | (3) | 0 | (0) | 0 | (0) |
| 50–59 | 11 | (6) | 0 | (0) | 0 | (0) |
| 60–69 | 8 | (4) | 0 | (0) | 1 | (0.5) |
| Total | 180 | (100) | 182 | (99.5) | 179 | (99.5) |

$\overline{X}$=32.5, $S$=11.3  $\overline{X}$=13.5, $S$=4.3  $\overline{X}$=19.3, $S$=6.4

represent a fairly wide age range. The age distribution of the questionnaire sample is shown on Table 1.

### COMING OUT

The term "coming out" is frequently used by homosexuals to refer to the identity change to homosexual. Hooker (1965) states: "Very often, the debut, referred to by homosexuals as the coming out, of a person who believes himself to be homosexual but who has struggled against it will occur when he identifies himself publicly for the first time as a homosexual in the presence of other homosexuals by his appearance in a bar" (p. 99). Gagnon and Simon (1968) refer to coming out as that ". . . point in time when there is self-recognition by the individual of his identity as a homosexual and the first major exploration of the homosexual community" (p. 356).

In this study it was found that the meaning that the informant attached to this expression was usually directly related to his own experiences concerning how he met other gay* people and how and when he decided he was homosexual. For purposes of this study the term "coming out" will mean identifying oneself as being homosexual.† This self-identification as being homosexual may or may not occur in a social context in which other gay people are present. One of the tasks of this paper is to identify the social contexts in which the self-definition of "homosexual" occurs.

## THE SOCIAL CONTEXTS OF COMING OUT

The child who is eventually to become homosexual in no sense goes through a period of anticipatory socialization (Merton, 1957); if he does go through such a period, it is in reference to heterosexuality, not homosexuality. It is sometimes said that the homosexual minority is just like any other minority group (Cory, 1951; Westwood, 1960); but in the sense of early childhood socialization it is not, for the parents of a Negro can communicate to their child that he is a Negro and what it is like to be a Negro, but the parents of a person who is to become homosexual do not prepare their child to be homosexual—they are not homosexual themselves, and they do not communicate to him what it is like to be a homosexual.*

The person who has sexual feelings or desires toward persons of the same sex has no vocabulary to explain to himself what these feelings mean. Subjects who had homosexual feelings during childhood were asked how they would have honestly

---

* In homosexual argot, "gay" means homosexual and "straight" means heterosexual. These terms are acceptable to homosexuals whether used by gay or straight persons.

† Sometimes homosexuals use the expression "to bring out" or "bringing out." The meaning attached to these expressions varies; they are sometimes used interchangeably with "coming out." However, as used by my informants, they usually refer to the first complete homosexual act which the subject found enjoyable. The statement, "He brought me out," usually means, "He taught me to enjoy real homosexual acts."

responded to the question "Are you a homosexual?" at the time just prior to their graduation from high school. Some typical responses follow:

SUBJECT 1: I had guilt feelings about this being attracted to men. Because I couldn't understand why all the other boys were dating, and I didn't have any real desire to date.

INTERVIEWER: Were you thinking of yourself as homosexual?

SUBJECT 1: I think I did but I didn't know how to put it into words. I didn't know it existed. I guess I was like everybody else and thought I was the only one in the world. . . . I probably would have said I didn't know. I don't think I really knew what one was. I would have probably asked you to explain what one was.

SUBJECT 2: I would have said, "No. I don't know what you are talking about." If you had said "queer," I would have thought something about it; this was the slang term that was used, although I didn't know what the term meant.

SUBJECT 3: I don't think I would have known then. I know now. Then I wasn't even thinking about the word. I wasn't reading up on it.

Respondents were asked the age at which they first became aware of any desire or sexual feeling toward persons of the same sex; subsequently they were asked when they decided they were homosexual. Results are presented in Table 1. On the average, there was a six-year interval between time of first sexual feeling toward persons of the same sex and the decision that one was a homosexual. The distribution of the differing time intervals

---

* Some homosexuals are parents. In the homosexual social networks that I am involved in, there are many persons who once played the role of husband and father—generally before they decided they were homosexual (Dank). In addition, there are homosexual couples who are raising children they adopted or children from a former heterosexual marriage; however, such couples tend to be lesbian. In some cases one parent has decided that he or she is homosexual, but both parents have remained together as husband and wife. "Front" marriages also occur, in which a male homosexual marries a female homosexual and they adopt children or have children of their own; such marriages are generally for purposes of social convenience. What the effects are, if any, of being raised by at least one homosexual parent have not been determined. In this sample, there were no cases in which a subject had a homosexual mother or father.

between a person's awareness of homosexual feelings and the decision that he is homosexual is presented in Table 2. As Table 2 indicates, there is considerable variation in this factor.†

The fact that an actor continues to have homosexual feelings and to engage in homosexual behavior does not mean that he views himself as being homosexual. In order for a person to view himself as homosexual he must be placed in a new social context, in which knowledge of homosexuals and homosexuality can be found; in such a context he learns a new vocabulary of motives, a vocabulary that will allow him to identify himself as being a homosexual. This can occur in any number of social contexts—

TABLE 2

Time Interval Between First Homosexual Desire and the
Decision That One Is a Homosexual

| Time Interval (years) | Distribution | |
|---|---|---|
| | N | % |
| 0 | 29 | (16) |
| 1–4 | 66 | (37) |
| 5–9 | 49 | (27) |
| 10–14 | 21 | (12) |
| 15–19 | 7 | (4) |
| 20–29 | 5 | (3) |
| 30–39 | 1 | (0.5) |
| 40–49 | 0 | (0) |
| 50–59 | 1 | (0.5) |
| Total | 179 | (100) |

$$\overline{X}=5.7, \quad S=6.4$$

† First sexual desire toward persons of the same sex was chosen instead of first sexual contact with persons of the same sex since it is quite possible for one to have homosexual desires, fight against those desires, and have no homosexual contacts of any type for an extensive period of time. The mean age of first homosexual contact of any type was thirteen, which was not significantly different at the .01 level from age of first homosexual desire. In reference to which came first, homosexual act or homosexual desire, 31% (56) had desire before the act; 49% (87) had act before desire; 20% (36) had first homosexual desire and first homosexual act at approximately the same time.

through meeting self-admitted homosexuals, by meeting knowledgeable straight persons, or by reading about homosexuals and
homosexuality. Knowledge of homosexuals and homosexuality
can be found in numerous types of physical settings: a bar, a
park, a private home, a psychiatrist's office, a mental hospital,
and so on (see Table 3). It is in contexts where such knowledge
tends to be concentrated that the actor will be most likely to
come out. It is therefore to be expected that an actor is likely to
come out in a context in which other gay people are present; they
are usually a ready and willing source of knowledge concerning
homosexuals and homosexuality. In the questionnaire sample, 50
percent came out while associating with gay people.

It is also to be expected that a likely place for an actor to come
out would be in one-sex situations or institutions. Sexually
segregated environments provide convenient locales for knowl-

TABLE 3

Social Contexts in Which Respondents Came Out

| Social Contexts | $N^*$ | (%) |
|---|---|---|
| Frequenting gay bars | 35 | (19) |
| Frequenting gay parties and other gatherings | 46 | (26) |
| Frequenting parks | 43 | (24) |
| Frequenting men's rooms | 37 | (21) |
| Having a love affair with a homosexual man | 54 | (30) |
| Having a love affair with a heterosexual man | 21 | (12) |
| In the military | 34 | (19) |
| Living in a YMCA | 2 | (1) |
| Living in all-male quarters at a boarding school or college | 12 | (7) |
| In prison | 2 | (1) |
| Patient in a mental hospital | 3 | (2) |
| Seeing a psychiatrist or professional counselor | 11 | (6) |
| Read for the first time about homosexuals and/or homosexuality | 27 | (15) |
| Just fired from a job because of homosexual behavior | 2 | (1) |
| Just arrested on a charge involving homosexuality | 7 | (4) |
| Was not having any homosexual relations | 36 | (20) |

*Total $N$ of social contexts is greater than 180 (number of respondents)
because there was overlap in contexts.

edge of homosexuality and homosexual behavior. Examples of these one-sex environments are mental institutions, YMCAs, prisons, the military, men's rooms, gay bars, and school dormitories. The first six case histories below illustrate the influence of such milieux.

The first example of an actor coming out in the context of interacting with gay persons concerns a subject who came out in a mental hospital. The subject was committed to a mental hospital at age twenty; his commitment did not involve homosexuality and the hospital authorities had no knowledge that the subject had a history of homosexual behavior. Prior to commitment he had a history of heterosexual and homosexual behavior, thought of himself as bisexual, had had no contact with self-admitted homosexuals, was engaged to marry, and was indulging in heavy petting with his fiancée. In the following interview excerpt the subject reports on his first reaction to meeting gay persons in the hospital:

SUBJECT: I didn't know there were so many gay people, and I wasn't use to the actions of gay people or anything, and it was quite shocking walking down the halls, going up to the ward, and the whistles and flirting and everything else that went on with the new fish, as they called it.

And there was this one kid who was a patient escort and he asked me if I was interested in going to church, and I said yes . . . and he started escorting me to church and then he pulled a little sneaky to see whether I'd be shocked at him being gay. There was this queen* on the ward, and him and her, he was looking out the hall to see when I'd walk by the door and they kissed when I walked by the door and this was to check my reaction. And I didn't say a word. So he then escorted me to the show, and we were sitting there and about halfway through the movie he reaches over and started holding my hand, and when he saw I didn't jerk away, which I was kind of upset and wondering exactly what he had in mind, and then when we got back to the ward, he wrote me a long love letter and gave it to me;

---

*In gay argot, the meaning of the term "queen" is variable. Depending on the context it can mean any homosexual or a homosexual on the feminine side.

before we knew it we were going together, and went together for about six months.

[After three weeks] he had gotten me to the point where I'd gotten around the hospital, where I picked up things from the other queens and learned how to really swish and carry on and got to be one of the most popular queens in the whole place. [About that same time] I'd gotten to consider myself—I didn't consider myself a queen. I just considered myself a gay boy; we sat down, a bunch of us got together and made out the rules about what was what as far as the joint was concerned, drew definitions of every little thing ... if someone was completely feminine, wanted to take the female role all the time, then they were a "queen," if they were feminine but butchy, then they were a "nellie-butch," and I was considered a "gay boy" because I could take any role. I was versatile.

INTERVIEWER: Before this bull session were you considering yourself gay?

SUBJECT: Yes, I had definitely gotten to be by this time; after three months my folks came down to see me and I told them the whole thing point blank.

INTERVIEWER: What would you say was the most important effect the hospital had on you?

SUBJECT: It let me find out it wasn't so terrible. . . . I met a lot of gay people that I liked and I figured it can't be all wrong. If so and so's a good Joe, and he's still gay, he can't be all that bad. . . . I figured it couldn't be all wrong, and that's one of the things I learned. I learned to accept myself for what I am—homosexual.

This subject spent a year and a half in the mental hospital. After release he did not engage in heterosexual relations, and has been actively involved in the gay subculture for the past four years.

The above example clearly demonstrates how a one-sex environment can facilitate the development of a homosexual identity. Although some one-sex environments are created for homosexuals, such as gay bars, any one-sex environment can serve as a meeting and recruiting place for homosexuals, whether or not the environment was created with that purpose in mind.

The YMCA is a one-sex environment that inadvertently functions as a meeting place for homosexuals in most large urban areas in the United States.* The following subject came out while living and working at a YMCA. He was twenty-four when he first visited a Y, never had had a homosexual experience, and had just been separated from his wife.

I became separated from my wife. I then decided to go to Eastern City. I had read of the Walter Jenkins case and the name of the YMCA happened to come up, but when I got to the city it was the only place I knew of to stay. I had just $15.00 in my pocket to stay at the Y, and I don't think I ever had the experience before of taking a group shower. So I went into the shower room, that was the first time I remember looking at a man's body and finding it sexually enticing.† So I started wondering to myself—that guy is good-looking. I walked back to my room and left the door open and the guy came in, and I happened to fall in love with that guy.

After this first experience, the subject became homosexually active while living and working at the Y and became part of the gay subculture that existed within the Y.

. . . I found that the kids who were working for me, some of them I had been to bed with and some of them I hadn't, had some horrible problems and trying to decide the right and wrong of homosexuality . . . and they would feel blunt enough or that I had the experience enough to counsel them along the lines of homosexuality or anything else. . . . Part of this helped me realize that one of the greatest things that you can do is to accept what you are and if you want to change it, you can go ahead and do it. . . .

This subject spent six months living in this Y; by the end of three months he had accepted himself as being homosexual and has been exclusively homosexual for the last two years.

---

*YMCAs have not been studied in their relation to homosexual society. It appears that YMCAs function as meeting places for homosexuals and for those desiring homosexual relations but defining themselves as straight. This is not a regional phenomenon but is, according to my informants, true for almost all YMCAs in large metropolitan areas. YMCAs are often listed in gay tourist guides.

†This subject later admitted that he had previously been attracted to other males.

The prison is another one-sex environment in which homosexual behavior is concentrated. Although there have been studies of situational homosexuality in prison (Giallombardo, 1966; Sykes, 1957; Tittle, 1969; Ward and Kassebaum, 1965), and of how homosexual activities are structured in prison, there have been no studies that have looked at the possible change of the sexual identity of the prisoner. In the following case the subject was sentenced to prison on a charge of sodomy at the age of thirty-two, and spent five years in prison. He had been homosexually active for twenty-two years, and before his arrest he had been engaging predominantly in homosexual behavior, but he had not defined himself as being a homosexual. He had had only peripheral contacts with the gay subculture before his arrest, largely because he was married and held a high socioeconomic position.

INTERVIEWER: In prison did you meet homosexuals?
SUBJECT: Yes.
INTERVIEWER: I'm not talking about people who are just homosexual while in prison.
SUBJECT: People who are homosexual, period. I became educated about the gay world, how you can meet people and not lay yourself open to censure, and how to keep from going to prison again. And still go on being homosexual. While in prison I definitely accepted myself as being homosexual. . . . I had frequent meetings with psychiatrists, various social workers. We were all pretty much in tacit agreement that the best thing to do would be to learn to live with yourself. Up until then, I rationalized and disillusioned myself about a lot of things. As I look back on it, I was probably homosexual from ten years on.

After his release from prison, this subject became involved in the gay subculture and has been exclusively homosexual for the last eight years.

The military is a one-sex environment that is a most conducive setting for homosexual behavior. In the military, a large number of young men live in close contact with one another and are deprived of heterosexual contacts for varying periods of time; it is not surprising that a homosexual subculture would arise. Given the young age of the military population, it should also be expected that a certain proportion of men would be entering military service with homosexual desires and/or a history of homosexual behavior, but without a clearly formulated homosexual identity. Approximately 19 percent of the sample came out while in military service. The following subject had a history of homosexual desires and behavior previous to joining the navy, but came out while in military service.

INTERVIEWER: How did you happen to have homosexual relations while in the navy?

SUBJECT: We were out at sea and I had heard that one of the dental technicians was a homosexual, and he had made advances toward me, and I felt like masturbation really wouldn't solve the problem so I visited him one night. He started talking about sex and everything. I told him I had never kissed a boy before. And he asked me what would you do if a guy kissed you, and I said you mean like this and I began kissing him. Naturally he took over then. . . . There were other people on the ship that were homosexual and they talked about me. A yeoman aboard ship liked me quite a bit, was attracted to me; so he started making advances toward me, and I found him attractive, so we got together, and in a short period of time, we became lovers. He started to take me to the gay bars and explain what homosexuality was all about. He took me to gay bars when we were in port.

INTERVIEWER: Did you start to meet other gay people aboard ship?

SUBJECT: The first real contact with gay people was aboard ship. . . .

INTERVIEWER: Was it while you were in the navy that you decided you were a homosexual?

SUBJECT: Yes. Once I was introduced to gay life, I made the decision that I was a homosexual.

Public rest rooms, another part of society which is sexually segregated, are known in the gay world as T-rooms, and some T-rooms become known as meeting places for gay persons and others who are looking for homosexual contacts (Humphreys, 1970). Sex in T-rooms tends to be anonymous, but since some nonsexual social interaction also occurs in this locale, some homosexuals do come out in T-rooms. In the sample studied here 21 percent came out while frequenting T-rooms for sexual purposes. The following subject came out in the context of going to T-rooms when he was fifteen. Previously he had been homosexually active, but had not thought of himself as being a homosexual.

I really didn't know what a homosexual was. In the back of my mind, my definition of a homosexual or queer was someone who wore girls' clothes and women's shoes, 'cause my brothers said this was so, and I knew I wasn't.

At the age of fifteen this subject had a sexual relationship with a gay man.

And he took me out and introduced me to the gay world. I opened the door and I went out and it was a beautiful day and I accepted this whole world, and I've never had any guilt feelings or hang-ups or regrets. . . . I was young and fairly attractive and I had men chasing me all the time. . . . He didn't take me to bars. We went to rest rooms, that was my outlet. He started taking me to all the places they refer to in the gay world as T-rooms, and I met other people and I went back there myself and so on.

After meeting other gay persons by going to T-rooms, this subject quickly discovered other segments of the gay world and has been exclusively homosexual for the last nine years.

Gay bars are probably the most widespread and well-known gay institutions (Achilles, 1967; Hooker, 1965). For many persons who become homosexual, gay bars are the first contact with organized gay society and therefore a likely place to come out. In this sample 19 percent came out while going to gay bars. Since gay bars apparently are widespread throughout the nation, this could be viewed as a surprisingly low percentage. However, it should be remembered that generally the legal age limit for entering bars is twenty-one. If the age limit is enforced, this would reduce the percentage of persons coming out in gay bars. T-rooms and gay private parties and other gatherings perform the same function as gay bars, but are not hampered by any age limit. Thus, it is not really surprising that the percentages of persons who came out in several other ways are higher than the percentage coming out in gay bars.

The following subject came out in the context of going to gay bars. He had been predominantly homosexual for a number of years and was twenty-three at the time he came out.

SUBJECT: I knew that there were homosexuals, queers and what not; I had read some books, and I was resigned to the fact that I was a foul, dirty person, but I wasn't actually calling myself a homosexual yet. . . . I went to this guy's house and there was nothing going on, and I asked him, "Where is some action?" and he said, "There is a bar down the way." And the time I really caught myself coming out is the time I walked into this bar and saw a whole crowd of groovy, groovy guys. And I said to myself, there was the realization, that not all gay men are dirty old men or idiots, silly queens, but there are some just normal-looking and acting people, as far as I could see. I saw gay society and I said, "Wow, I'm home."

INTERVIEWER: This was the first time that you walked into this gay bar that you felt this way?

SUBJECT: That's right. It was that night in the bar. I think it saved my sanity. I'm sure it saved my sanity.

This subject has been exclusively homosexually active for the last thirteen years.

Even after an introduction to gay bars, labeling oneself as homosexual does not always occur as rapidly as it did in the previous example. Some persons can still, for varying periods of time, differentiate themselves from the people they are meeting in gay bars. The following subject came out when he was twenty-two; he had been predominantly homosexual before coming out. He interacted with gay people in gay bars for several months before he decided he was a homosexual. He attempted to differentiate himself from the other homosexuals by saying to himself, "I am not really homosexual since I am not as feminine as they are."

Finally after hanging around there for so long, some guy came up to me and tried to take me for some money, and I knew it, and he said, "You know, you're very nellie."* And I said I wasn't, and he said, "Yes, you are, and you might as well face facts and that's the way it is,

---

* In gay argot, "nellie" means feminine or feminine-appearing. The word is not usually used in a complimentary manner.

and you're never going to change." And I said, "If that's the case, then that's the way it's going to be." So I finally capitulated.

This subject has been predominantly homosexually active for the last twenty-one years.

It should be made clear that such a change in sexual identity need not be accompanied by any change in sexual behavior or any participation in homosexual behavior. It is theoretically possible for someone to view himself as being homosexual but not engage in homosexual relations just as it is possible for someone to view himself as heterosexual but not engage in heterosexual relations. Approximately 20 percent of this sample came out while having no homosexual relations. The following subject is one of this group; he came out during his late twenties even though he had had his last homosexual experience at age twenty.

I picked up a copy of this underground newspaper one day just for the fun of it . . . and I saw an ad in there for this theater, and after thinking about it I got up enough nerve to go over there. . . . I knew that they had pictures of boys and I had always liked boys, and I looked at the neighborhood and then I came home without going in. . . . I went back to the neighborhood again and this time I slunk, and I do mean slunk through the door . . . and I was shocked to see what I saw on the screen, but I found it interesting and stimulating and so I went back several more times.

Eventually this subject bought a copy of a gay publication, and subsequently he went to the publication's office.

I visited with the fellows in the office and I had time on my hands and I volunteered to help and they were glad to have me. And I have been a member of the staff ever since and it was that way that I got my education of what gay life is like. . . . For the last ten years, I had been struggling against it. Back then if I knew what homosexuality was, if I had been exposed to the community . . . and seen the better parts, I probably would have admitted it then.

This subject has been very active socially but not sexually in the gay subculture for the last year.

In contrast to the previous examples, there are cases in which the subject has no direct contact with any gay persons, but yet comes out in that context. Fifteen percent (twenty-seven) of the sample came out upon first reading about homosexuals or homosexuality in a book, pamphlet, etc.; ten of these (about 6 percent of the sample) were not associating with gay people at the time they came out. The following subject came out in this context. He was fourteen at the time, had just ended a homosexual relationship with a person who considered himself to be straight, and had had no contact with gay society.

I had always heard like kids do about homosexuals and things, but that never really entered my mind, but when I read this article, when I was in the eighth grade, and it had everything in it about them sexually, not how they looked and acted and where they go. It was about me and that was what I was thinking. I just happen one day to see a picture of a guy, and thought he was kind of cute, so I'll read the article about him. But before that I didn't realize what was happening. I didn't even realize I wasn't right as far as heterosexuals were concerned. I didn't realize that what I was thinking wasn't kosher. . . . If people don't like it I'll keep my mouth shut. The article said people wouldn't like it, so I decided to keep my mouth shut. That's the way I was, so I accepted it.

This subject has been active sexually and socially in the gay subculture for the last five years.

Another context in which a subject can come out is that of having a homosexual relationship with a person who defines himself as being heterosexual; 12 percent (twenty-one) of the sample came out in such a context. Of these, twelve (about 7 percent of the sample) had never met any self-admitted homosexuals and had never read any material on homosexuality. The following case involves a subject who came out in such a context. At the age of twenty-one he was having an intense love affair with a serviceman who defined himself as straight. The subject also became involved in a triangular relationship with the serviceman's female lover.

This got very serious. I told him I loved him. . . . He wanted me for a sex release; I didn't admit it then, but now I see, through much heartbreak. He liked me as a person. . . . At the same time he was dating a married woman; he was dating her and having sex with her. . . . She couldn't admit to having a relationship with him 'cause she was married, but he told me and I was extremely jealous of her. [We worked together] and privately she was a very good friend of mine. So I started feeling hatred toward her because she was coming between he and I, competition. I was strong competition, 'cause I frankly dominated it, and she sensed this; so one day she said, "I bet he'd be very good in bed." So I said, "You know he is." She said, "What did you say?" and I said, "Oh, I guess he would be." And I wanted to tell her; so I finally acted like I just broke down and I told her everything in order to make her not like him. So she got on his tail and told him to stop seeing me or she wouldn't have anything to do with him. . . . I taped all their phone conversations and told her if she wouldn't leave him alone, I'd play them for her husband. She got furious, so she said if I tried to blackmail her she would go to the police with the whole thing . . . it all backfired on me and I really didn't want to hurt her, but my love for him was so strong; I'd hurt anybody to keep him, so I erased the tape. And later I bawled and bawled and cried about it to her because I was very sensitive at this time and I told her I was sorry, didn't want to hurt her, but I loved him so much. . . . After I fell in love with him I knew I was homosexual. I talked to my brother about it and he said I wasn't really in love. He said you're just doing it cause you want to; it's not right, boys don't fall in love with boys. He wasn't nasty about it. . . . I really loved him; he was my first love; I even dream about him once in a while to this very day. . . . It was during this time that I came out, and I was extremely feminine, not masculine in any way. I wore male clothing, but dressed in a feminine way, in the way I carried myself, the way I spoke. . . . I realized that I was homosexual because I loved him. I was afraid of gay people; heard they did all kinds of weird things from straight people talking about them.

Before this relationship, the subject had engaged in both homosexual and heterosexual petting. Shortly after the relationship terminated the subject became involved in the gay subculture and has been almost exclusively homosexual since that time.

## COGNITIVE CHANGE

What is common to all the cases discussed is that the subject placed himself in a new cognitive category (McCall and Simmons, 1966), the category of homosexual. In some cases, such placement can occur as soon as the person learns of the existence of the category; an example of this is the boy who placed himself in that category after reading about homosexuals in a magazine. However, probably most persons who eventually identify themselves as homosexuals require a change in the meaning of the cognitive category *homosexual* before they can place themselves in the category.

The meaning of the category must be changed because the subject has learned the negative stereotype of the homosexual held by most heterosexuals, and he knows that he is no queer, pervert, dirty old man, and so on (Simmons, 1965). He differentiates himself from the homosexual image that straight society has presented to him. Direct or indirect contact with the gay subculture provides the subject with information about homosexuals that will challenge the "straight" image of the homosexual. The subject will quite often see himself in other homosexuals, homosexuals he finds to be socially acceptable. He now knows who and what he is because the meaning of the cognitive category has changed to include himself. As one subject said: "Wow, I'm home"; at times that is literally the case since the homosexual now feels that he knows where he really belongs.

A person's identification of himself as being homosexual is often accompanied by a sense of relief, of freedom from tension. In the words of one subject:

I had this feeling of relief; there was no more tension. I had this feeling of relief. I guess the fact that I had accepted myself as being homosexual had taken a lot of tensions off me.

Coming out, in essence, often signifies to the subject the end of a search for his identity.

## IDENTIFICATION AND SELF-ACCEPTANCE

Identifying oneself as being homosexual and accepting oneself as being homosexual usually come together, but this is not necessarily the case. It can be hypothesized that those who identify themselves as being homosexual but not in the context of interacting with other homosexuals are more likely to have guilt feelings than those who identify themselves as being homosexual in the context of interacting with other homosexuals. Interaction with other homosexuals facilitates the learning of a vocabulary that will not simply explain but will also justify the homosexual behavior.

Identifying oneself as homosexual is almost uniformly accompanied by the development of certain techniques of neutralization (Sykes and Matza, 1957).* In this self-identification, it would be incorrect to state that the homosexual accepts himself as being deviant, in the evaluative sense of the term. The subject may know he is deviant from the societal standpoint but often does not accept this as part of his self-definition. Lemert (1951) has defined secondary deviation as the situation in which "... a person begins to employ his deviant behavior or a role based upon it as a means of defense, attack or adjustment to the overt and covert problems created by the consequent societal reaction to him" (p. 76). Once the subject identifies himself as being homosexual, he does develop means, often in the process of the change in self-definition, of adjusting to the societal reaction to the behavior. The means employed usually involve the denial, to himself and to others, that he is really deviant. Becker (1963) explained the situation when he stated:

But the person thus labeled an outsider may have a different view of the matter. He may not accept the rule by which he is being judged and may not regard those who judge him as either competent or legitimately entitled to do so [pp. 1–2].

The societal reaction to homosexuality appears to be ex-

---

* Particularly, denial that there is a victim and denial of injury.

pressed more in a mental health rhetoric (Bieber et al., 1965; Hadden, 1967; Ovesey, 1969; Socarides, 1970; Szasz, 1970) than in a rhetoric of sin and evil or crime and criminal behavior. In order to determine how the subjects adjusted to this societal reaction to homosexuality, they were asked to react to the idea that homosexuals are sick or mentally ill. With very few exceptions, this notion was rejected.

SUBJECT 1: I believe this idea to be very much true, if added that you are talking from society's standpoint and society has to ask itself why are these people sick or mentally ill. . . . In other words, you can't make flat statements that homosexuals are sick or mentally ill. I do not consider myself to be sick or mentally imbalanced.

SUBJECT 2: That's a result of ignorance; people say that quickly, pass quick judgments. They are not knowledgeable, fully knowledgeable about the situation.

SUBJECT 3: I don't feel they are. I feel it's normal. What's normal for one person is not always normal for another. I don't think it's a mental illness or mental disturbance.

SUBJECT 4: Being a homosexual does not label a person as sick or mentally ill. In every other capacity I am as normal or more normal than straight people. Just because I happen to like strawberry ice cream and they like vanilla, doesn't make them right or me right.

It is the learning of various ideas from other homosexuals that allows the subject to in effect say, "I am homosexual, but not deviant," or, "I am homosexual, but not mentally ill." The cognitive category of *homosexual* now becomes socially acceptable, and the subject can place himself in that category and yet preserve a sense of his self-esteem or self-worth.

It should be emphasized that coming out often involves an entire transformation in the meaning of the concept of homosexual for the subject. In these cases the subject had been entirely unaware of the existence of gay bars or an organized gay society, of economically successful homosexuals, of homosexually "married" homosexuals, and so on. In the words of one subject:

I had always thought of them as dirty old men that preyed on ten-, eleven-, twelve-year-old kids, and I found out that they weren't all that way; there are some that are, but they are a minority. It was a relief for me 'cause I found out that I wasn't so different from many other people. I had considered consulting professional help prior to that 'cause at the time I thought I was mentally ill. Now I accept it as a way of life, and I don't consider it a mental illness. It's an unfortunate situation. . . . I consider myself an outcast from general society, but not mentally ill.

## PUBLIC LABELING

It should be made clear that the self-identification as a homosexual does not generally take place in the context of a negative public labeling, as some labeling theorists imply that it does (Garfinkel, 1956; Lemert, 1951; Scheff, 1966). No cases were found in the interview sample in which the subject had come out in the context of being arrested on a charge involving homosexuality or being fired from a job because of homosexual behavior. In the questionnaire sample, 4 percent (seven) had just been arrested and 1 percent (two) had just been fired from a job. A total of eight respondents or 4.5 percent of the sample came out in the context of public exposure.

It can be hypothesized that the public labeling of an actor who has not yet identified himself as being homosexual will reinforce in his mind the idea that he is not homosexual. This is hypothesized because it is to be expected that at the time of the public labeling the actor will be presented with information that will present homosexuals and homosexuality in a highly negative manner. For example, the following subject was arrested for homosexual activities at the age of eleven. Both before and after the arrest he did not consider himself to be a homosexual. His reaction to the arrest was:

SUBJECT: The officer talked to me and told me I should see a psychiatrist. It kind of confused me. I really didn't understand any of it.

INTERVIEWER: And were you thinking of yourself at that time as a homosexual?

SUBJECT: I probably would have said I wasn't. 'Cause of the way the officer who interrogated me acted. It was something you never admit to. He acted as if I were the scum of the earth. He was very rude and impolite.

If the actor has not yet identified himself as being homosexual, it can probably be assumed that to a significant degree he already accepts the negative societal stereotype; the new information accompanying the public labeling will conform to the societal stereotype, and the actor consequently will not modify his decision not to place himself in the homosexual category. This is not to say that public labeling by significant others and/or official agents of social control does not play a significant role in the life of the homosexual; all that is hypothesized is that public labeling does not facilitate and may in fact function to inhibit the decision to label oneself as being homosexual.

### THE CLOSET QUEEN

There are some persons who may continue to have homosexual desires and may possibly engage in homosexual relations for many years, but yet do not have a homosexual identity. Self-admitted homosexuals refer to such persons as "closet queens."* Such persons may go for many years without any contact with or knowledge of self-admitted homosexuals. The subject previously cited who came out in prison was a closet queen for twenty years.

An interval of ten or more years between first awareness of sexual attraction toward males and the decision that one is a homosexual would probably classify one as having been a closet queen. As Table 2 shows, the questionnaire sample included thirty-five respondents (20 percent of the sample) who at one time were closet queens.

It is the closet queen who has most internalized the negative

---

* In gay argot, the meaning of the term "closet queen" varies, but usually it is applied to one who does not admit to being homosexual. However, the term is sometimes used to refer to a self-admitted homosexual who does not like to associate with other homosexuals, or who may be trying to pass as being straight most of the twenty-four hours of the day

societal stereotype of the homosexual. It is to be expected that such persons would suffer from a feeling of psychological tension, for they are in a state of cognitive dissonance (Festinger, 1957)—that is, feelings and sometimes behavior are not consistent with self-definition.

The following subject was a closet queen for over fifty years. He had his first homosexual experience at the age of twelve, has had homosexual desires since that time, and has been exclusively homosexual for fifty-three years. At the time the subject was interviewed, he expressed amazement that he had just come out during the last few months. Over the years, his involvement with the gay subculture was peripheral; at the age of twenty-nine, for about one year, he had some involvement with overt homosexuals, but otherwise he had had only slight contact with them until recently. During that earlier involvement:

I was not comfortable with them. I was repressed and timid and they thought I was being high hat, so I was rejected. It never worked out; I was never taken in. I felt uncomfortable in their presence and I made them feel uncomfortable. I couldn't fit in there, I never wanted to, never sought to; I was scared of them. I was scared of the brazen bitches who would put me down.

During the years as a closet queen he was plagued with feelings of guilt; for varying periods of time he was a patient in over twenty mental hospitals. His social life was essentially nil; he had neither gay friends nor straight friends. His various stays in mental hospitals relieved continuing feelings of loneliness. At the age of sixty-five he attended a church whose congregation was primarily homosexual. It was in the context of interacting with the gay persons who were associated with this church that after fifty-three years this subject came out.

SUBJECT: I had never seen so many queens in one place; I was scared somebody would put me down, somebody would misunderstand why I was there. I had this vague, indescribable fear. But all this was washed away when I saw all were there for the one purpose of fellowship and community in the true sense of the term. . . . I kept going and then I got to be comfortable in the coffee hour. . . . Then out in the lobby a young fellow opened his heart to me, telling me all his troubles and so forth, and I listened patiently, and I thought I made a couple of comforting remarks. Then I went out to the car, and when I got in the car I put my hand out to shake hands and he kissed my hand . . . it's hard for you to understand the emotional impact of something like this—that I belong, they love me, I love them.

Until the last few weeks, in all my life I had never been in a gay bar for more than a few minutes, I was acutely uncomfortable. But now I can actually go into it; this is the most utterly ludicrous transformation in the last few weeks . . . there's no logic whatsoever. I'm alive at sixty-five.

It's a tremendous emotional breakthrough. I feel comfortable and relieved of tensions and self-consciousness. My effectiveness in other fields has been enhanced 100 percent. I have thrown off so many of the prejudices and revulsions that were below the surface. . . . I'm out of the closet. In every way, they know, where I work, in this uptight place where I work; I've told them where I live; I've written back east. What more can I do?

INTERVIEWER: Do you think you are now more self-accepting of yourself?

SUBJECT: Brother! I hope you're not kidding. That's the whole bit. How ironical it would come at sixty-five. The only thing that I wouldn't do now is to go to the baths. I told the kids the other day; it's the only breakthrough I cannot bring myself to.

One can only speculate why after all these years this subject came out. The reason may have been that he had had a very religious upbringing and could not conceive of homosexuals in a religiously acceptable manner. The church he attended for the first time at age sixty-five presented homosexuals as being religiously acceptable, and presented to the subject highly religious homosexuals.* Contact with this church may have helped change the meaning of the category homosexual so that he could now include himself.†

---

* It may be that among closet queens, or those who have been closet queens for many years, one would find a disproportionately high number of very religious persons; the traditional negative religious reaction would probably prevent highly religious persons from easily placing themselves in the homosexual category. It would therefore be expected that clergymen have a more

In a sense the closet queen represents society's ideal homosexual, for the closet queen accepts the societal stereotype of the homosexual and feels guilt because he does the same sort of things that homosexuals do, yet believes he is really different from homosexuals in some significant way. This inability of the closet queen to see himself in other homosexuals prevents him from placing himself in the cognitive category of *homosexual*, and he will not come out until some new information is given to him about homosexuals which permits him to say, "There are homosexuals like myself" or "I am very much like them."

There may be significant differences between ex-closet queens and those closet queens who never come out. Of course, I had contact only with ex-closet queens, and they uniformly reported that their own psychological adjustment has been much better since coming out. Their only regret was that they had not come out sooner. Possibly the closet queen who remains a closet queen reaches some sort of psychological adjustment that ex-closet queens were unable to reach.

**THE ROLE OF KNOWLEDGE**

The change of self-identity to *homosexual* is intimately related to the access of knowledge and information concerning homosexuals and homosexuality. Hoffman (1968) has observed:

---

difficult time in resolving problems of guilt, but also interaction with other homosexuals could lead to their losing their jobs. In this sample, there were ten respondents who were ministers or who were studying for the ministry at the time they came out. Their mean age for coming out was twenty-two, and the mean time interval between first homosexual desire and the homosexual self-identification was 10.4 years. I hope to publish a report in the near future on the social life of homosexual ministers.

† There have been some recent actions that challenge the traditional religious reaction against homosexuality and homosexuals. Particularly, see: John Dart, "Church for Homosexuals," *Los Angeles Times*, December 8, 1969, Part 2, pp. 1–3; Edward B. Fiske, "Homosexuals in Los Angeles . . . Establish Their Own Church," *New York Times*, February 15, 1970, Sec. 1, p. 58; "The Homosexual Church," *Newsweek*, October 12, 1970, p. 107. Some churches have openly accepted homosexuals; I am currently preparing an article on such a church.

Society deals with homosexuality as if it did not exist. Although the situation is changing, this subject was not even discussed and was not even the object of scientific investigation until a few decades ago. We just didn't speak about these things; they were literally unspeakable and so loathsome that nothing could be said in polite society about them ... [p. 195].

The traditional silence on this topic has most probably prevented many persons with homosexual feelings from identifying themselves as being homosexual. Lofland (1969) has noted that the role of knowledge in creating a deviant identity is an important one. If significant others or the actor himself does not know of the deviant category, his experience cannot be interpreted in terms of that category; or if his experience appears to be completely alien from that category he will not interpret his experience in terms of that category. If the societal stereotype of homosexuals is one of dirty old men, perverts, Communists, and so on, it should not be surprising that the young person with homosexual feelings would have difficulty in interpreting his experience in terms of the homosexual category.

The greater tolerance of society for the freer circulation of information concerning homosexuality and homosexuals has definite implications in reference to coming out. The fact that there is greater overt circulation of homophile magazines and homophile newspapers, that there are advertisements for gay movies in newspapers, and that there are books, articles, and movies about gay life, permits the cognitive category of homosexuals to be known to a larger proportion of the population and, most important, permits more information to be circulated that challenges the negative societal stereotype of the homosexual.

Since there has been a freer circulation of information on homosexuality during the past few years, it can be hypothesized that the development of a homosexual identity is now occurring at an increasingly earlier age. Indeed, older gay informants have stated that the younger homosexuals are coming out at a much earlier age. In order to test this hypothesis, the sample was dichotomized into a thirty-and-above age group and a below-thirty age group. It can be seen in Table 4 that the below-thirty mean age for developing a homosexual identity was significantly lower (at the .01 level) than the above-thirty mean age; the drop in mean age was from approximately twenty-one to seventeen.*

Indications are that the present trend toward greater circulation of information that is not highly negative about homosexuals and homosexuality will continue. The fact that a mass circulation magazine such as *Time* gave its front cover to an article entitled "The Homosexual in America" (October 31, 1969) and that this article was not highly negative represents a

TABLE 4

Relationship of Respondent Age to Age
at Homosexual Self-Identification

| Age at Homosexual Self-Identification | Age of Respondents | | | |
|---|---|---|---|---|
| | 30 and above | | Below 30 | |
| | N | (%) | N | (%) |
| 5–9 | 0 | (0) | 1 | (1) |
| 10–14 | 8 | (9) | 19 | (22) |
| 15–19 | 35 | (38) | 44 | (50) |
| 20–24 | 29 | (32) | 23 | (21) |
| 25–29 | 10 | (11) | 1 | (1) |
| 30–39 | 7 | (8) | 0 | (0) |
| 40–49 | 1 | (1) | 0 | (0) |
| 50–59 | 0 | (0) | 0 | (0) |
| 60–69 | 1 | (1) | 0 | (0) |
| Total | 91 | (100) | 88 | (100) |
| Mean | 21.4* | | 17.2* | |
| Standard Deviation | 7.7 | | 3.8 | |

* It can be argued that this was not a meaningful test because of sample bias, since the sample could not include subjects of the younger generation who had still not come out. However, the age of thirty was chosen as the dividing point because only nine respondents (5%) had come out after the age of thirty. Any remaining bias in the sample from this source should presumably be insignificant.

*Means significantly different at .01 level.

significant breakthrough. The cognitive category of homosexual is now being presented in a not unfavorable manner to hundreds of thousands of people who previously could not have been exposed to such information through conventional channels. This is not to say that more information about homosexuals and homosexuality will lead to a significantly greater prevalence of persons engaging in homosexuality. What is being asserted is that a higher proportion of those with homosexual desires and behavior will develop a homosexual identity, and that the development of that identity will continue to occur at an increasingly younger age.

## CONCLUSION

This study has suggested that the development of a homosexual identity is dependent on the meanings that the actor attaches to the concepts of homosexual and homosexuality, and that these meanings are directly related to the meanings that are available in his immediate environment; and the meanings that are available in his immediate environment are related to the meanings that are allowed to circulate in the wider society. The commitment to a homosexual identity cannot occur in an environment where the cognitive category of homosexual does not exist. Hoffman (1968) in essence came to the same conclusion when he hypothesized that the failure to develop a homosexual identity is due to a combination of two factors:

... the failure of society to make people aware of homosexuality as an existent way of life (and of the existence of the gay world), and the strong repressive forces that prevent people from knowing what their real sexual feelings are. One might consider this a psychological conspiracy of silence, which society insists upon because of its belief that it thereby safeguards existent sexual norms [p. 138].

In an environment where the cognitive category of homosexual does not exist or is presented in a highly negative manner, a person who is sexually attracted to persons of the same sex will probably be viewed and will probably view himself as sick, mentally ill, or queer.

It can be asserted that one of the main functions of the viewpoint that homosexuality is mental illness is to inhibit the development of a homosexual identity. The *homosexuality-as-mental-illness* viewpoint is now in increasing competition with the *homosexuality-as-way-of-life* viewpoint. If the homosexuality-as-way-of-life viewpoint is increasingly disseminated, one would anticipate that the problems associated with accepting a homosexual identity will significantly decrease, there will be a higher proportion of homosexually oriented people with a homosexual identity, and this identity will develop at an earlier age.*

If the homosexuality-as-way-of-life philosophy does become increasingly accepted, the nature of the homosexual community itself may undergo a radical transformation. To have a community one must have members who will acknowledge to themselves and to others that they are members of that community. The increasing circulation of the homosexuality-as-way-of-life viewpoint may in fact be a self-fulfilling prophecy. It may lead to, and possibly is leading to, the creation of a gay community in which one's sex life is becoming increasingly less fragmented from the rest of one's social life.

## REFERENCES

ACHILLES, NANCY. "The Development of the Homosexual Bar as an Institution." In John H. Gagnon and William Simon, eds., *Sexual Deviance*. New York: Harper & Row, 1967.

BECKER, HOWARD S. *Outsiders: Studies in the Sociology of Deviance*. New York: Free Press, 1963.

BERGLER, E. *Neurotic Counterfeit-Sex*. New York: Grune & Stratton, 1951.

BIEBER, IRVING, et al. *Homosexuality: A Psychoanalytic Study of Male Homosexuals*. New York: Vintage Books, 1965.

CORY, DONALD W. *The Homosexual in America*. New York: Greenberg, 1951.

---

* Weinberg (1970) has recently reported that younger homosexuals have on the whole a worse psychological adjustment than older homosexuals. As the age for the development of a homosexual identity drops, the psychological adjustment of younger homosexuals may significantly improve.

DANK, BARRY M. "Why Homosexuals Marry Women." In *Medical Aspects of Human Sexuality* 6, no. 8 (August 1972): 14–23.

FESTINGER, LEON. *Theory of Cognitive Dissonance.* New York: Harper & Row, 1957.

FREUD, SIGMUND. *Three Contributions to the Theory of Sex.* New York: Dutton, 1962.

GAGNON, JOHN H., and WILLIAM SIMON. "Homosexuality: The Formulation of a Sociological Perspective." In Mark Lefton et al., eds., *Approaches to Deviance.* New York: Appleton-Century-Crofts, 1968.

GARFINKEL, HAROLD. "Conditions of Successful Degradation Ceremonies." *American Journal of Sociology* 61 (1956): 420–424.

GEBHARD, PAUL, et al. *Sex Offenders: An Analysis of Types.* New York: Hoeber-Harper, 1965.

GIALLOMBARDO, ROSE. *Society of Women: A Study of a Women's Prison.* New York: Wiley, 1966.

HADDEN, SAMUEL B. "A Way Out for Homosexuals." *Harper's Magazine,* March 1967, pp. 107–20.

HOFFMAN, MARTIN. *The Gay World: Male Homosexuality and the Social Creation of Evil.* New York: Basic Books, 1968.

"Homosexual in America, The." *Time,* Oct. 31, 1969, p. 56.

HOOKER, EVELYN. "Male Homosexuals and Their 'Worlds.' " In Judd Marmor, ed., *Sexual Inversion: The Multiple Roots of Homosexuality.* New York: Basic Books, 1965.

————. "Parental Relations and Male Homosexuality in Patient and Non-Patient Samples." *Journal of Consulting and Clinical Psychology* 33 (1969): 140–42.

HUMPHREYS, LAUD. *Tearoom Trade: Impersonal Sex in Public Places.* Chicago: Aldine, 1970.

KRICH, A. M., ed. *The Homosexuals.* Secaucus, N.J.: Citadel Press, 1954.

LEMERT, EDWIN M. *Social Pathology.* New York: McGraw-Hill, 1951.

LOFLAND, JOHN. *Deviance and Identity.* Englewood Cliffs, N.J.: Prentice-Hall, 1969.

McCALL, C. J., and J. L. SIMMONS. *Identities and Interactions.* New York: Free Press, 1966.

MERTON, ROBERT K. *Social Theory and Social Structure*. Rev. ed. New York: Free Press, 1957.

OVESEY, LIONEL. *Homosexuality and Pseudohomosexuality*. New York: Science House, 1969.

POLSKY, NED. *Hustlers, Beats and Others*. Chicago: Aldine, 1967.

RUITENBEEK, HENDRIK, ed. *The Problem of Homosexuality in Modern Society*. New York: Dutton, 1963.

SCHEFF, THOMAS. *Being Mentally Ill*. Chicago: Aldine, 1966.

SCHOFIELD, MICHAEL. *Sociological Aspects of Homosexuality*. Boston: Little, Brown, 1965.

SIMMONS, J. L. "Public Stereotypes of Deviants." *Social Problems* 13 (1965): 223–32.

SOCARIDES, CHARLES W. "Homosexuality and Medicine." *Journal of American Medical Association* 212 (1970): 1199–1202.

STOLLER, ROBERT. *Sex and Gender*. New York: Science House, 1968.

SYKES, GRESHAM M. *Society of Captives*. Princeton, N.J.: Princeton University Press, 1958.

———, and DAVID MATZA. "Techniques of Neutralization: A Theory of Delinquency." *American Sociological Review* 22 (1957): 664–70.

SZASZ, THOMAS. *The Manufacture of Madness*. New York: Harper & Row, 1970.

TITTLE, CHARLES R. "Inmate Organization: Sex Differentiation and the Influence of Criminal Subcultures." *American Sociological Review 34* (1969): 492–505.

WARD, DAVID A., and GENE G. KASSEBAUM. *Women's Prison: Sex and Social Structure*. Chicago: Aldine, 1965.

WEINBERG, MARTIN S. "The Male Homosexual: Age-Related Variations in Social and Psychological Characteristics." *Social Problems* 17 (1970): 527–37.

WEST, DONALD J. "Parental Figures in the Genesis of Male Homosexuality." *International Journal of Social Psychiatry* 5 (1959): 85–97.

WESTWOOD, GORDON. *A Minority: A Report on the Life of the Male Homosexual in Great Britain*. London: Longmans, Green, 1960.

# Exodus and Identity: The Emerging Gay Culture

## LAUD HUMPHREYS

### THE CLOSET CULTURE OF THE SIXTIES

Describing the world of homosexuals as "an impoverished cultural unit," Simon and Gagnon (1967) point out that "in contrast to ethnic and occupational subcultures the homosexual community, as well as other deviant subcommunities, has very limited content. This derives from the fact that the community members often have only their sexual commitment in common." Others who did research on the gay world before 1970 (Hoffman, 1968; Sagarin/Cory, 1969; West, 1967) or in relatively small and isolated communities (Lindquist, 1976) reached similar conclusions:

The homosexual is caught up in a world in which there are no guides for conduct. Homosexuality in America is an anomic situation. The individual doesn't know what to do; there are no structures of social rules to help govern his behavior [Hoffman, 1968:195].

Leaving aside the question of whether any cultural subdivision can be said to be totally lacking in rules governing behavior, it is understandable that observers of a decade ago might have interpreted the gay world as relatively impoverished or anomic. At least to the outsider, that community appeared as little more than a clandestine confederation of sexual marketplaces.

Seen as the central institution of the homosexual subculture (Hooker, 1965), the gay bar was characterized as transitory, requiring payoffs to the police, and subjected to frequent raids (Achilles, 1967). Sympathetic observers, such as Churchill (1967), saw them as "little worlds" that were "restricting" although essential as refuges from social oppression. Less sympathetic writers emphasized the predatory cruising patterns and the effeminacy of gay bar patrons (Stearn, 1962). These institutions were the shabby, nocturnal clues to a world that was largely hidden from public view. With gay bars as the nicotine-encrusted windows through which outsiders peeked at the homosexual world, it is little wonder that only stereotypical images were seen.

With coverage of gay events and concerns excluded from the mass media, communication between members of the hidden group was limited to underground newspapers and quarterlies with tiny circulations, in addition to the oral transmission of the grapevine. The latter was characterized as "bitchy" and dominated by gossip and rumor. Gay bookstores were no more than specialized erotica shops; and, apart from the "muscle mags," literature directed to or about homosexuals would have done well to fill a two-foot bookshelf.

It is shocking to look back on the books available before 1965, the year in which I began work on my doctorate: three volumes by Donald Webster Cory, a handful of psychoanalytic studies, Peter Wildeblood's *Against the Law,* Stearn's *The Sixth Man,* Ruitenbeek's *The Problem of Homosexuality in Modern Society.* At the time, I thought of all but the psychoanalytic works as relatively "advanced, liberal, and positive"; but their contents now appear surprisingly negative, replete with stereotypical descriptions of the gay world. Even the homosexual authors were given to self-loathing commentary on the tragedy of gay life.

Analyzed as "deviants," homosexuals were assumed to have but one thing in common: "their deviance. It gives them a sense of common fate," out of which commonality "grows a deviant subculture" (Becker, 1963:38). There were no openly gay religious congregations and no publicized centers to provide social services for the gay community. Homophile organizations were almost exclusively anonymous in terms of membership and visibility. Gay student unions did not exist. The gay world was an underground phenomenon, governed chiefly by considerations of secrecy and self-preservation. With all their energy focused upon the exigencies of present existence, gays remained largely oblivious to their common history and evidenced little hope for future liberation. They huddled in back-biting cliques and moved stealthily between bars and cruising areas.

## TRANSFORMATION THROUGH GAY LIBERATION

With the beginning of gay liberation in the Christopher Street riots, a marked transfiguration became observable in the gay world. The caterpillar began to shed its cocoon of fear, self-hatred, and defensiveness. What had been described, with much justification, as a deviant subculture of "bitchiness" and "camp effeminacy" began to emerge in a greatly altered form. In *Out of the Closets* (1972), I have described the grounding of this movement in the youth and antiwar contraculture of the late 1960s:

Development of this counter culture on America's streets and campuses was an essential condition for the gay revolution. It supplied special skills, an ideology, and the necessary reinforcement to increase autonomy for the youthful gays. Older homosexuals had a subculture, a frightened, exploited and exploitative community with which they might identify—if they so desired. It was just beginning to develop a distinctive ideology, apart from that dictated by the straight society, and its patterns of interaction were so furtive and competitive that it often drove its members back into the closet. All that was "prerevolutionary," for, beginning in 1969, the counter culture intruded upon that scene [p. 113].

If protest movements of the sixties provided the dynamics behind gay liberation, they also contributed a methodological framework for transforming the deviant subculture into a different sort of cultural unit. Protest marches, sit-ins, fasts, and zapping were all familiar strategies of other liberation movements. The homosexual community, however, added distinctive features to these techniques. There was not only a characteristically creative flair in the way gays worked to gain public attention (an accentuation of elements of humor and irony in their confrontations, for example), but the gay movement also emphasized methods of consciousness raising that were essential for a people whose egos had been systematically assaulted.

Having been subjected to blanket labeling as "pathological," homosexual women and men stressed the importance of counseling centers, encounter therapy, crisis hot lines, and public commitment in order to develop gay pride. The homosexual community drew on the examples of ethnic minorities, who shared their experience of centuries of psychological as well as social oppression, to encourage its members in "coming out" with a proud self-image.

In an article (1971) written early in 1970, I predicted the emergence of a new, masculine image on the male homosexual scene. The image of the post-Stonewall gay male is, as I foresaw, distinctly virile and light years away from "the effete martini sippers" of preliberation times (see page 291). This emphasis on masculinity has proved as important to the elevation of consciousness for gay men in the movement as the feminist cause is for lesbians. Members of stigmatized minorities must not only counter stereotypes in their struggle for freedom but must overcome what I have discussed previously as the self-hatred that afflicts "all oppressed groups. It is a tenet of social psychology that we appropriate the image of ourselves that others project" (1972:40).

After nearly a decade of gay liberation, the changes are remarkable: Monthly magazines aimed at the gay public may be purchased at newsstands; and *The Advocate* boasts a readership in excess of 100,000, 70 percent of whom have college degrees, 9 percent doctoral degrees, and 35 percent with annual incomes in excess of $25,000. With more than half of its readers having contributed to a political campaign in the past year, 83 percent report having voted in the latest election. This not only signifies a high degree of political participation by readers of the nation's leading publication for gays but helps in explaining the impact of homosexual voters in such cities as San Francisco, Los Angeles, and New York. Openly gay candidates have been elected to city councils and state legislatures, and endorsement by gay political organizations is sought by candidates in several American cities.

Twelve years after Simon and Gagnon (1967) described the homosexual community as "an impoverished cultural unit,"

aspiring entertainers covet billing in the Back Lot of Hollywood's Studio One, a gay disco, while Bette Midler has soared to
fame through appearances in a Manhattan gay bath. Supporters
of the gay community fill the Hollywood Bowl for a star-studded
benefit concert. Both educational and commercial television now
offer programs with nonstereotypical characters identified as
homosexual, features and news items of interest to gays, and
high-quality productions on homosexual themes, such as *The
Naked Civil Servant* and *The War Widow.*

From 1976 to 1979, leading publishers offered books by such
prominent authors as Christopher Isherwood, Tennessee Williams, Charles Reich, and Rod McKuen in which they discuss
their homosexuality. John Rechy's *The Sexual Outlaw* and
Dave Kopay's autobiography of a gay athlete may be purchased
in paperback at the checkout stand of supermarkets, along with
a copy of *People* that features a gay couple. Few books are more
popular with student readers than Rita Mae Brown's *Rubyfruit
Jungle. A Gay American History* by Jonathan Katz and *Homosexuals in History,* by the noted literary authority A. L. Rowse,
are typical of scholarly works appearing on the shelves of
bookstores. Courses in homosexuality are taught in dozens of
American universities. *Falconer,* the best-selling novel of 1977,
featured on the cover of *Newsweek* as "A Great American
Novel," portrays the redemption of its hero as springing from a
love affair with a younger prison inmate.

This partial portrait of the homosexual world as it steps out of
the closet in the 1970s is not meant to indicate that homosexuality has lost its stigma or become acceptable to the American
public. Voters in Dade County, Florida, and several other
jurisdictions, encouraged by religious fundamentalists and a
number of right-wing organizations, deny the right of employment in certain occupations to openly gay persons; and leading
pollsters reveal that most Americans continue to fear homosexuals, although they would grant them all civil rights except that
of serving as schoolteachers. Homosexual identities are still
formed against the background of a hostile society, and openly
gay women and men must continue to cope with rejection and
social oppression.

## FROM SUBCULTURE TO SATELLITE CULTURE

What is important in the catalog of gay accomplishments is that it demonstrates an emergence of gay culture in the United States. What even astute sociologists could describe as only a limited and fearful "deviant subculture" in the 1960s must now be viewed as a rich and diverse cultural entity. Homosexually oriented women or men, forced until recently to patronize bars, baths, or clandestine cruising areas in order to find others like themselves, may now meet them in rap groups, social clubs, political meetings, or in a wide variety of religious organizations. The dozen largest urban areas of North America now have readily identifiable gay neighborhoods with heavy populations of same-sex couples. Each of these districts features not only openly gay bars and restaurants, but clothiers, bookstores, laundromats, a variety of shops, doctors, lawyers, dentists, and realtors that cater to a gay clientele (Levine, 1977).

Although it would be appropriate to write of "gay subcultures" in the limited sense of primary groups that are smaller than, and derivative from, the larger cultural entities of Western Europe or North America, I choose to depart from my earlier practice (1970:132–33, 165–66; 1972:72–73) of referring to "the homosexual subculture" in analyzing the gay world. This change results from my research and teaching in the area of subcultural theory during the past five years, as well as from my observations of significant transformation within the gay world.

A sound, operational definition of subculture includes not only the presence of a distinctive set of norms that are refracted and derived from those of the parent cultural system, a distinctive argot, and the training of its members in special skills—all of which are present in larger cultural groups—but also necessitates a high degree of face-to-face interaction among its participants. In addition, because subcultural theory has developed almost exclusively from studies of violent offenders, delinquent gangs, and other criminal or "deviant" groups, it will be some time before it can be divorced from the pejorative sense of "sub" as implying inferior, esoteric, and deviant. Finally, there are a number of well-defined subcultures operating *within* the gay world: a diverse array that includes lesbian feminists, gay academics, suburban couples, street hustlers, drag queens, and gay bikers.

When a cultural entity becomes extensive and diverse—when it is seen to spawn subcultures of its own—Eliot (1949) suggests that we use the term "satellite culture" to designate it. Thus we are able to differentiate it from subcultures with their specific foci and differential association, on the one hand, and from a nationwide, societal culture, on the other. When dealing with large, geographically dispersed ethnic or social-class groups, for instance, it is far more accurate to speak of satellite cultures than of subcultures. Just as there is no single "black subculture" in the United States, there is no single gay subculture. Certainly, there is a large and diverse catalog of subcultures with almost exclusively black memberships, all of which relate to the nation's satellite culture of Afro-Americans and to a black culture that transcends national boundaries. The same may be said of the gay cultural system as it now becomes visible: It, too, extends beyond class and national divisions, includes a wide range of subcultures, and can claim a distinguished heritage of traditions and accomplishments.

Another characteristic of satellite cultures is that each has a history of persecution, an exodus out of bondage into the promised land. Indeed, the common experience of oppression and movement toward freedom may be seen as essential for development of a distinct cultural entity. At some time in its history, every satellite culture, be it religious, ethnic, or sexual in origin, was viewed by the dominant majority as a "dangerous class," constituting a threat to the decent citizenry. Its members were viewed as immoral, heretical, sinful, traitorous, criminal, insane, and/or genetically inferior. Had sociologists been present to provide descriptive analyses in the relatively powerless stages of its development, every satellite culture would have been defined as a "deviant subculture," having "limited content," as "impoverished" and "anomic." This is as true of gays, Mormons, Catholics in Northern Ireland, and coal miners as it is of Jews, blacks, Quakers, and French Canadians. A glance at that list, incidentally, should dispel the idea that one must be born into a cultural minority. Sympathy for its adherents may be greater in times of persecution if they are seen as having become such "through no fault of their own"; but membership may be achieved by migration, occupational choice, or initiation, as well as birth.

The intolerable reality of social oppression, taken alone, cannot account for the emergence of a satellite culture. According to Cohen (1955), the "effective interaction with one another of a number of actors with similar problems of adjustment" (p. 59) gives rise to the formation of subcultures. As I have indicated earlier (1972), if the intolerable reality is accompanied by concerted action to bring about conceivable change, we have a liberation movement. Once freedoms have been tasted, even in part or for short periods of time, the tendency is toward the emergence of a satellite culture.

By the use of "emergence," I do not mean to imply that the culture lacked a heritage prior to liberation. Rather, I would emphasize the appearance, actualization, and development of hidden potentialities. Gay culture was present, even on the American scene, prior to 1970, but it was so covert and fractionated as to be unrecognizable to most observers. It is essential to realize a degree of freedom from oppression before a cultural entity can be recognized as such.

The tendency of dominant cultures is to suppress, bowdlerize, distort, ban, and obliterate the literary and historical records of "dangerous classes." Alex Haley's *Roots* would have been classified as a presumptuous underground document in America of the 1950s. Although impossible in 1968, a decade later so many new books on homosexuality appeared on the market that *Publishers Weekly* referred to it as "this remarkable phenomenon." As problematic as it is to piece together the history of blacks, gays, or Jews from charred rubbish piles of the dominant society, it is far more difficult to publish the accounts thus resurrected until some degree of media influence and freedom from censorship has been achieved. The power to write and disseminate history is the keystone maintaining cultural privilege and exclusivity.

Satellite cultures do not just emerge; they break free. As the bonds of oppression are broken, the shabby garments of deviant subcultures are also shed, revealing rich garments of the hidden culture. While organizing for power, gays have also facilitated emergence of a proud satellite culture by raising consciousness.

## THE EMBODIMENT OF CULTURE

Cultures emerge from ghettos and closets in personified, bodily forms rather than as disembodied sets of values or works of literature. It is essential that role models emerge from the anonymity and disrepute of persecution to give material and personal expression to the cultural heritage. Although often preceded by a flurry of anonymous pamphlets, emerging cultures are inevitably incarnate phenomena. Every emerging satellite culture threatens the moral standards of the dominant group, otherwise it could not be classified as a distinct cultural entity. Guardians of the old morality make last-ditch stands by attacking the role models who appear to "flaunt their immorality." In this sense, Anita Bryant does not differ from members of the Ku Klux Klan or inquisitors throughout history: Their goal is to push those who embody the threatening culture back into their closets and prison cells. The existence of flagrant role models cannot be tolerated; and that is precisely the reaction that creates martyrs, whose lives further illustrate and enrich the emerging value system.

In order to transmit and exemplify the pride of a cultural tradition, role models must not only flaunt their differentness but demonstrate that they differ from others in the society by virtue of their cultural characteristic of race, religion, or sexual orientation and not by any lack of success, occupational diversity, stability, or personal happiness. To personify the negative stereotypes of queens and hustlers endemic to the old deviant subculture may promote bitter nostalgia and anger toward the oppressors, but it does not inspire cultural pride. Such images are valuable as reminders of the injustice we have suffered but not as examples of types of lives most of us would like to lead. Openly gay schoolteachers and professors, swimmers and baseball players, physicians, policemen, and judges are the sort of persons necessary to convey the pride of gay culture. Without such role models, it is not possible to escape the oppressive self-hatred and impoverishment.

On the wall of my study hangs a copy of an advertisement by the Gay Student Union which recently filled half a page of a large university newspaper. It lists the names of a hundred homosexual notables, from Alexander the Great and Horatio Alger to Virginia Woolf and Zeno. A "Gay Engagement Calendar" lists important events in the long story of persecution of homosexuals and the short history of our liberation, along with the dates of birth and death of famous writers, musicians, statespersons, religious leaders, scholars, and rulers now known to have been gay. Such publications are the artifacts of a rich cultural heritage. Deviant subcultures, intent on protecting their members from stigma and stereotype, display only the more conforming and respectable of their members—if able to make any display at all. Satellite cultures, on the other hand, publish richly diverse lists of role models that include more innovators than conformists.

## CULTURE AND IDENTITY

Creation and maintenance of valid identity is the most important task with which we occupy ourselves. In a relatively affluent, welfare-oriented society such as our own, this search for identity probably demands far more of our time and energy than the acquisition of essential food and shelter. It is what we do when we comb (or blow dry) our hair in the mornings, when we dress, purchase the automobile we drive to work, choose and decorate our residence, interact with friends and office mates, walk down the street, court our lovers, and engage in the rituals of lovemaking. It is the chief determinant of the patterns—and much of the content—of our conversations and other communication. Most of us do not work merely for money. We work for status, and that is an important ingredient of identity.

Rainwater (1970) expresses this process of identity construction as clearly as any writer:

A valid identity is one in which the individual finds congruence between who he feels he is, who he announces himself to be, and where he feels his society places him. Individuals are led to announce a particular identity when they feel it is congruent with their needs, and the society influences these needs by its willingness to validate such announcements by a congruent placement. As individuals seek to build identities valid in terms of their own needs, they use the resources— the values, norms, and social techniques—which their culture makes available to them. *Each individual tries on identities that emerge from the cultural material available to him and tests them by making appropriate announcements* [p. 375; italics mine].

If the identity one tries on and proclaims is recognized by others in the person's social world as "a valid expression of the human condition" (p. 374), the person in search of identity believes that s/he is essentially human and significant. Only in this way do we come to "be somebody." Lacking such positive validation, we suffer the pain of an identity crisis.

Without becoming involved in extensive discussion of voluntarism versus determinism, we should note that all individuals are severely limited by a number of factors in the range of possible identities available to them. There are obvious physiological, intellectual, economic, social class, and cultural limitations upon each of us. I lack the physical capabilities of being a blond decathlon champion, the educational resources necessary for winning a prize in nuclear physics, the economic conditions essential to being a member of the jet set, or the class requirements for becoming an intimate friend to the queen of England. Of even greater importance is that I am unlikely to desire an identity that is foreign to the "values, behaviors, outlooks, imagery, expectations, definitions of reality, and meanings" that constitute the cultural milieu in which I am situated (Curtis, 1975:7). Some identities we cannot have; some we do not want; but each of us must have a valid identity in order to feel important enough to survive.

To the extent that the cultural womb in which identity is formed is impoverished or limited, personal construction of a valid identity will be thwarted and circumscribed. No one is completely free to choose the cultural environment in which the identity search takes place: ethnic, religious, and socioeconomic backgrounds are highly determinative, as is a factor as basic as sexual orientation. People can depart from any of these only at severe social and psychological cost. Unless such resources as great wealth or exceptional ego strength are available, movement to another cultural milieu is precluded. Even under exceptional conditions, migration from the cultural heritage that provides the raw material for identity construction tends to isolate the person from those significant others who must validate the ventured identity.

The emergence of a rich and varied satellite culture profoundly affects the quality and range of identities formed by its members. If its central values are made clear, its role models viewed as successful and fulfilled, its heritage described as noble, if its members manifest pride, then strong identities will form within it. As Hooker points out (1965:104), identities constructed by members of oppressed minorities tend to be characterized by "ego-defensive traits." When the cultural heritage is made manifest, cultural roots are discovered, and positive role models appear, identities nurtured by the emerging culture tend to be less ambivalent and defensive.

Several predictions should follow the recognition of a developing gay culture in America. Young women and men who come to think of themselves as homosexual during adolescence, when identity construction is an all-consuming preoccupation, should manifest fewer individual problems and fewer attempts at suicide. They will suffer less from a perceived lack of power and significance. Since the construction of valid identity is a lifelong process, others of homosexual orientation will also benefit. With an increased capacity for finding significance and personal fulfillment in the gay culture, lesbians and gay men will be less inclined to pass as "straight" or to flee into heterosexual marriage (Miller, 1978).

Evidence already exists to demonstrate that more highly committed and acculturated homosexual persons, who see homosexuality as "normal" rather than pathological, report greater psychological well-being than those who are more closeted

(Weinberg and Williams, 1974; 160–61). Thomas Weinberg (1977) found a similar tendency to greater ego strength among respondents who were active in gay liberation organizations. With continuing enrichment of the cultural milieu and the proliferation of positive role models, gay subjects of future studies should reflect few of the ego-defensive traits observed by Hooker and other researchers of past decades.

Because the dominant culture is slow in ridding itself of prejudice, one cannot predict that self-hatred will disappear from those of us with homosexual orientation, but it will cease to be *characteristic* of the gay world. Gay women and men will be more intent on defining and expressing the innovative, humane, and nonviolent values that characterize our culture at its best. We shall expend less of our energy in self-defense. Perhaps we shall even help social scientists learn to recognize an emerging culture when they encounter one.

## REFERENCES

ACHILLES, NANCY. "The Development of the Homosexual Bar as an Institution." In John H. Gagnon and William Simon, eds., *Sexual Deviance*. New York: Harper & Row, 1967.

BECKER, HOWARD S. *Outsiders: Studies in the Sociology of Deviance*. New York: Free Press, 1963.

CHURCHILL, WAINWRIGHT. *Homosexual Behavior Among Males: A Cross-Cultural and Cross-Species Investigation*. Englewood Cliffs, N.J.: Prentice-Hall, 1967.

COHEN, ALBERT K. *Delinquent Boys: The Culture of the Gang*. New York: Free Press, 1955.

CURTIS, LYNN A. *Violence, Race, and Culture*. Lexington, Mass.: D. C. Heath, 1975.

ELIOT, T. S. *Notes Toward the Definition of a Culture*. New York: Harcourt Brace Jovanovich, 1949.

HOFFMAN, MARTIN. *The Gay World: Male Homosexuality and the Social Creation of Evil*. New York: Basic Books, 1968.

HOOKER, EVELYN. "Male Homosexuals and Their 'Worlds.'" In Judd Marmor, ed., *Sexual Inversion: The Multiple Roots of Homosexuality*. New York: Basic Books, 1965.

HUMPHREYS, LAUD. *Tearoom Trade: Impersonal Sex in Public Places*. Chicago: Aldine, 1970.

———. "New Styles in Homosexual Manliness." In *Trans-Action*, March–April 1971, pp. 38–46, 64–65.

———. *Out of the Closets: The Sociology of Homosexual Liberation*. Englewood Cliffs N.J.: Prentice-Hall, 1972.

LEVINE, MARTIN. "Gay Ghetto." In this volume, pp. 182–204.

LINDQUIST, NEIL. "Adaptation to Marginal Status: The Case of Gay Males." Ph.D. dissertation, Department of Sociology, University of Alberta, Edmonton, Canada, 1976.

MILLER, BRIAN. "Adult Sexual Resocialization: Adjustments Toward a Stigmatized Identity." In *Alternative Lifestyles* 1, no. 2 (May 1978).

RAINWATER, LEE. *Behind Ghetto Walls: Black Families in a Federal Slum*. Chicago: Aldine, 1970.

SAGARIN, EDWARD. *Odd Man In: Societies of Deviants in America*. New York: Quadrangle Books, 1969.

SIMON, WILLIAM, and JOHN H. GAGNON. "Homosexuality: The Formulation of a Sociological Perspective." In *Journal of Health & Social Behavior* 8, no. 3 (September 1967): 177–85.

STEARN, JESS. *The Sixth Man*. New York: Macfadden Books, 1962.

WEINBERG, MARTIN S., and COLIN J. WILLIAMS. *Male Homosexuals: Their Problems and Adaptation*. New York: Oxford University Press, 1974.

WEINBERG, THOMAS S. "On 'Doing' and 'Being' Gay: Sexual Behavior and Homosexual Self-Identity." Paper delivered at meetings of the Society for the Study of Social Problems, Chicago, September 1977.

WEST, DONALD J. *Homosexuality*. Chicago: Aldine, 1967.

Scene

# Inside the Colossal Closet

## WAYNE SAGE

Gay bars are not what they used to be—clandestine hideaways where a few of the more brazen gay people sought one another out in secret. At Cabaret, currently the most popular spot in the Los Angeles gay world, about 1,500 people pack in on a Saturday night. At nearby, but more exotic, Studio One, such Hollywood heavyweights as Burt Reynolds and Liza Minnelli drop in to see and be seen. Richard Chamberlain, Candice Bergen, Johnny Mathis, Fred Astaire, Carol Channing, Steve Allen, Carol Burnett, Gene Kelly, and Jack Haley, Jr., filed in for the opening of the Chita Rivera Show and, on the dance floor, Raquel Welch could be seen dancing with her boyfriend among the crowds of men dancing with men and women dancing with women.

To encounter a celebrity incognito in a gay bar would be nothing new. For them to parade in, unconcerned by—or even because of—the fact that the place is gay, is a testament to the new status of gay establishments.

Ten years ago, Cabaret and Studio One could not have existed. Seven years ago, only one in ten gay people had ever been to a gay bar. But greater honesty about sex generally, the gay liberation movement, and the realization by even the psychiatric and psychological establishments that homosexuality is not an "illness" have had their impact on the gay scene. Sex researchers who demonstrated that homosexual experiences are common among a large percentage of the population also made apparent the potential market for gay entertainment. As best as can be determined by what research data are available and the crude polls of their readerships by gay publications, most predominantly or exclusively homosexual people still do not go to bars, and it seems most of those who do fade back into the straight world by the light of day. But by night, the market is at last being realized. "The gay liberation movement hasn't done much to break down the door to the closet," complains a former gay activist who has "mellowed" in the bars and whose lover is a policeman on the vice squad, "but it may have expanded the domain of closetdom to include the bars."

If Cabaret and Studio One are closets, they are colossal ones. A former bomb factory revamped to look like a motion picture sound stage, cavernous Studio One includes four bars, a restaurant, a movie theater, a discotheque the size of a basketball court, a game room with pool tables and pinball machines, a television lounge, and a nightclub where such top acts as Joan Rivers and Ruth Buzzi play to a packed house. Well over 800 people crowd in every night. Housed in a space-age architectural landmark on L.A.'s restaurant row, Cabaret outdoes Studio One (and every other discotheque, gay or straight, on the West Coast), with five bars, tiered dance floors, balconies, a showroom, underground caverns with soft lights and low music for conversation, and a double-decker restaurant and discotheque at its second building nearby.

Perhaps the crowds and plush surroundings are reassuring. "Gay people like to be awed by their own numbers," explains the manager of a gay bar in the South that fills to its capacity of 1,100 and turns people away, and as they overflow the bars, the gay world of old is straining to accommodate them. Across the country, gay entrepreneurs have torn down walls, expanded into adjacent buildings, purchased warehouses and auditoriums, and realized the ascendance and staggering success of "superbars" in Atlanta, Washington, D.C., San Franciso, Houston, New York, Chicago, Dallas, Miami, and Boston. The trend has at least begun in most other major cities.

For all their bloated capacities, the superbars are only one of many signs of a booming gay capitalism. They are the type of establishment that is, and long has been, an American institution. In the East, all indications are that the Mafia's grip on gay-bar ownership is still strong, although more subtle. But in other areas, especially on the West Coast, "there is a big desire for gay people to support gay businesses," according to Bob Dameron, publisher of the most reliable gay-bar guidebook available. "Ten years ago maybe 25 to 30 percent of the [gay] bars in San Francisco were gay owned," Dameron estimates. "Today, they're probably 75 to 80 percent gay owned." Using the four current major bar guides printed through gay channels, one can compile a list of 166 gay bars in the Los Angeles area and still miss some that have gone unreported. More can be discovered in gay-publication ads and through the gay grapevine. There are at least a hundred gay bars in New York City, over ninety in Chicago and around four thousand in the continental United States.

The trend is still being stifled in more conservative areas. "Even today, the only way you'll run a gay bar in the Deep South is to have a connection or you won't last one day," says the manager of a San Francisco bar who migrated from Alabama. "But it's a good system," he says. "You just pay off the cops. The corruption is tremendous." Even in the most unlikely locales, the major cities are catching up fast. Ten years ago, there were four gay bars in Houston; today, there are forty. The number of gay bars in Atlanta has gone from five to thirty-one in the same period.

Although gay bars tend to concentrate in major population centers, they are by no means just a big-city phenomenon. They are as ubiquitous as the people who patronize them. Many of the small-town bars that dot the map of mid-America, like a few in the major cities, have been well established for twenty years or more and are virtual local landmarks. There are gay bars in Pocatello, Idaho; Tupelo, Mississippi; Burlington, Vermont; Anchorage, Alaska; Aquas Buenas, Puerto Rico.

Overwhelmingly, gay bars are a male phenomenon. Gay men, true to the male role, venture out when and where they choose; and wherever there is a large concentration of males to support them, gay bars sprout and thrive. They can be found near every large military base and every major university.

Contrary to popular misconception, gay bars vary tremendously in character, atmosphere and clientele and usually reflect the character of their local surroundings far more than that of a distinctive subculture. There are gay bars in the South where farm hands listen to country-western music, gay bars in the Midwest where truck drivers stop over on long hauls across the country, just as there are gay bars in the East dominated by a social elite. At Santa Barbara's The Pub, sandy-haired surfer boys gather; at Fort Lauderdale's The Poop Deck, college students from schools throughout the East converge for Easter break; and at a gay bar near Capitol Hill, government employees meet discreetly to talk.

Nestled in the Blue Ridge Mountains of Virginia is Roanoke, where the local gay bar fills on weekends with young professionals, students from nearby Virginia Tech and Roanoke College as well as gay people from a dozen isolated hamlets for a fifty-mile radius. As is usual for small-town gay bars, the atmosphere is more like that of a private club than a public bar—in this case, a gathering of young southern gentlemen and local townspeople.

Strangers who wander into the ground-level bar at Roanoke's The Tradewinds see only two or three people chatting lazily with the bartender and could easily wander out again without realizing that in the café downstairs, around sixty people are sharing a fellowship that is possible in their locale only because of a covenant of mutual trust.

Most of the local patrons have grown up together and share a common cultural background. Also, many have known one another for many years, or at least continue their long-standing friendships with others in the bar year after year. A stranger is accepted with southern hospitality and finds almost anyone he wants to meet responsive and friendly. In small-town bars, this usually leads to long talks in the bar that develop into dating much like that straights practiced in the 1950s, and the attitude toward sex is anything but cavalier. Sexual relationships require trust and an understanding of the life circumstances of one's partner.

Discretion is all pervasive in small-town bars, where one does not have the option to drift between the gay world and the straight world with anonymity. A large number of the patrons have girl friends, and many are married, mostly for the sake of appearances in a social milieu in which anyone over thirty who is not married is automatically suspect. And in a town where probably no one would believe that people such as those in the bar are homosexual and where many of the townspeople probably do not even know what a gay bar is, most of the patrons seem content and not even remotely moved to change the situation.

Significantly, such bars sometimes contain a far more diverse crowd than is visible in urban gay bars, and in more cosmopolitan areas, the gatherings are motley indeed. Like comrades under social flak, gay people gather at The Clubhouse in Pasadena, California, for example, where the regular crowd includes both men and women, blacks and whites, young and old from widely varied walks of life.

Even more diverse is the patronage at the Whitehorse Inn, located near the border between Berkeley and Oakland, California. A steady stream of street people from Telegraph Avenue and intellectuals from the nearby University of California assert a strong influence, as do middle-class residents from Bay Area suburbs and blacks from the adjacent ghetto of East Oakland. The music alternates from the symphonies of Shostakovich and Mahler to the classics of Frank Sinatra and Tony Bennett to the rock of The Jackson Five, and students readily break off discussions of international politics to join groups of middle-class lesbians in talks about bridge hands and everybody talks to everybody about the weather.

In the urban gay scene, the trend is strong toward variety and segregation. In all large cities, the crowds vary from bar to bar according to age, sex, ethnic background, status, and character. Although the process can be seen anywhere in the country, it is most highly evolved on the West Coast. In San Francisco, for example, where it sometimes seems "the love that dares not speak its name" is shouted from the rooftops, there are bars for young male collegiates (The End Up, for one); bars for blacks (Bo Jangles's); bars for the discreet business executive (Gold Street); bars for bohemian women (The Bacchanal); bars for middle-class women (The Carnation Club); bars for the rich

(The Woods); and a bar for transsexuals, drag queens, and hustlers (The Thousand and One Nights). There are bars to chat in, bars to dance in, bars to cruise in, and bars to have sex in. Probably for gay people, as for all people, city life increases the need to search out and be with one's own kind.

That need, and not sex, is the most fundamental reason for the existence and increasing popularity of different gay bars, which are at present the major social institutions where people can be honest about an important aspect of human sexual and emotional nature.

For people who are exclusively or predominantly homosexual, one of the most important functions of today's gay bar is to provide gay people with a way of finding one another—despite what amounts to a conspiracy to keep them apart—and to provide them the peer group support with which to break down the stereotypes and prejudice that society instills in us all. "Gay people are raised in straight society and are taught its phobias as well as its values. They end up hating 'queers' just like everybody else does. They hopefully know those things [the myths] aren't true of themselves, but each thinks he's the only 'normal' person who feels that way, until he begins to find other gay people like himself," says one gay person who used to go to bars before he found a lover and established a circle of gay friends.

For many gay people, the first step inside a gay bar is the first chance to see through the facade of universal heterosexuality that society tries to maintain. An example is a young medical student who drove nearly one hundred miles from his university [he was afraid to go to a gay bar only five miles from campus for fear of being discovered] to a bar in Los Angeles. "I never went home with anybody," he remembers. "I'd drive two hours to get there, hang around for the evening and then drive two hours back home. Just to be able to stand around and talk with [gay] guys who were stable, successful, and happy was worth the drive," he says. "I [had] thought I was all alone." Ironically, one of the first people he met there was a fellow student at his medical school.

That was seven years ago. Today, the gay student has far more places to go. One of the most popular and elite types of gay bars is the collegiate dance bar. Such discotheques are found in all major cities and many small ones, from Seattle to Denver to Hartford. On the West Coast, a prime example is L.A.'s Oil Can Harry's, where all-American-boy types dressed in jeans, tennis shirts, and football jerseys dance with one another like fraternity boys glad to be free from pretenses with sorority girls. Most seem to be in their early twenties, with the top age around twenty-five. Observes one of the waiters there: "The typical Oil Can Harry's goer drives a Volkswagen, goes to whatever state college his family can afford, and works summers at a department store or gas station. He likes Mom, apple pie, and the boy next door."

At The End Up, San Francisco's counterpart, young, good-looking, clean-cut, masculine guys who look as if they just stepped out of the pages of a Sears catalog crowd in literally by the hundreds. On a Saturday night, The End Up is so packed it sometimes becomes impossible to move. The rock music is loud and constant, and the dancing and socializing are carried on with a fine high cheerfulness that is hard not to get caught up in, if you qualify.

Not unlike the straight world's swinging-singles bars, the urban gay scene puts a high premium on youth, good looks, and, in men, masculinity. Those who don't measure up seem to get the message and stay away.

Otherwise, they are kept away. The crowd is under strict quality control by the management. Near the entrance of such a bar, there is invariably a sign saying Three Pieces of Acceptable ID Required. Since the management takes the prerogative of defining what an "acceptable" piece of identification is, anyone who is asked for three such IDs quickly learns that the requirement is impossible to meet. The "acceptable identification" is demanded of most women and blacks and all straights or people the management considers "freaks"—such as transsexuals, drag queens, and others of shifting or dubious gender identity—with whom "gay people are loath to be reminded that they are associated" in the minds of the population at large, as one owner explains the reasons for his policy.

That association is an oppressive one, both within and without the gay scene. This, as with so much of society's intolerance of homosexuality, hinges on our culture's traditional ideas about what is masculine and what is feminine. The sexism of American society is such that the most degrading thing that can be said about a man is that he is like a woman. Perhaps as a result, the fastest proliferating type of establishment in the gay bar business is a place where gay men can declare with gusto that they are not like women.

Folsom Street in San Francisco is a district of warehouse loading docks frequented by belching semis and factories that grind to a halt at five o'clock. At night, the gay bars there, as they do everywhere, take on something of the atmosphere of their surroundings. Bikers in black leather, studs in faded Levis, and grizzly musclemen with shaved heads crowd into such places as Folsom Prison, The No Name Bar, The Lumberyard and, most macho of all, The Boot Camp. These are examples of the leather and western bars that, with their black walls, dim red lights, and dirty interiors, represent one of the most important trends in gay bars, and perhaps in gay life, throughout the country.

Beyond the door of The Boot Camp, a black leather curtain holds back stray beams from the headlights of passing cars on the rarely used (by night) roadway beneath the maze of freeway offramps where cars roar constantly overhead. Past the curtain, the darkness seems total except for the island of light surrounding the bar. As your eyes adjust to the rest of the room, you begin to see the bulging muscles, bearded faces, and tatooed skin you feel rubbing against you as you try to move about. Logging chains hang from the ceiling, and barrels and huge spools from coils of steel cable provide the only furnishings. No one speaks and no one moves to get out of your way as you try to pass. The air seems stale, the walls and floor are grimy, and the men look mean. The crowd becomes increasingly dense toward the rear of the room, where the men press themselves together and back toward the grope room, a doorway that looks like the entrance to a tool shed into which people disappear as though swallowed.

At a time when the straight world shows signs of drifts toward androgyny, the gay world seems to be moving toward strict sexual identity. Nationwide, the number of supermasculine bars has increased 40 percent in five years, a rate faster than that for any other type of gay bar. For the men, this means a hard-core affirmation of our culture's traditional concept of masculinity. "Gay men are discovering their manhood," theorizes one bartender. "Or each other's manhood," he grinned, nodding toward the grope room.

Perhaps this is male chauvinism's last stand. "Gay men are the ultimate male chauvinists," comments one lesbian on hearing a description of such a bar. And the appreciation is deeply rooted. She adds: "They prefer men physically and that naturally carries over into their emotional selves. They're enraptured by maleness, their own and that of other men. Being gay, I can understand that."

Some of the patrons of such scenes are bargoers from the old days who have reached middle age perhaps feeling cheated by what they were looking for in the bars when they were younger but could not find. Occasionally, a hairdresser locks his poodle into his purple Cadillac and trips off toward such a bar in black leather and chains. But for many others, if the machismo is a mask, the mask is as much a part of them as it is for any heterosexual male. Many of the men not only look like, but in fact are, truck drivers, mechanics, and hardhat construction workers. "Guys are going to bars who would have never gone before. Some of them need some reassurance that going to a gay bar is a manly thing to do. Here, there's no doubt of that," explains the owner of a similar bar in Southern California, where men from the nearby oil drills drop in after work wearing the insignia of their respective oil companies on their work shirts.

Many men, well over one-third of the male population even by the most conservative measures, have had some homosexual experience, research has shown. But for a man to identify himself as "a homosexual" in our society traditionally has meant his condemnation as a sexual loser, since part of the male role includes laying women. To step inside a gay bar has traditionally meant such an admission, and if society labels him half a man for taking that step, perhaps some of those now doing so feel they must be a man and a half to compensate. But for a growing number of bargoers, the need for a man and the need to be a man is not a contradiction.

"The idea that men relate to one another sexually by playing male-female roles is nonsense," says a psychologist who frequents a gay bar in Pasadena. Indeed, what one observes in gay bars would not support such an idea. The attractions and rejections usually follow a distinct pattern: masculine men are attracted to masculine men. The more masculine and handsome a man is, the more masculine and handsome must be another man to interest him. Effeminate men go home either with each other or alone. "If I wanted a woman," says a patron of Mike's Corral in Long Beach, "I wouldn't be here."

Among the intricate communication subtleties that have evolved in men's bars, one of the most salient is the expression of sexual preference. Contrary to popular misconceptions, the degree of one man's masculinity relative to another's is no indication of whether he prefers the active or passive role in specific sex acts. In search of a compatible partner, the message comes across through certain conventions. The most generally recognized of these is the position of a man's keys worn on a metal ring and hooked through his belt. If the keys are worn on the right, the man prefers to be passive; if the keys are on the left, he prefers to be active. Though such insignia are common in the macho bars, most gay bargoers do not wear keys because their preferences are flexible.

Whether for reasons of biology, socialization, or social reinforcement, or some combination of all three, sexual encounters between two men seem to have a distinct character compared with those between two women, at least to the extent that such encounters are visible in the bars.

"The essence of homosexuality is two men relating to one another sexually and emotionally as men and two women relating to one another sexually and emotionally as women," theorizes a veteran gay barroom philosopher. Mark Freedman, a member of a research group of gay psychologists, adds, "Gay men are socialized as men in our society so the emphasis is more on sexual conquest than long-term relationships. Lesbians, socialized as women, focus more on love and long-term relationships."

Certainly society's reaction to intimate relationships between two women is different from the hostility with which it reacts to physical expressions of affection between two men, as data for barroom arrests for "lewd conduct" clearly show. Until recently, and still in some areas of the country, "lewd conduct" arrests have been made in male gay bars on incidents of two men holding hands, hugging, kissing, or even touching one another. As one gay woman explains the dearth of lesbian bars compared to the multitude of bars for men: "Women are already able to hug each other in public without getting shot. We don't need bars as much."

Of course, if two men were to relate to one another on a purely sexual level (assuming it is possible for humans ever to relate sexually without emotional interplay, which is doubtful), they would necessarily cast off one of society's most puritanical dictums: that nice people should not enjoy sex as such. Probably the simple facts that such hindrances as pregnancy, birth control, and courting etiquettes are not in the way is more significant. "As all that changes for heterosexuals, their relationships are becoming more and more like ours," says one gay male whose fourteen-year relationship with his lover closely resembles what is currently termed an open marriage. And if it is the case that male-to-male sex is more physical and direct, as such it grates against our culture's most cherished ideas. Sex "must be ennobled with love"—and only with love as it is presently socially condoned. Perhaps such dilemmas exist only for those, including traditional theorists, who insist on judging homosexual relationships in heterosexual terms.

Something of the nature of man-to-man trysts can be seen in the cruising habits of the gay male.

Flanked by gay bars, Ventura Boulevard makes its way along the edge of the hills that separate Los Angeles from its commuters' homes in the San Fernando Valley. The bars along the boulevard's course in Sherman Oaks, Studio City, and North Hollywood have taken on some of the character of the Valley and its residents. Most are conservative and homey. Of special note is The Hayloft—all of its patrons are men. The average age is about thirty, and most seem to be clean-cut, conservative, and well educated, with comfortable jobs, homes, cars, and lives. The Hayloft is generally recognized as one of the "cruisiest" bars for a hundred miles in any direction.

Its reputation is well deserved in that virtually everyone there on a given night seems intensely attuned to one another's moves and glances. The place is crowded every night by 10:30, and on weekends—especially Sundays—it's packed. Free movies, extremely good ones (most recently *Day of the Jackal, Jesus Christ Superstar,* and *The Lion in Winter)* are shown on the front wall, and the crowd stares at them intently, although sometimes it seems no one is really aware of what he is watching. Concentration is almost totally absorbed in what is going on in the bar.

Until one learns what to look for, an observer would probably wonder why eighty men would stand around watching a movie they could see at home on cable TV. Side glances away from the film have tremendous significance, as do where one stands or sits and, especially, the casual nudge.

The goal of the cruise game is to find someone—the right person—to leave with. The right person is so judged by strict physical and personality requirements. But the incredibly intricate subtleties of communication with which the search is carried out are finely tuned by an overriding concern—to avoid rejection.

Usually, interest in one another is expressed through very brief eye contact, and the slightest sign of disinterest on either man's part will end things at that point. If the exchange continues, the progression to longer glances and tentative smiles of approval can take half an hour before one or the other makes an approach. Even at this point, they may stand or sit beside one another for another fifteen minutes to an hour as they tune into one another, perhaps occasionally nudging shoulders or knees, sensing one another's reaction before one or the other finally speaks. The conversation usually begins with offhand, noncommittal talk, and, if each continues to feel good about the other, progresses to friendly conversation that seems to engross the two to the exclusion of everyone else in the bar.

Oddly, at one of the "cruisiest" spots within one hundred miles of Los Angeles, the atmosphere is not one of promiscuity, but of extreme selectivity. Encounters that go even so far as long glances are not frequent, and those that lead to conversation occur only now and then. On a typical weekend, in the course of two consecutive nights, The Hayloft was filled with at least eighty men at any given time, and the crowd continually changed as new arrivals came in and others left. From nine o'clock in the evening till four in the morning on those two nights, only three or four times each night could encounters that led to two men leaving together be observed.

"Promiscuity as such has no place in The Hayloft," explained a young attorney as he described the goings on with a certain gay romanticism. "There are places in the gay world for that, but not here. Guys here are looking for someone. Sometimes a lover (a permanent or long-term mate), but always somebody they can relate to deeply both physically and emotionally."

"Do you really think they find that this way?" I asked, after sitting engrossed for nearly two hours.

"It's the most efficient way imaginable," he said.

"But how long does it last when they do find each other?"

"For as long as they both want it to. They're looking for something that's meaningful to them. That doesn't mean spending thirty years raising kids in the suburbs. . . ."

One of the most quiet, but probably the strongest, influences on the gay world comes, as usual, from the middle class. What may be an emerging silent majority is beginning to make its influence felt. Illustrative is The Riviera Room in Redondo Beach, California, and The Ripples, a dance bar that overlooks the ocean in Long Beach, California. The crowds there are suburban and middle class and, significantly, outnumber by ten to one the combined patronage of Long Beach's half-dozen gay dives. Bars in most locales are cleaning themselves up, putting in thickly upholstered leather chairs, fireplaces, and richly furnished lounges in the hope that such patrons may be tempted.

"Being gay doesn't mean taking on the values and life-styles of any group or even imitating the one straight society has. I make my own rules," said a high school teacher at The Ripples. "Those just aren't my kind of people," he added, referring to the patrons of other bars.

That attitude, on the part of both straight and gay people, probably is at the root of our society's oppression of gay people. Objective research on homosexuality, begun only within the last twenty years, has demonstrated that not even psychologists and psychiatrists can tell a homosexual personality from a heterosexual one, and virtually every psychoanalytic theory and social stereotype on the subject has been forced into serious question. In society at large, gay people are invisible by the standards by which they are labeled. Research has shown that only one in twenty is detectable—95 percent of all gay people do not fit the stereotypes. As a result, drag queens, transsexuals, effeminate men, masculine women, sex offenders, and mental patients who are visible to society or come in conflict with its norms and laws make up the highly unrepresentative sample from which society develops its concept of what a gay person is like. This has resulted in the view of "the homosexual" as a deviant rather than a human being whose sexual and emotional needs differ from those of a heterosexual person and the association of homosexuality with a freakie subculture rather than its recognition as a common variation of sexual affectionate conduct.

To say that the patrons of gay bars, as they are now visible, make up a representative sample of gay people is nonsense. As sex researchers have finally realized, there is simply no way of knowing what a representative sample of homosexual people would be like, even if it were possible to collect such a sample— which it isn't. But the ongoing migration from the closets to the bars is making one fact obvious: There is no such thing as a homosexual type. Gay people differ from one another in at least as many ways as do straight people. "That's right," says a young bar owner who was the student body president at his alma mater and is now an executive with a California bank and plans to run for the state legislature. "The truth would be visible," he says, "if all gay bars were made of glass."

But some are, or nearly so. Fort Lauderdale's The Poop Deck has huge glass windows overlooking the street and is located on the ground floor of the Marlin Beach Hotel, one of the finest and most touristy hotels on Fort Lauderdale's beach-front strip. Tourists staying there exchange smiles with the well-mannered young people passing through the lobby as they head for the discotheque off to the left. Were the tourists ever to take a look beyond the doorway, they would see men dancing with men and women dancing with women.

In the past, invisibility has been an asset in that predominantly gay people have escaped much of the oppression that would otherwise have been thrust upon them. Apparently most gay people still cling to the security of their anonymity. Talking to people in the bars, one encounters much apathy, little sympathy, and some outright hostility toward the struggling gay rights movement.

"I've got my rights as a human being right now," insists one bargoer. "Why worry about the rights of a homosexual?" "You can have a good life and enjoy your homosexuality. What more do you want?" says another. "It's not hypocrisy," says a third, "just pragmatism. The way things are, you make the most of your own situation."

Of over fifty people interviewed in bars during the course of researching this article, only three would allow their names to be used, and those three preferred anonymity. A member of the gay students' union at a California university agreed that the super-bars are "just colossal closets," and asked that his name be withheld to keep his parents from seeing it.

Perhaps such attitudes are understandable. But as the bars fill and their patrons dance and fraternize happily in same-sex pairs, society outside seethes with hostility. . . . As long as people continue to fear homosexuality in their children, in others, and in themselves, and as long as the most powerful gay people remain silent, such attitudes will maintain. Says a young oil company executive: "Other minorities have everything to gain by demanding their rights; we have everything to lose." And as long as that situation maintains, gay bars will thrive.

"There is a certain element of people that's conducive to

making a [gay] bar work," says Tim Manning of the Cabaret. That element is the young, sociable, successful, handsome gay men who have a lot of money to spend, who draw in the fringe crowds, and who are among our society's most desirable men by both straight and gay standards. Said one heterosexual young female model after an evening at a gay superbar, "I fell in love eight times tonight and they're all gay!"

"They're there to socialize and be with friends and meet people and they do a lot of drinking while they are doing this," says Manning. "That's the bar business. When you get right down to it, the rest is fringe. It's the five bars we have here and the booze that's behind them."

Thus it seems the people who have made the gay bars boom are also those who might be able to do the most to change the stereotypes that necessitate the ghettoization of their private lives. "You're too naive," says a producer of industrial films who frequents The Hayloft. "Some people might be surprised to find out their son or their brother goes here, but they wouldn't particularly care if they found out we're actually good citizens and pretty nice people. There will always be prejudice against people who are different in some way. It's better this way. You live the way you see fit, and what they don't know won't hurt us."

# Gay Baths and the Social Organization of Impersonal Sex

MARTIN S. WEINBERG AND
COLIN J. WILLIAMS

The methods employed in gathering data for this paper were fieldwork observation and informal interviews. Five gay baths—all relatively new and modern—were studied in cities in the southeastern, midwestern, and western parts of the United States. Observations were conducted at different times (e.g., afternoons and late in the evening, weekdays and weekends) in order to obtain as broad a picture as possible. Field notes were taken in private areas or immediately after leaving the bath, and observations were interpreted and validated by interviews with bath patrons contacted and interviewed away from that setting. In addition, we attended a week-long convention of owners and managers to learn more about the operation of gay baths.

In formulating our ideas, we utilized other sources of data as well. We had considerable knowledge of the gay world from our previous research. (Williams and Weinberg, 1971; Weinberg and Williams, 1974); and we also drew on our fieldwork and interviews from other contexts of impersonal sex. These contexts included massage parlors, tearooms (men's rest rooms where homosexual sex takes place), pickups, Sexual Freedom League (group sex) parties, and prostitution. Finally, materials in the Institute for Sex Research collections were consulted, further confirming our impressions.

*Social Problems* 23, no. 2 (December 1975): 124–36. Reprinted by permission of the publisher and authors.

The authors are grateful to Sue Kiefer Hammersmith, Stuart Hadden, Karen Ruse Struch, Odis Bigus, Marilyn Lester, Alan Bell, and the two anonymous *Social Problems* referees for their invaluable comments and suggestions.

## IMPERSONAL SEX—CHARACTERISTICS, CONCERNS, AND IDEAL CONDITIONS

A pure case of impersonal sex would be sexual activity without any personal involvement whatsoever between the sexual partners (Downie, 1971:129–31). In effect, none of the aspects of a primary relationship would appear. The interchange would be easily transferable from one partner to another and narrowly confined in its social depth and breadth (Broom and Selznick, 1963:135–39); the partner would be a means to an impersonal, purely sexual, objective. (This description is ideal-typical, exaggerating the impersonality commonly surrounding sex in such contexts as gay baths, prostitution, massage parlors, pickups, and tearooms.)

Male participants generally construe the meaning of such sex within the framework of "easy sex"—i.e., sex without commitment, obligation, or a long-term social relationship. Ordinarily, they do not regard impersonal sex as qualitatively better than personal sex, but simply as more expedient given their circumstances (Humphreys, 1971:372; Piro, 1973). Not all participants, however, interpret impersonal sex as a substitute for personal sex. Indeed, impersonal sex may be pursued as an end in itself—e.g., for variety in sexual experience—rather than as a way of compensating for a lack of personal sex. Moreover, the attendant sexual enjoyment can, at times, be a catalyst in the development of a more personal relationship.

From the standpoint of male participants, however, the effective social organization of impersonal sex can be difficult to achieve. (For example, in tearooms there is almost constant fear of intrusion or arrest [Humphreys, 1970]; in massage parlors, patrons often pay exorbitant prices to be masturbated, or find after paying a considerable amount that the parlor provides no sex at all [Hong et al., 1975]; in pursuing sex with pickups [especially heterosexual], because there may be nonsexual as well as sexual aims and modes of relating, participants may experience anomie, misunderstandings, or resentment [Davis, 1973]; men patronizing prostitutes are sometimes robbed or treated in a demeaning manner [Ross, 1959; Gray, 1973]; and the settings available for impersonal sex can be unpleasant and sleazy [e.g., smelly tearooms, cheap hotels].) Thus, male participants (whether homosexual or heterosexual) voice a number of concerns regarding the pursuit of impersonal sex, and they recognize some circumstances as more ideal than others for that pursuit. As noted, these concerns and ideal conditions point primarily to social organization.*

1. Male participants are often concerned about sanctions and dangers. Thus, ideal conditions include features that protect the participant—e.g., a safe setting with low public visibility and with arrangements that inhibit intrusion and facilitate anonymity.

2. Male participants often consider the opportunities for impersonal sex inadequate. Thus, ideal conditions provide ample access to good sexual partners and settings at a reasonable cost—e.g., a field of attractive and potential partners who will be amenable to and readily available for the desired sexual acts, at minimal expense.

3. Anomie and conflict often occur in soliciting and carrying out impersonal sex. Thus, ideal conditions promote a known, shared, and organized reality within the opportunity structure—e.g., the existence of a known and shared intent and of clear and simple "road maps" for transforming the intent into interaction.

4. Male participants often have a singular purpose. Thus, ideal conditions bound the experience—e.g., limiting nonsexual interaction as well as the horizons of the relationship.

5. Abrasive interaction is often experienced as demoralizing or degrading. Thus, ideal conditions include a congenial atmosphere—e.g., the masking of rejection, and nonabrasiveness in the solicitation, acceptance/nonacceptance, sexual process, and departure.

6. Uncomfortable physical settings decrease enjoyment. Thus,

---

* In many instances these conditions overlap, relate to, or exacerbate one another. They are kept distinct in this paper for analytic purposes, and each is elaborated in later dicussion. These conditions are not applicable solely to the pursuit of impersonal sex. They are often relevant (though less highlighted) in more personalized forms of sex and in nonsexual activities as well.

ideal conditions include physical settings that promote relaxation and convenience—e.g., cleanliness, facilities for relaxation, and the availability of desired sundries.

## GAY BATHS AND IMPERSONAL SEX

Gay baths are licensed men's health clubs that provide a setting for impersonal homosexual sex. Traditionally, baths offered little to their patrons except sex (Young, 1973; Bates, 1972). Most of the owners were not themselves homosexual, and they were generally lax about the upkeep or development of facilities.

In recent years, however, the bath scene has begun to change. In larger cities, homosexuals have themselves become bath owners, and there is a nationwide chain of baths run by gay businessmen. Homosexual owners have improved the baths to better meet the needs of their clientele. Some of the older baths have been upgraded because of this new competition. Increasingly popular, baths are becoming better maintained and better able to meet a variety of needs in addition to the traditional sexual one—e.g., many now provide entertainment and recreational facilities. Thus, at present, the bath scene is in a state of flux. Coexisting are plush baths, dilapidated baths, and baths somewhere between these extremes. (As noted above, this study was conducted in baths of the newer, more modern variety.)*

While the physical arrangements may vary from bath to bath, certain features are common. Gay baths have a steam room or sauna (used more as a legal facade than for its standard function), and they usually contain private bedrooms (for which one pays extra), lockers, shower and toilet facilities, and a "dormitory" or "orgy room."

---

* As the bath scene changes, so does the meaning of the baths for homosexuals. Some claim that the newer, more famous baths are at the forefront of the gay movement. Others claim that baths, no matter how luxurious, still ghettoize the homosexual and, by promoting *impersonal* sex, retard the development of social relationships among homosexuals. Between these ideological extremes is the traditional clientele who more or less simply accept the sexual function of the baths.

After paying for admission, the patron goes to either the locker room or a private room. Here he leaves his clothes and valuables and dons a towel around his waist. He may then utilize whatever amenities the particular bath offers (snacks, showers, TV), or he may begin his search for a sexual partner. If he has a private room, he may simply leave the door open and lie on the bed waiting for an interested passerby. If he finds a passerby attractive, he may invite that person in. Private rooms also serve as home bases for ventures into other areas where sex may occur, as places to return to with a partner, or as convenient places to rest after sexual activity. If the patron does not have a private room, he may walk through the hallways around the rooms, looking for a sexually desirable partner. Thus, the hallways adjacent to the private rooms are characterized by a continual parade of towel-clad men who glance into the rooms and occasionally stop to smile at, or briefly chat with, an occupant. Cruising, in the form of eye contact, a smile, or a gentle grope, also occurs between the men walking through the hallways.

Another center of sexual activity is the "orgy room." This dimly lit room, sometimes designed with recesses and cubbyholes, usually contains mattresses, water beds, or benches. Patrons rarely talk in the orgy room. They typically stand against the wall, sit or lie on a bed or bench, or circulate in pursuit of sexual activity. Group sex is a common occurrence here, and patrons sometimes join in sexual activity already in progress. In this room, one also finds spectators who are not, at the moment, attempting to participate in sexual activity.

In addition to these two areas for sexual activity, sex can occur in most other areas of the bath, especially on a crowded night. The following is a description of a large bath late on a Saturday night.

The whole bath is extremely crowded, with all facilities—bar, discotheque, TV—utilized. The hallways around the private rooms are full of people, and it is difficult to circulate because sexual activity has begun in one of the corridors. Group sex involving at least five persons has also begun in another corridor, and the covey of spectators makes passage even more difficult. Few words are spoken, but the air is filled with grunts and moans, exacerbated by a great deal of sexual activity going on in a concentrated space.

The orgy room is equally crowded. Two males are engaging in anal intercourse on a central bed, surrounded by some 15–20 spectators. Throughout the room, cruising and sexual activity are taking place. When they come into the room, patrons move clockwise around the room, squeezing through the crowd. The room is very hot and humid, with a great deal of traffic and no conversation.

Upstairs in the discotheque, an audience of towel-clad males roar their appreciation of an elderly female burlesque star doing a strip-tease.

Now we consider how the social organization of the baths succeeds or fails in meeting the ideal conditions for impersonal sex.

## Protection

Given contemporary proscriptions against homosexual sex, gay baths and their patrons are usually liable to both legal and social sanctions. Since official intervention into "deviant" institutions is often prompted by public pressure or notoriety, the very survival of such institutions may depend upon their ability to operate without attracting public attention. Furthermore, the ability of such institutions to attract customers depends in large part on the security they can offer their patrons against public embarrassment and legal harassment. This aim is accomplished in a number of ways.

First, gay baths tend to be inconspicuous. They are not often found in smaller cities, and in larger cities they are often located in nonresidential, interstitial areas. Gay baths are usually muted in appearance, with no external indication of what they are except a cryptic sign such as "Men's Health Club." In addition, advertisements for gay baths ordinarily appear only in gay and underground publications.

Second, gay baths take other precautions to reduce their vulnerability to intrusion by authorities or by heterosexuals. One national chain of baths requires that each member bath must be operated as a private membership club. This gives some safeguard against police intrusion on the grounds of invasion of privacy. For baths in this chain, other rules that limit the possibility of legitimate intrusion by authorities include compliance with health and safety regulations, the actual existence of a steam room or sauna to give the semblance of a health club, keeping an orderly place, and prohibiting drug use. In one bath, a sign notes that police have received complaints about bath patrons' parking illegally on residential streets and concludes, "Please do not let parking endanger the ————— Baths."

Attempting to enter a gay bath can involve some screening, including such questions as where one heard about the bath and whether one knows what type of place it is. In addition to "homosexual" credentials (such as familiarity with gay newspapers), IDs are sometimes requested. Also, in case a raid should occur, there is often a series of locked doors to delay intrusion and to allow time for patrons to stop sexual activity.

Third, the baths protect their patrons by fostering anonymity. For example, patrons wear only a towel, leaving behind such social identifiers as clothing and uniforms. In addition, in dimly lit areas (such as the orgy room, the steam room, and recesses) it is often difficult to identify participants. Most important, though, is a custom that exists in many baths against conversation, even in such areas as the TV room or snack bar. When there is conversation, there is an informal rule against prying.

The baths also alleviate another anxiety sometimes associated with the pursuit of impersonal sex—the fear of theft or assault. Among male homosexuals this fear is exacerbated by the isolated places (e.g., parks) sometimes used for sexual activity, and by the limited protection and recourse offered to homosexuals by legal authorities. In the baths, the patron locks up his valuables when he arrives, and—although violence is almost unknown—others are near enough to be summoned if needed.

While baths provide considerable protection for their clientele, however, they are not completely successful. In their day-to-day operation, gay baths face numerous problems of survival in a hostile environment. There are, for example, occasional police raids (*The Advocate*, 1971, 1972, 1975), and the owners and managers we interviewed made it clear that the police are well aware of which baths are gay and of what goes on inside them. Thus, many owners concentrate on maintaining good relationships with the local authorities in charge of safety, health, fire, and zoning regulations. We have been informed of some direct payoffs to the police, as well as indirect payoffs in the form of contributions to such things as police-run charities.

Also, anonymity is far from complete. As noted above, in some baths one must take out membership, and in many one must provide an ID. In baths with parking lots, license plates could be used to identify those inside. And in smaller baths, the limited clientele makes it possible to recognize "regulars" whom one would also recognize outside the bath. Recently, one large, popular bath with its own nightclub adopted the policy of allowing nongays into the nightclub. This threat to anonymity upset many of the bath patrons, and the policy has since been discontinued.

Nonetheless, insofar as protection is concerned, gay baths do fairly well. The rules promoting anonymity contribute to a sense of concealment and ease. In addition, participants appreciate the protection offered by a location that is relatively safe, inconspicuous, private, and unknown to "outsiders."

## A Good Opportunity Structure

As with any other behavior, in order to engage in impersonal sex one needs not only the motivation, but also the opportunity. The ideal opportunity structure is one where everyone is attractive and available at minimal expense. To a large degree, the baths are territories that provide such an opportunity structure. Their clienteles include many attractive men, with enough diversity in physical types to satisfy customers' varying notions of attractiveness. Moreover, everyone at a gay bath is a potential partner. (We observed few "couples" and few situations in which a person could not be approached.) In addition, the orgy room provides an area where sex can usually be obtained. Finally, the baths are not expensive. Prices ordinarily range from two to twelve dollars, depending on the time of day and day of the week, the lavishness and popularity of the bath, and whether or not one rents a private room.

At the same time, the opportunity structure is not perfect, with disappointments sometimes arising at the level of face-to-face interaction—namely, acceptance and reciprocity on the part of the prospective partner. Thus, while the bath patron can probably find a partner, he may not get the one he desires. In addition, the partner may limit the range of sexual acts, or he may fail to reciprocate sexual acts (e.g., some patrons will receive but not perform fellatio). Moreover, the standards of the wider homosexual culture, in which youth and physical attractiveness are highly valued, pervade the baths. Thus, older or very overweight patrons may spend much of their time cruising with little success.

Certain features of gay baths, however, mitigate these potential problems. For example, because of the ample field of partners, there is a high probability of eventually finding a partner interested in the same type of activity. In addition, in areas that are poorly lit, it is difficult to fully ascertain the attractiveness of a partner. Indeed, the very anonymity of these places appears to generate a high level of sexual excitement—so much so that the physical characteristics of participants seem to recede in importance. (In one bath, there is a particularly dark corridor known as "Pig Alley" because it reputedly is a place for the old and unattractive. This is, however, a very popular place for sex, and our impression was that the participants entering and leaving this corridor differed little from participants elsewhere in the bath.)

## A Known, Shared, and Organized Reality

Soliciting and carrying out impersonal sex often makes participants uneasy. Anomie is inherent when one person does not know whether or not the other recognizes and shares the intent to have impersonal sex, and participants may fear embarrassment or the other person's anger. Also, in most settings there are no simple, institutionalized rules for transforming the intent into various stages of interaction (from solicitation on). Thus, awkwardness may prevail, and considerable time and energy may be expended without any sexual outcome.

Ideally, then, the sexual intent would be known and shared by all parties, and there would be some kind of organized "road map" for transforming the intent into various stages of interaction. Gay baths meet these conditions fairly well.

Regarding a known and shared intent, baths are well known among homosexuals as territories for impersonal sex. Furthermore, the open and continuous cruising, the orgy rooms, and the sale of such sundries as KY lubricant leave no doubt about the interests to which the baths cater.

Because of the known and shared intent, cruising is much less furtive in the baths than in most other settings. At the baths, "road maps" for transforming the intent into interaction are manifest in the form of interactional rules involving body language and other nonverbal signals. For instance, one patron may signify sexual interest in another by displaying his room key. More generally, an open door to a private room usually indicates the occupant's availability. He may signify a desire for anal intercourse by lying on his stomach, a desire to receive fellatio by lying on his back and displaying an erection. A potential partner indicates interest by lounging in the doorway to the room, perhaps engaging in small talk, and waiting for an invitation to come in.

Invitation in the orgy room consists primarily of touching another person (usually, but not always, on the genitals) or sitting next to someone on a water bed, mattress, or bench. One then waits for some indication of reciprocal interest. If group sex is occurring, one may simply attempt to join the gathering.

A system of body language continues to orient behaviors throughout the sexual activity. (These "road maps" are usually an import from the wider homosexual culture.) A rule of experimentation exists whereby one partner explores the other with his fingers, which the latter removes from those areas he does not want stimulated or penetrated. We have also observed one partner's attempting to motion the other into a particular position, as well as mutual repositioning. Communication is usually restricted to body language, especially in the orgy room, where talking is uncommon. In the private rooms, a limited amount of talking is more likely, and sexual requests are sometimes verbalized.

Although less clear in its details, the "road map" for departure provides for a simple exit. Participants sometimes use verbal scripts like "Thank you," or "Time for a shower." Often they leave with a friendly clasp of the partner's shoulder or with no ritual at all.

Despite all of the above, interaction at the baths is not totally free from awkwardness. Interactional rules are, of course, incomplete guidelines. For example, a number of informants say they use the orgy rooms because they are shy and reluctant to initiate sexual contact with persons in private rooms. Likewise, in the orgy room, we have often seen a number of persons apparently waiting for something to happen without being quite sure who should do what. In the orgy room, there are also occasions where departure seems problematic. A common observation, for example, is uncertainty after one partner has brought the other to orgasm. Confusion centers around whether or not there will be reciprocation. A person who has been fellated often just stands still while his partner does a backward and forward step movement, undecided as to whether to go or stay. (In such cases, usually nothing develops and the pair dissolves.)

Thus, in the baths we have a culture of impersonal sex, fed and sustained by the wider homosexual culture. One implication is that homosexuals from one part of the country can easily use baths in another area, although they must orient themselves to minor variations among baths and get a sense of what is "normal" for each bath.

## Bounding of the Sexual Experience

Because of the singular purpose often involved in impersonal sex, many males do not want a complex or broad social relationship. Thus from their perspective it is desirable to limit nonsexual, social interaction. This desire is often related to the wish to conceal the activity or to avoid involvements that could compete with established relationships (e.g., romantic relationships). It also is sometimes related to shyness or a wish psychologically to compartmentalize the activity. With regard to the latter, for many males involved in homosexual activity, their self-image does not easily commit them to any more of a relationship than is required by the sexual goal itself (Hoffman, 1968:177–78).

In the baths, social relationships can be curtailed in a number of ways. In the first place, the baths are not regarded in the homosexual world as a place to develop a lasting relationship; thus, few persons go there with that intent. Also, even though many of the newer baths contain social-recreational facilities, there is no pressure on patrons to use these facilities. Furthermore, there are subterritories (such as the orgy room) that limit socializing and "road maps" that can supply simple means for transforming the sexual intent into appropriate interaction within these subterritories.

In short, bounding of the sexual experience is described by many male participants as a desirable condition for impersonal sex. It is facilitated by interactional rules and territories that clearly define sex as an outcome, that limit socializing, and that sustain the expectation of closed horizons regarding the future of the relationship.

## Congenial Interaction

In situations of impersonal sex, the absence of a known and shared intent, "road maps," and rules of bounding can make for awkward, demoralizing, or hostile interaction. Even situations that have such features, however, may fail to promote congeniality. In gay baths, additional rules exist that make for relatively congenial interaction.

Sexual invitations follow an etiquette involving simple and nonabrasive rituals (already described) that are characterized by their gentleness; usually they are not forceful or persistent. Nonacceptance is ordinarily communicated in a way that is nonabrasive and that masks rejection. In the hallways, one declines another's invitation by avoiding eye contact or by smiling but not sustaining eye contact. In private rooms, such simple scripts as "I'm just resting," "Sorry, I've just come," or "Not now," accompanied by a smile, are customary forms of not accepting an invitation. In the orgy room, one gently removes the hands of the solicitor and/or moves on. If group sex is occurring, a participant merely turns his head, shifts his body, or raises his arm to signify that a newcomer is not welcome.

During the sexual activity itself, concerns over sexual performance do not disrupt an atmosphere of congeniality to the degree that they often do in other contexts. For example, since trial-and-error positioning is routinized, it does not communicate rejection or a sense of incompetence. In addition, erection and orgasm (which are often demanded for heterosexual performance) are not much of an issue in the baths. An erection is not necessary to fellatio or receive anal intercourse, and the possibility that one has recently experienced an orgasm can mask impotency problems. Moreover, anxiety about gossip regarding one's sexual performance is reduced by the relative lack of conversation. Participants also note that after sexual episodes verbal and nonverbal communications of congeniality are not uncommon (e.g., an embrace or expression of thanks).

Since participants expect the interaction to be restricted to sexual activity, departures after a sexual episode are also simple, routine, and nonabrasive. Participants melt away with little or no ceremony. And since participants expect as much, such departures do not ordinarily engender feelings of disappointment or emptiness.

Although the atmosphere in the baths is courteous and relatively congenial, it does not quite reach the level of friendliness that some patrons would consider ideal. Many of the rules of interaction (e.g., against conversation) that contribute to meeting other ideal conditions (e.g., bounding) limit that degree of friendliness.

Moreover, we occasionally did observe open breaches of congeniality, usually directed at participants who had themselves broken other interactional rules. For example, contrary to the rules of etiquette in one bath, a person cruising in the corridors between the rooms clumsily groped at passersby, who looked indignant and quickly walked away. We also observed

negative reactions toward occasions of open rejection of people
who persistently tried to join sexual episodes already in progress.
(Again, overweight or older patrons sometimes complain of
uncongenial treatment.)

## Physical Settings

Important features of the physical settings for impersonal sex
are the facilities, cleanliness, and decor. A lack of facilities that
provide comfort for the sexual act may impede the sexual
episode. Also, participants may avoid or hasten their departure
from settings that lack provisions for their nonsexual comfort
(e.g., air conditioning, bathrooms). Moreover, if the physical
surroundings are dirty or unattractive, participants are more
likely to experience the episode as degrading and to fear that
they might "catch something." Finally, attention-focusing facilities such as a television set may prevent boredom or self-
consciousness in the time surrounding the sexual episode. Thus,
social and psychological, as well as physical, comfort are affected by the physical setting.

The greatest change in gay baths during recent years has been
the improved quality and scope of their physical facilities and
layouts. The newer, more modern baths are, as a rule, very clean
and attractive. Lounges are carpeted and comfortable, and
attendants continuously sweep, empty ashtrays, and change
sheets in private rooms. Facilities that enhance relaxation include steam and sauna rooms, showers, whirlpool baths, TV
rooms, snack bars, swimming pools, movies, pool tables, and
libraries. In some baths, there are dance floors and live entertainment. A variety of sundries and services are available for the
convenience of patrons, including towels and mouthwash. There
are also notice boards advertising events in the gay community.*

Too many recreational facilities, however, are evaluated negatively by some patrons. They are seen by these participants as
detracting from the traditional focus of the baths (the pursuit of

---

* In the most plush baths, there are also massage and manicure services,
laundry and valet services, hair dryers, hair stylists, weight-lifting and body-
building instructions, and yoga classes.

impersonal sex) and/or as a threat to anonymity.

In general, though, impersonal sex, like probably any other social activity, is more positively evaluated when it takes place in physical settings that are clean, relaxing, and solicitous of the participants' needs.

## CONCLUSIONS

The ideal conditions presented in this paper can be effectively utilized for identifying and delineating—from the male participants' perspective—the areas in which other contexts besides the baths succeed or fail in the social organization of impersonal sex. Tearooms, for example, fail to provide protection and a pleasant physical setting. Massage parlors often exploit an unknown reality to "con" their customers, and the cost/reward ratio of most parlors is too high to constitute a good opportunity. With pickups, there may be confusion and awkwardness about whether or not one's intentions are shared, how to transform the situation, or the degree to which the experience will be bounded. And, as a final illustration, streetwalkers are often denounced for failures with regard to protection, congeniality, and the physical settings to which they take their patrons. . . .

In the course of our research, it became clear that what sociologists label "social organization" is at times recognized and experienced by the participants. In effect, they recognize what we call social organization as existing to the degree that social arrangements promote a *sense of ease* for at least some class of participants.*

Regarding this sense of ease, both environmental and individual referents are invoked (Merton, 1957:161–2 on anomie vs. anomy). In terms of environment, the sense of ease usually refers to an easily locatable and accessible setting, the layout and program of which promote a controlled and efficient achieve-

---

* Participants may recognize, however, that they themselves are not included in the class of participants for whom there is successful organization. (For example, con victims often recognize, in retrospect, that the con was remarkably well organized for the operators but not for the victims.)

ment of goals. In this sense, gay baths are seen to provide "easy sex" in the same way that neighborhood shopping centers provide "easy shopping." In terms of the individual, the sense of ease refers to a related state of mind—an absence of confusion and aggravation. For example, a sense of ease may mean that, for at least some class of participants, social organization coordinates activities in a way that requires relatively little psychological effort on their part. Known, shared, and organized rules of interaction, thus, decrease confusion vis-à-vis sexual as well as other activities. Who intends to do what, how, and with whom can be taken for granted, at least in its general form.

The emphasis placed by our subjects on ease and efficiency in obtaining a variety of sexual partners also relates to a second theme in general social theory—the concept of the market mentality. Tonnies, Marx, Weber, Simmel, Wirth, Fromm, Slater, and other commentators represent a long tradition that has addressed the topics of the market mentality and the depersonalization of relationships. This tradition describes people as objectified "things," considered solely in terms of the way they serve as impersonal means to ends.

Depersonalization and objectification are salient features of our participants' ideals regarding impersonal sex. Note, for example, their construction of an ideal opportunity structure—"where everyone is attractive and available at minimal expense." From this point of view, sex partners should be there for the picking with nonsexual interaction and the horizons of the relationship kept to a minimum. Thus, the market mentality is demonstrated not simply as a theorist's conceptualization but also as an empirical finding (Becker, 1974).

At the same time, our findings suggest a modification of the traditional "market mentality" concept. For example, it was clear throughout our research that human beings often have a difficult time sustaining complete impersonality, even given optimal conditions. Also, participants sometimes feel shy and embarrassed, hurt and rejected, envious and jealous, friendly and intimate—emotions that call into question the image of complete detachment that we usually associate with the market mentality. Such emotions attest to the capacity of humans to attribute a variety of meanings to their experiences and to react emotionally rather than in the simple and solely cognitive manner often depicted by sociology (Douglas, 1971:Chapter 1). Thus, as other empirical studies of impersonal situations have also shown (e.g., Jacobs, 1969; Zimmerman, 1970), the "market mentality" should be regarded more as a sensitizing concept or variable than as a strict and literal description of the phenomena to which it is applied.

In addition, sociology traditionally conceptualizes impersonal relationships as superficial, tawdry, depressing, or pathological. This conception ignores the fact that such relationships may be defined as positive by the people involved. It ignores the fact that participants may interpret the impersonal experience as fun, enjoyable, or satisfactory, and that a market-type social organization may indeed be the best for facilitating such experiences.

## REFERENCES

*The Advocate* 60 (May 26–June 18, 1971): 2, 100; (December 6, 1972): 4; 172 (March 26, 1975): 5.

BATES, AARON. "Eversoft at the Everard." *Gay* 3 (January 24, 1972):5.

BECKER, HOWARD S. "Art as Collective Action." *American Sociological Review* 39 (December 1974): 767–76.

BROOM, LEONARD, and PHILIP SELZNICK. *Sociology*. New York: Harper & Row, 1963.

DAVIS, MURRAY S. *Intimate Relations*. New York: Free Press, 1973.

DOUGLAS, JACK D. *"Existential Sociology."* Unpublished manuscript, 1971.

DOWNIE, R. S. "Personal and Impersonal Relationships." Proceedings of the Annual Conference, Philosophy of Education Society (Great Britain) 5 (July 1971, supplementary issue): 125–38.

GARY, DIANA. "Turning Out: A Study of Teenage Prostitution." *Urban Life and Culture* 1 (January 1973): 401–25.

HOFFMAN, MARTIN. *The Gay World: Male Homosexuality and the Social Creation of Evil*. New York: Basic Books, 1968.

HONG, LAWRENCE K., WILLIAM DARROUGH, and ROBERT DUFF. "The Sensu ous Ripoff: Customer Fraud Turns Blue." *Urban Life and Culture* 4 (January 1975): 464–70.

HUMPHREYS, LAUD. *Tearoom Trade: Impersonal Sex in Public Places*. Chicago: Aldine, 1970.

―――. "Impersonal Sex and Perceived Satisfaction." In James M. Henslin, ed., *Studies in the Sociology of Sex*. New York: Appleton-Century-Crofts, 1971.

JACOBS, JERRY. "Symbolic Bureaucracy: A Case Study of a Social Welfare Agency." *Social Forces* 47 (June 1969):413–22.

MERTON, ROBERT K. *Social Theory and Social Structure*. Rev. ed. New York: Free Press, 1957.

PIRO, RICHARD. "The Ritch Street Baths: An Alternative to the Alternative." *Vector* 9 (April 1973):4–6.

ROSS, H. LAURENCE. "The Hustler in Chicago." *Journal of Student Research* 1 (September 1959):13–19.

WEINBERG, MARTIN S., and COLIN J. WILLIAMS. *Male Homosexuals: Their Problems and Adaptations*. New York: Oxford University Press, 1974.

WILLIAMS, COLIN J., and MARTIN S. WEINBERG. *Homosexuals and the Military: A Study of Less Than Honorable Discharge*. New York: Harper & Row, 1971.

YOUNG, PERRY DEANE. "So You're Planning to Spend a Night at the Tubs?": Here's Some Advice Your Mother Never Gave You." *Rolling Stone* 128 (February 15, 1973): 48, 50.

ZIMMERMAN, DON H. "The Practicalities of Rule Use." In Jack D. Douglas, ed., *Understanding Everyday Life: Toward the Reconstruction of Sociological Knowledge*. Chicago: Aldine, 1970.

# Gay Ghetto

## MARTIN P. LEVINE

We are refugees from Amerika. So we
came to the ghetto.
  —Carl Wittman

Gays have claimed that there exist within major cities "gay
ghettos," neighborhoods housing large numbers of gays as well
as homosexual gathering places, and in which homosexual behavior is generally accepted, designating as such certain sections
of Boston, New York, Chicago, San Francisco, and Los Angeles
(Aiken, 1976; Altman, 1971:42; Brill, 1976; Chicago Gay Liberation, 1970:3–4; Kantrowitz, 1975:48; Nassberg, 1970:1; Russo,
1976; Shilts, 1977:20; Whitmore, 1975:45; Wittman, 1972:167–
68). Sociologists have picked up the term, repeatedly using it in
homosexual research. For example, Humphreys (1972a:80–81)
labels as "gay ghetto" a neighborhood characterized by marked
tolerance of homosexuality and a clustering of gay residences
and bars. Weinberg and Williams (1974:43) use the term
"lavender ghetto" for districts with large numbers of homosexuals and their institutions.* Typically, however, these authors
offer no observations to support their use of the term.

This paper analyzes the validity of "gay ghetto" as a sociological construct, limiting the discussion to the male homosexual
community.

An abbreviated version of this paper appears in the *Journal of Homosexuality* 4, no. 4 (1979), in press. Reprinted by permission of The Haworth Press
and the author.

I am grateful to Margot Abel, Dr. Edgar W. Butler, Dr. Carol Corden, Dr.
Claude S. Fischer, Kenneth Rosow, and especially Dr. Wagner Thielens, Jr.,
for their invaluable comments and suggestions. I would like to thank Fredric
Bell for translating the street maps into spot maps.

* The color lavender has been traditionally used to symbolize homosexuality.

## THE GHETTO

The term "ghetto" has been employed by sociologists in varied and sometimes inconsistent ways. Most sociologists consider a ghetto to be an area of the city housing a segregated cultural community, but there is marked disagreement about the particular features of the community that qualify it as a ghetto. The term was first used in accordance with its historical connotation, as applicable only to the Jewish community (Wirth, 1928:4). In the 1920s, sociologists from the Chicago School, notably Robert E. Park (1928:vii–ix) and Louis Wirth (1928:1–10), began to use it to describe any urban neighborhood inhabited by a people socially segregated from the larger society and bearers of a distinctive culture. Noting that the circumstances of immigrant groups often did fit these requisites, Park and Wirth applied the term to neighborhoods inhabited by Jews, Poles, blacks, and Italians. They also suggested its suitability as a depiction of areas dominated by such moral deviants as bohemians, hobos, and prostitutes (Park, 1928:vii-viii; Wirth, 1928:6, 20, 286). Disregarding Park's and Wirth's more general formulation, contemporary usage of the term has in some instances restricted the concept to communities inhabited by racial and ethnic groups, particularly those that are poverty stricken and socially disorganized (Butler, 1977:121; Kerner Commission, 1968:12). In other cases, the word "ghetto" is applied to any area inhabited by a minority group (Fischer, 1976:13; Theodorson and Theodorson, 1969:174). Even affluent minority communities are said to live in ghettos, these being called "gilded ghettos" (Michelson, 1970:65).

Park's and Wirth's notion is superior to the other formulations because it removes "ghetto" from its historical connotation and translates it into a construct useful to the study of urban ecology. Wirth (1928:6) recognizes this advantage when he notes that a ghetto epitomized ecological segregation in the sense that it is a spatial indicator of the extent to which a community is isolated from the surrounding society. Unfruitfully grounded in the ghetto's historical meaning, the other formulations limit the term to racial and ethnic communities, obscuring the generalizability of its features and thus hiding its important implication for urban ecology. For these reasons, I will use Park's and Wirth's conceptualization.

The classic exposition of Park's and Wirth's formulation appears in Wirth's well-known study *The Ghetto*. In the book's foreword, Park (p. vii) defines a ghetto as an area of the city that houses a segregated cultural community. Wirth develops the concept further by specifying as key elements of a ghetto four features: institutional concentration, culture area, social isolation, and residential concentration. Institutional concentration denotes the centralization of the ghettoized people's gathering places and commercial establishments in the ghetto. For example, in the Jewish ghetto are concentrated large numbers of synagogues, religious schools, ritual bathhouses, kosher butchers and restaurants, and Yiddish theaters and bookstores.

Wirth (p. 286) means by "culture area" that the culture of a particular people dominates the geographic area, a dominance reflected in the spatial centralization of the ghettoized people's cultural traits. Inside the Hebrew quarter, for example, Wirth observes a concentration of Jewish traits. He finds mainly Yiddish written on store signs, restaurant menus, and billboards; he hears mainly Yiddish spoken in conversations and speeches. The distinctive attire of the Jews also prevails in this neighborhood. Most of the men have long sidelocks and flowing beards, and wear long black coats and hats or skullcaps. Most of the women wear kerchiefs, long dresses, aprons, and shawls. Wirth also records the widespread adherence to the special customs of the Jewish people, such as the closing of stores on the sabbath and high holy days.

The third key element of the ghetto, social isolation, denotes the segregation of the ghettoized people from meaningful social relations with the larger community. To Wirth (p. 287), this isolation is produced by the prejudice that is typically heaped upon the ghettoized people or by the social distance different cultural practices create between the group and the larger community. Wirth (pp. 222–26) illustrates this type of social isolation by showing how anti-Semitism and/or the social distance caused by Jewish subcultural practices are responsible for the restriction of the ghettoized Jews' social lives to other Jews.

Residential concentration, the last key element, signifies that the ghetto is a residential area with a concentration of the homes of the ghettoized people. Wirth (pp. 205–10) demonstrates, with population statistics, that the majority of the people living in Chicago's Jewish ghetto are Jewish.

Following Park and Wirth, an urban neighborhood is a "gay ghetto" if it possesses the attributes Park and Wirth have put forth. It must contain gay institutions in number, a conspicuous and locally dominant gay subculture that is socially isolated from the larger community, and a residential population that is substantially gay. The rest of the paper presents exploratory research findings which show that some metropolitan subcommunities are indeed "gay ghettos." To prove this, I used a multifaceted research strategy. First I limited my inquiry to metropolises commonly reputed to have large numbers of homosexuals. Then I developed procedures to demonstrate the degree to which gay institutions concentrate in each metropolis, to measure the extent of concentration, and to determine the boundaries and the names of the areas in which the institutions cluster. Finally I carried out exploratory fieldwork in the areas of concentration to study the degree to which they fulfilled the other requisites.

## PARK'S AND WIRTH'S FIRST REQUISITE: INSTITUTIONAL CONCENTRATION

This section locates neighborhoods with large numbers of homosexual institutions. My strategy for the research was the ecological method (Michelson, 1970:11). I first plotted the location of gay institutions on maps of five cities. I then studied the maps for concentrations of these institutions, and ascertained the names and boundaries of the districts in which they occur.

The data used in constructing the maps came from a national directory of gay gathering places, *Bob Damron's 1976 Address Book*. This directory contains the names and addresses of bars, bookstores, steam baths, churches, restaurants, and movie theaters catering to the gay community. It also lists cruising locations, indoor or outdoor places such as beaches, parks, or street corners where homosexuals go to meet each other, often to set up sexual encounters. Places listed within this directory are coded as to the type of patrons who frequent them (e.g., youths, hustlers, western) and as to the kinds of activities available there (e.g., dancing, entertainment, overnight accommodations).* *Bob Damron's Address Book* is one of several available gay directories, all of which vary in the accuracy of their listings. *Bob Damron's* is the most current and accurate, according to the personnel of New York's Oscar Wilde Memorial Bookshop, the nation's oldest, largest, and best-known gay bookstore.†

Cities selected for study were Boston, New York, Chicago, San Francisco, and Los Angeles. They were chosen because the available literature makes reference to areas in these cities housing large numbers of homosexuals and their institutions.

Maps were constructed by plotting the location of the directory listings on city street maps. The street maps used contain street indexes and are labeled by neighborhood and house number. The plotting was done city by city, by locating with the street index and the house numbers the position of every directory listing on each map. This procedure placed each listing on its appropriate block. The institutional listings such as bars, restaurants, and steam baths are indicated by solid black dots. The cruising areas are represented by solid black lines. The street maps were then simplified and reduced into spot maps.

The spot maps (see maps) indicate a definite distribution pattern of gay gathering places in these cities.‡ They show that large numbers of these places are concentrated in small areas,

---

* "Western" denotes, in gay argot, that patrons dress in western attire: chaps, cowboy hats, leather vests (Warren, 1974:20).

†This opinion is shared by Weinberg and Williams (1974:41n, 58n). Warren (1974:19) is of the opinion that all the directories are out of date. Harrys (1974:241) formed a different guide, the *Guild Guide,* to be the most current and up to date.

‡The map of New York City omits Staten Island because the directory contains no listings there.

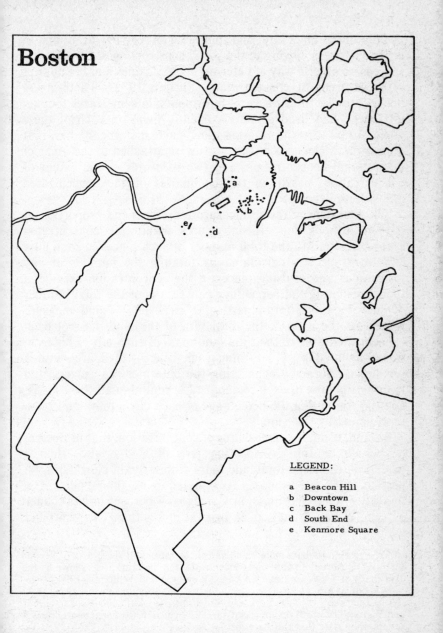

# Boston

LEGEND:

a  Beacon Hill
b  Downtown
c  Back Bay
d  South End
e  Kenmore Square

usually in the inner city, and that none or very few are found in other city areas. Owing to the social construction of community, there is no precise way of determining the names and boundaries of these areas of concentration (Suttles, 1972). Therefore, I decided to ask this of several informants, in some cases sociologists, who had lived or were currently living in each of these cities. From the information they gave me, the names that appear on the legends of the maps were attached to the areas of institutional concentration, and two measures of the extent of concentration, based on the boundaries of the concentrated areas, were developed.*

The first concentration measure represents the proportion of gay institutions and cruising places within the concentrated areas compared to the total number of such places in each city. This measure was calculated by totaling the number of gay institutions and cruising places in the concentration areas and then calculating the percentage this sum is of the total number of such locations for a particular city. The second measure represents the ratio of the total sum of the land mass of each concentrated area to the total land mass of each city. This ratio was calculated by (1) turning each concentrated area into a rectangular form by connecting the outermost gay places; (2) figuring the area of each rectangle; (3) summing all these areas; and (4) computing the percentage of each city's total land mass represented by this sum.

I found, using these measures of concentration, that in Boston, 83 percent of the gay locations are situated on less than 2 percent of the city's total land mass. Similarly, in New York, 86 percent of the gay locations are situated in less than 2 percent of this city's total land mass; in Chicago, 64 percent in less than 1 percent; in San Francisco, 64 percent in less than 1 percent; and

---

* Other authors have noted similar concentrations in these areas. Newton (1972:22) observed institutional concentrations in the same areas shown by the spot maps of New York and Chicago. Weinberg and Williams (1974:41–46, 56–61) cite as areas housing large numbers of gay locations the districts shown on the spot maps of New York and San Francisco. Although Hooker (1967) and Warren (1974:20) do not specify areas in which institutional concentration occurs, they state that this happens in the cities they studied.

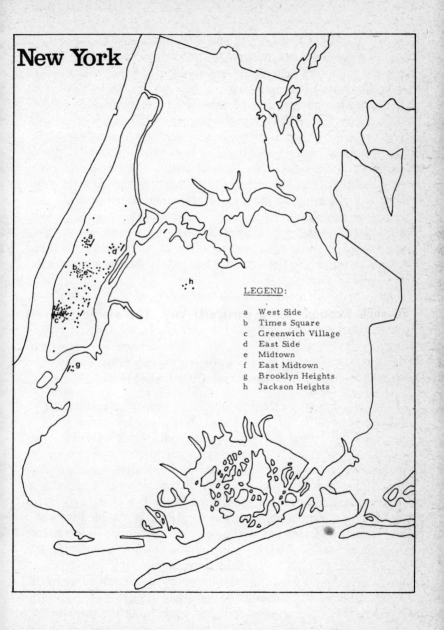

# New York

LEGEND:

a   West Side
b   Times Square
c   Greenwich Village
d   East Side
e   Midtown
f   East Midtown
g   Brooklyn Heights
h   Jackson Heights

in Los Angeles, 78 percent in less than 3 percent. The spot maps thus clearly demonstrate that gay institutions and cruising areas are not randomly distributed but in each case are concentrated in specific city districts.

Areas of concentration revealed by these maps also tend to vary as to what kinds of establishments are housed within them. The majority of these districts are comprised mainly of restaurants, cruising areas, and bars. A few, however, shelter places that cater to a specialized interest within the gay community. Gay-oriented movie theaters and bookstores and bars or street corners frequented by male prostitutes tend to concentrate only in one of these districts, usually in the downtown public entertainment districts, e.g., Times Square or the Tenderloin. Bars catering to western or sadomasochistic gays also are centralized in a particular district, usually an industrial warehouse area, e.g., Folsom Street.

The maps demonstrate the existence of gay institutional concentration in areas of each city. This is one indicator that there may indeed be gay ghettos.

### PARK'S AND WIRTH'S OTHER REQUISITES: CULTURE AREA, SOCIAL ISOLATION, RESIDENTIAL CONCENTRATION

To determine the extent to which the twenty-seven districts on the spot maps fulfill Park's and Wirth's other criteria for a ghetto, I conducted exploratory research, which entailed informal fieldwork and a literature survey. Fieldwork was carried out in New York and to a lesser degree in Boston, Chicago, San Francisco, and Los Angeles. The fieldwork was conducted in each of the neighborhoods indicated in the five cities' spot maps as housing a large number of gay locations. It included informal and formal interviews as well as observations made in the course of lengthy walks. Walks were oriented toward discovering the social characteristics of these areas by noting the types of institutions, land use, and populations within each community. The interviews were conducted with gay residents of each city. In interviews, questions were asked concerning the residence of the interviewee and his gay friends and the character of the interviewee's social network. Observations were conducted on main thoroughfares, from a place where I could both see and hear street activity, usually a street corner or in front of the popular bars, as well as in restaurants and stores.

The survey of the literature included both the professional literature and a national publication of the gay community, *The Advocate*. The professional literature search was confined mainly to literature on homosexuality and produced material that was generally impressionistic. *The Advocate* was utilized because it is widely recognized as a leading gay publication (Humphreys, 1972a:133; Warren, 1974:178). A scan of issues dated from September 1975 to June 1977 uncovered articles on the gay community in each of the five cities under consideration, all written by local correspondents.* The results of this research are presented below, broken down in terms of Wirth's other requisites of the ghetto—culture area, social isolation, and residential concentration.

## Culture Area

The culture of these districts was partially determined in the course of the fieldwork and literature search. The method used to ascertain this has been employed by many other sociologists (Park, 1925:6; Zorbaugh, 1929:4). This technique determines the culture of an area by examining the cultural traits that appear within it. A neighborhood's culture, according to this method, is that of the group whose cultural traits are most prevalent in the area.

The results of this research indicate that only certain sections—those sheltering places of the local gay scene—of seven of these districts are homosexual culture areas. The districts in which these sections occur are the West Side, Greenwich Village, New Town, Polk Street, Folsom Street, Castro Village, and West Hollywood. The boundaries of the homosexual cultural areas within these districts are ambiguous because of the social

---

* I was informed of this in a conversation with Mr. Joe Richards, director of public information at *The Advocate,* on June 7, 1977.

construction of community (Suttles, 1972). Generally, these sections consist of the streets housing a cluster of gay locations and the blocks proximate to them. For example, on New York's West Side, the homosexual culture area is comprised on the blocks surrounding the concentration of gay places between Broadway and Central Park in the low West Seventies. Similarly, in Greenwich Village, the homosexual culture area consists of the blocks encircling the cluster of gay establishments in the vicinity of the West Village's Christopher Street; in New Town, the intersection of Broadway and Clark Street; in Polk Street, Polk between Eddy and Broadway; in Folsom Street, Folsom between 4th and 12th Streets; in Castro Village, the intersection of Castro and 18th Streets; and in West Hollywood, Santa Monica Boulevard between Doheny Drive and La Cienega Boulevard.

These homosexual culture areas are typified by an extraordinarily high concentration of gays and their culture traits. This concentration is so extensive that the scene on many of the major commercial streets in these areas seems predominantly gay. Large numbers of gay men are present on the street, while women and children are conspicuously absent. Streets are lined with bars, bookstores, restaurants, and clothing stores catering to homosexuals, and many stores are gay-owned (Shilts, 1977; Thompson, 1976).

The most prevalent culture traits in these sections are those of the homosexual community. Gay language is widely used in these places.* For example, I frequently overheard conversations between gay men in which they referred to each other or other men with female names and pronouns. Many billboards, posters, and store signs also utilize this argot. Two oversized billboards towering over the intersection of Christopher Street and 7th Avenue South advertise a homosexual steam bath (Weinberg and William, 1975) by showing a drawing of the head of a cowboy and the message, "Come! to Man's Country." The billboards use knowledge common to gay men, the sexual

---

* Warren's (1974:100–121) conceptualization of gay language is used in this paper. She sees it as the linguistic aspect of the gay world, including vocabulary, ideology, mythology, and a symbolic universe.

implications of the word "come," and the western motif (Humphreys, 1972b) to imply that sex with desirable partners is available at the steam bath. There are also bars called Boot Hill, Numbers, Chaps, and stores called Boys' Market and Spike Liquors.

Gay fashion is a ubiquitous element of homosexual culture in these sections. The vast majority of men on the streets are dressed in the fashion currently favored by gays. This style, called "butch" in homosexual argot, includes four major looks: working man, lower-class tough, military man, and athlete (St. Clair, 1976). To illustrate, one variant of the lower-class tough look entails a tight black T-shirt, faded, skin-tight, straight-legged Levis, work boots, and a black leather motorcycle jacket. All of these looks call for short hair, muscular bodies, mustaches, closely cropped beards, and such accessories as key chains and handkerchiefs. These looks are so prevalent on these blocks that for a minute one gets the distinct impression of being in a union hall, army camp, or locker room. A few men in these areas wear the attire of sadomasochists—complete black leather outfits. Gay fashion is also sold in many of the local retail establishments, several specializing in it.*

Many social conventions within these areas are distinctly homosexual. Gestures of affection are exchanged openly between men, as well as eye contact and other gestures of sexual interest. For example, two men are frequently seen walking with their arms around each other's waists or holding hands. These open displays of affection rarely evoke sanctions; for the most part, people either accept or ignore them. Even police patrols through these sections pay little attention to such behavior. In light of the societal aversion to homosexuality, this tolerance is remarkable. In other places, such behavior quickly elicits harsh sanctions.

The scene in the homosexual culture areas shifts with the time of day. On weekday mornings and afternoons, bars and streets

---

* In these culture areas are found stores specializing in leather clothes, work clothes, western outfits or military gear. West Hollywood's Intermountain Logging Company is an example of a store that caters to the western look; Greenwich Village's The Leather Man, the sadomasochist look.

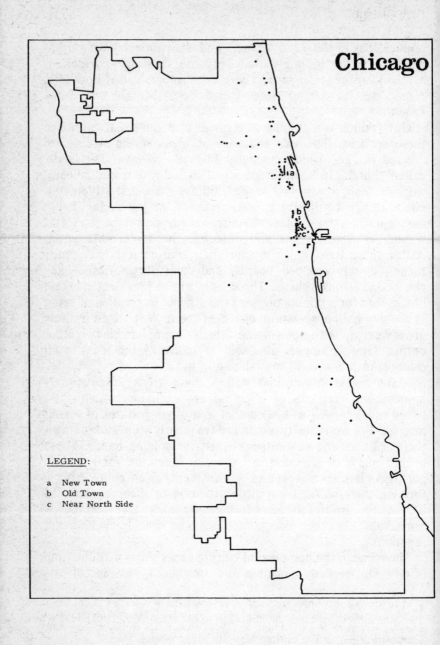

# Chicago

LEGEND:

a  New Town
b  Old Town
c  Near North Side

are relatively quiet. At night and on weekends, however, streets and bars are crowded, because participation in the gay world, for most homosexuals, occurs after normal working hours (Achilles, 1967; Hooker, 1967; Warren, 1974). At such times the areas are flooded with resident gays, as well as gays from surrounding neighborhoods and suburbs who come in to participate in the scene.

Gays recognize the culture areas as their quarters. These sentiments are reflected in the special names they give each area, names that are part of gay argot. For example, the homosexual culture area in West Hollywood is called Boy's Town (Stone, 1977). They are also reflected in the following statements made by gay residents of these areas (field notes):

I feel like an alien in other places. But in the Castro, I feel like I belong because I do.

For me, leaving the Village means pulling myself together and straightening up my act.

## Social Isolation

The literature on homosexuality reveals that most homosexuals are socially isolated (Gagnon, 1977:244; Hooker, 1967; Humphreys, 1972a:13–41; Leznoff and Westley, 1967; Warren 1974; Weinberg and Williams, 1974:18–30). Americans, strongly prejudiced against homosexuality, perceive it as a loathsome deviation (Levitt and Klassen, 1974; Weinberg and Williams, 1974:19–21). This societal antipathy creates an "intolerable reality" for gays, a reality in which homosexuals are confronted with a host of stringent sanctions (Humphreys, 1972a:13). Gays are discriminated against in employment and often fired upon discovery of their sexual orientation; they are criminals under various laws and thus subject to police surveillance; and they are frequently treated by those with whom they interact with ridicule, condemnation, ostracism, and even violence (Humphreys, 1972a:13–41; Weinberg and Williams, 1974:17–30). This prejudice and accompanying sanctions make it extremely difficult for homosexuals and heterosexuals to be socially and emotionally involved with each other. Gays, whether their condition is known or hidden, are always aware that most heterosexuals regard them as socially unacceptable. As a reaction to this, many homosexuals have withdrawn from meaningful social relations with members of conventional society and have restricted their social life and primary relations to other homosexuals (Hooker, 1967: 180–81; Leznoff and Westley, 1967: 193–95; Saghir and Robins, 1973: 170; Warren, 1974). Thus, gays are socially isolated from the larger society.

My research indicates that this is the case for many of the homosexuals I encountered. Some of my informants told me that their interaction with heterosexuals was restricted to their jobs or sporadic family visits. Aside from this, social relations were confined mainly to other homosexuals. Their friends and acquaintances were usually gay residents of the district in which they lived. Roommates, if they had them, were also homosexuals. A few informants told me they had even less contact with the heterosexual world. These individuals managed to live within an almost exclusively gay world by limiting their social relations to fellow homosexuals and working in either stereotypical gay jobs or businesses catering to gays. The extent of some gay men's social isolation is underscored in the following remarks (field notes):

The people at work are real friendly, always asking me out for drinks or inviting me to parties. I never go. It's too much of a hassle. They don't know I am gay, so I avoid seeing them outside of work. I'd much rather spend my free time with other gay men, hanging out on Polk Street.

I live on the West Side with two gay men, work in a gay restaurant, and spend my summers on Fire Island. I never relate to straight people.

Residential Concentration

Normally, the determination of residential segregation patterns is a relatively simple affair. Data are collected, usually from the census, on the addresses of all the members of the

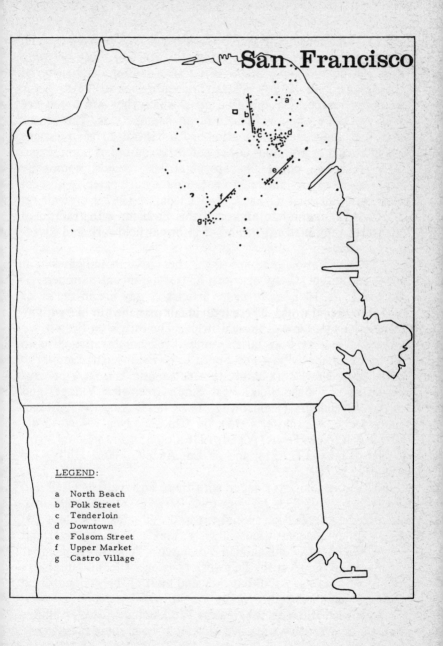

San Francisco

LEGEND:

a  North Beach
b  Polk Street
c  Tenderloin
d  Downtown
e  Folsom Street
f  Upper Market
g  Castro Village

group under consideration. The residential location of the group is then ascertained by analyzing data through one of three possible methods: spot maps, social area analysis, and factorial ecology (Timms, 1971). These procedures cannot be used for homosexuals because the data upon which they are based are lacking, namely, the addresses of all homosexuals. The census does not supply such information because it fails to ask questions about sexual orientation. Other potential sources of homosexual addresses (e.g., police files, psychiatrists' records, homophile organizations) are inadequate because they are patently misrepresentative of gays (Kitsuse and Cicourel, 1963:9; Weinberg, 1970). My inability to approach this problem with traditional measures prompted utilization of informal fieldwork and literature search.

The information obtained from the research indicates that only certain of these districts house significant numbers of homosexuals. In *The Advocate* articles of gay life in the cities under consideration, references are made to the large gay populations in a few of these districts. The article on Boston, for example, asserts that large numbers of homosexuals live in Beacon Hill, Back Bay, and South End (Brill, 1976). Similarly, articles on New York imply that substantial numbers of gays reside on the East Side, West Side, Greenwich Village, and Brooklyn Heights (Kantrowitz, 1975:48; Russo, 1975; Stoneman, 1975; Whitmore, 1975); on Chicago, Near North Side, Old Town, New Town (Aiken, 1976); on San Francisco, Castro Valley (Shilts, 1977:21); and on Los Angeles, West Hollywood (Stone, 1977).

Several sociologists concur with these observations (Bell and Weinberg, 1978:233–35, Newton, 1972:22; Starr and Carns, 1973:282). In addition Weinberg and Williams (1974:46, 60) find similar concentrations in New York's East Midtown and Jackson Heights, and on San Francisco's Polk Street. Similar results were found in the fieldwork. The overwhelming majority of my informants stated that they and most of their friends lived in these neighborhoods.

Greenwich Village's subarea the West Village, Castro Village, and the Boy's Town area of West Hollywood seem to have the largest concentrations of homosexual residents. In fact, judging from the available material, the latter two areas may even be predominantly homosexual (Shilts, 1977; Stone, 1977). The gay concentration in all these areas is so extensive that entire blocks and buildings are inhabited exclusively by gays, many of whom own the buildings in which they live (Shilts, p. 21; Stone, 1977):*

Almost everyone in the West Village Houses [a large housing development in Greenwich Village's homosexual culture area] is gay, my neighbors across the hall, upstairs, downstairs [field notes].

## CONCLUSION

This paper examined the validity of "gay ghetto" as a sociological concept. I have argued that its validity is contingent upon the existence of urban homosexual communities that meet Park's and Wirth's requisites for a ghetto.

Three communities in the cities studied, the West Village, Castro Village, and Boy's Town, fulfill all these requisites. All communities are characterized by large numbers of gay institutions and cruising places, a marked gay culture, socially isolated gay residents, and a substantially gay population. The West Village, Castro Village, and Boy's Town are thus gay ghettos. Their existence, in turn, validates "gay ghetto" as a sociological construct.

Twelve communities are partially developed gay ghettos. These communities partly satisfy the ghetto requisites. Three of them (West Side, New Town, Polk Street) house a concentration of gay locations, a homosexual culture area, and socially isolated gay residents. Their lack of a markedly gay population prevents them from being fully developed ghettos. Nine of the communities (Beacon Hill, Back Bay, South End, East Side, Brooklyn Heights, East Midtown, Jackson Heights, Old Town,

---

*I noted this in my fieldwork in Castro Village. My informants and Roy Tacker, owner of Paul Langley Real Estate, a major real estate agency in the area, concurred with this observation. Hooker (1967:172) and Warren (1974:20) also discovered predominantly gay blocks but they fail to specify their location.

**Los Angeles**

LEGEND:

a   San Fernando Valley
b   West Hollywood
c   Hollywood
d   Downtown

Near North Side) are marked by large numbers of gay institutions and socially isolated residents. These communities are not fully developed gay ghettos because they lack a salient homosexual culture area and a substantially gay populace. The remaining twelve spot map districts are probably not ghettos because they meet only one requisite—institutional concentration.

When considered together, it is possible that these communities represent different stages in ghetto development. Societal antipathy toward homosexuality sets the stage for their formation. Conditions of total suppression and zealous persecution inhibit ghetto development, but with a modicum of tolerance, the process begins. At first gay institutions and cruising places spring up in urban districts known to accept variant behavior, resulting in a concentration of such places in specific sections of the city, as shown on the spot maps. This concentration attracts large numbers of homosexuals, causing a centralization of gay culture traits, turning the districts into homosexual culture areas. Tolerance coupled with institutional concentration make the areas desirable residential districts for gays. Many homosexuals, especially those publicly labeled as gay or open about their orientation, settle in these areas. At this point, the areas have become partially developed gay ghettos.

Recent modifications of social attitudes toward homosexuals explain the transformation of the West Village, Castro Village, and Boy's Town into fully developed gay ghettos. A growing acceptance of homosexuality in the more liberal parts of the country signifies that gays can now practice an openly gay lifestyle without fear of penalization. Once out of the closet, gays may be drawn to the partially developed ghettos, to be near others like them and the places of gay life, increasing the number of gay residents in such districts. In cities like New York, San Francisco, and Los Aneles, with large gay populations, this increase coupled with a possible "heterosexual flight" (withdrawal from the community) may turn the areas into markedly gay neighborhoods, that is, fully developed gay ghettos.

This discussion of the development of gay ghettos is speculative. The actual process by which gay ghettos evolve can only be ascertained through longitudinal research of fully developed ghettos. Further research is thus needed on the West Village, Castro Village, and Boy's Town.

## REFERENCES

ACHILLES, NANCY. "The Development of the Homosexual Bar as an Institution." In John H. Gagnon and William Simon, eds., *Sexual Deviance*. New York: Harper & Row, 1967.

AIKEN, DAVID. "Chicago." *The Advocate* 198 (September 8, 1976):27–28.

ALTMAN, DENNIS. *Homosexual Oppression and Liberation*. New York: Avon Books, 1971.

BELL, ALAN P., and MARTIN S. WEINBERG. *Homosexualities: A Study of Diversity Among Men and Women*. New York: Simon & Schuster, 1978.

BRILL, DAVID. "Boston." *The Advocate* 184 (February 25, 1976):27.

BUTLER, EDGAR W. *The Urban Crisis: Problems and Prospects in America*. Santa Monica, Calif.: Goodyear Publishing Company, 1977.

CHICAGO GAY LIBERATION. "Working Paper for the Revolutionary Peoples Constitutional Convention." Gay Flames Pamphlet No. 13. New York: Gay Flames, 1970.

FISCHER, CLAUDE S. *The Urban Experience*. New York: Harcourt Brace Jovanovich, 1976.

GAGNON, JOHN H. *Human Sexualities*. Oakland, N.J.: Scott, Foresman, 1977.

HARRYS, JOSEPH. "Urbanization and the Gay Life." *The Journal of Sex Research* 10 (August 1974):238–47.

HOOKER, EVELYN. "The Homosexual Community." In John H. Gagnon and William Simon, eds., *Sexual Deviance*. New York: Harper & Row, 1967.

HUMPHREYS, LAUD. *Out of the Closets: The Sociology of Homosexual Liberation*. Englewood Cliffs, N.J.: Prentice-Hall, 1972a.

———. "New Styles in Homosexual Manliness." In Joseph A. McCaffrey, ed., *The Homosexual Dialectic*. Englewood Cliffs, N.J.: Prentice-Hall, 1972b.

KANTROWITZ, ARNIE. "I'll Take New York." *The Advocate* 175 (October 22, 1975):48–51.

KERNER COMMISSION. *Report of the National Advisory Commission on Civil Disorders.* New York: Bantam Books, 1968.

KITSUSE, JOHN I., and AARON V. CICOUREL. "A Note on the Use of Official Statistics." *Social Problems* 11 (Fall 1963): 131–139.

LEVITT, EUGENE E., and ALBERT D. KLASSEN, JR. "Public Attitudes Toward Homosexuality: Part of the 1970 National Survey by the Institute for Sex Research." *Journal of Homosexuality* 1 (Fall 1974): 29–43.

LEZNOFF, MAURICE, and WILLIAM A. WESTLEY. "The Homosexual Community." In John H. Gagnon and William Simon, eds., *Sexual Deviance.* New York: Harper & Row, 1967.

MICHELSON, WILLIAM. *Man and His Urban Environment: A Sociological Approach.* Reading, Mass.: Addison-Wesley, 1970.

NASSBERG, GUY. "An Introduction to Gay Liberation." In *Revolutionary Love,* Gay Flames Pamphlet no. 11. New York: Gay Flames, 1970.

NEWTON, ESTHER. *Mother Camp: Female Impersonators in America.* Englewood Cliffs, N.J.: Prentice-Hall, 1972.

PARK, ROBERT E. "The City: Suggestions for the Investigation of Human Behavior in the Urban Environment." In Robert E. Park and Ernest W. Burgess, *The City.* Chicago: University of Chicago Press, 1925.

———. "Foreword." In Louis Wirth, *The Ghetto.* Chicago: University of Chicago Press, 1928.

RUSSO, VITO. "The Village." *The Advocate* 175 (October 22, 1975): 47.

SAGHIR, MARCEL T., and ELI ROBINS. *Male and Female Homosexuality: A Comprehensive Investigation.* Baltimore: Williams & Wilkins, 1973.

STARR, JOYCE R., and DONALD E. CARNS. "Singles and the City: Notes on Urban Adaptation." In John Walton and Donald E. Carns, eds., *Cities in Change: Studies on the Urban Condition.* Boston: Allyn & Bacon, 1973.

ST. CLAIR, SCOTT. "Fashion's New Game: Follow the Gay Leader." *The Advocate* 186 (March 26, 1976): 18–19.

SHILTS, RANDY M. "Mecca or Ghetto? Castro Street." *The Advocate* 209 (February 9, 1977): 20–23.

STONE, CHRISTOPHER. "West Hollywood. Where the Boys Are." *The Advocate* 214 (April 20, 1977): 23–24.

STONEMAN, DONNELL. "East Side." *The Advocate* 175 (October 22, 1975): 44–45.

SUTTLES, GERALD D. *The Social Construction of Communities.* Chicago: University of Chicago Press, 1972.

THEODORSON, GEORGE A., and ACHILLES G. THEODORSON. *A Modern Dictionary of Sociology.* New York: Thomas Y. Crowell, 1969.

THOMPSON, MARK. "Small Business Owners Experiencing a Natural Progression of Liberated Consciousness." *The Advocate* 192 (June 16, 1976): 12–13.

TIMMS, DUNCAN. *The Urban Mosaic: Towards a Theory of Residential Differentiation.* New York: Cambridge University Press, 1971.

WARREN, CAROL A. B. *Identity and Community in the Gay World.* New York: Wiley, 1974.

WEINBERG, MARTIN S. "Homosexual Samples: Differences and Similarities." *The Journal of Sex Research* 6 (November 1970): 312–25.

WEINBERG, MARTIN S., and COLIN J. WILLIAMS. *Male Homosexuals: Their Problems and Adaptations.* New York: Oxford University Press, 1974.

———. "Gay Baths and the Social Organization of Impersonal Sex." *Social Problems* 23 (December 1975): 124–36.

WHITMORE, GEORGE. "West Side." *The Advocate* 175 (October 22, 1975): 44–45.

WITTMAN, CARL. "Refugees from Amerika: A Gay Manifesto." In Joseph A. McCaffrey, ed., *The Homosexual Dialectic.* Englewood Cliffs, N.J.: Prentice-Hall, 1972.

WIRTH, LOUIS. *The Ghetto.* Chicago: University of Chicago Press, 1928.

ZORBAUGH, HARVEY WARREN. *The Gold Coast and the Slum.* Chicago: University of Chicago Press, 1929.

# Camp

## VITO RUSSO

*To talk about Camp is therefore to betray it.*
　　　　　—Susan Sontag, *Notes on Camp*

There is a church on New York's West Side which has come to be known, in limited circles, as a "campy place to go to church." The reason for this sudden exodus to worship by essentially all-night diner types is unclear all week, when the church ritual is pretty tame. Aside from a few house jewels and some fancy gold robes, nothing flashier than a satin pump is in evidence.

No, the real show is on a hot holiday like Easter Sunday. Suddenly it's Josef von Sternberg's *The Scarlet Empress* and Dietrich is marrying the mad prince amidst the ornate splendor of a Russian cathedral. The choir is belting out Gregorian chants as if they were auditioning for the pope, and the gowns lack only feathers to be contenders for the Edith Head Gives Good Costume Awards. The killer, though, is the incense. You can't see two feet ahead of you, and as it hangs in the air, a few discreet gays give way to barely controlled giggling. Welcome to the church some of us know as Smoky Mary's.

As Susan Sontag noted in her famous essay, camp is the love of the extravagant, the exaggerated, converting the serious into the frivolous (or vice versa). It's a sensibility rather than an idea and exists in a rarefied atmosphere of esoterica. Religion, because of its serious preoccupation with ritual and spirit of grand extravagance, has always been a target of camp. When Francis Spellman was cardinal in New York City, there was a widely circulated story about the time Spellman was bearing the incense, which hangs on a chain, at high mass in St. Patrick's Cathedral. Another cardinal seated near the altar leaned over as

*The Advocate,* May 19, 1976. Copyright © 1976, Liberation Publications, Inc. Reprinted by permission of the publisher and author.

Spellman approached and whispered, "Pssst! Frannie! The hat is divine and your coat is heavenly, *but your pocketbook is on fire!"*

It's a way of deflating the pomp and making the most of the circumstance at the same time, for camp is also a sensibility best understood by select groups who are privy to a special view from their rarefied position. To discuss camp, therefore, is like smashing a toy to see what makes it run. The essence of camp is the unspoken amusement derived from knowing something is camp without having to explain why. Nobody asked Carmen Miranda why she wore 10-inch heels and danced around with a dozen bananas on her head. Carmen Miranda was just "too much."

To gay men, camp has been both a lifeline and an anchor. Camp humor is not necessarily gay humor. Paintings of Jesus in which the eyes follow you across the room are a camp. Peter Lemongello is a camp. Even John Wayne is camp, but the reason for that is his exaggeration of the masculine role, bringing him closer to gay camp than he'd feel comfy with, if he knew what it was. No, camp is not *necessarily* gay humor, but it has been discreetly noted that gay people have been in its vanguard. Gay humor, or that famous "gay sensibility," has often been a form of camp. Since camp flourishes in urban cliques and is something of a secret code, it has become one of the mainstays of an almost ethnic humor which has been formed for defense purposes over the years. Because camp seeks to comfort and is largely a generous rather than a selfish feeling, it has also operated in a human sense, aiding people in forming images with which they feel comfortable in a hostile culture.

A look at some gay camp expressions finds that they neutralize any threat or ignore disturbing reality. Police become "Alice blue gown" or "Tillie law." It's not only a way of minimizing the danger, but couches it in feminine (nonthreatening) terms. It is not by accident that the phrase "Get you, Mary!" is always directed at gay men.

It's easy to see why a covert society would take a sensibility glorifying artifice and the "unnatural" and use it to parody its own image. For this reason, camp is often sexist. The American Heritage Dictionary defines the verb *to camp* as "to act in an outlandish or effeminate manner." According to *The Queens' Vernacular,* a gay lexicon by Bruce Rodgers, the word comes from sixteenth-century England, where *camping* meant men working in a theatrical play in women's costumes. Camping it up, therefore, became a play on what society said all gay men were like, implying that gay men were effeminate (like women) and less than "real" men.

In Fire Island's Cherry Grove there is a large man called The Infanta. The Infanta presides over The Monster restaurant with a devastating invective and the largest collection of day-glo caftans on the East Coast. The Infanta's favorite movie is *Cobra Woman* and he is always screaming, "Geeve me dose cobra jewels!" at unsuspecting straight tourists. The Infanta teaches high school during the winter. The Infanta is a camp.

In the early 1960s in Paterson, New Jersey, there was a man called David Kerwin. David was a little hard of hearing, but he never let it get in his way. One evening David was stopped by a policeman while driving a car containing several drag queens named Brandy and some rough trade. By the way, David always talked like Judy Holliday in *Born Yesterday.* The conversation went something like this:

"What's your name?"

"David Kerwin."

"Where do you live?"

"I told you, David Kerwin!"

"What are you, a wiseguy?"

(David, turning to the other passengers) "*Who's* she calling a cocksucker?"

David Kerwin was a camp.

The relation of camp to gay humor is the same as the relation of guilt to being Jewish. It's by reputation only. And just as there are some guilty Portnoys, there are campy homosexuals. The real issue is one of vision. Because of the rarefied position of gay people, camp has seemed intrinsic to gay humor. Gay people are born into a heterosexual world and spend a lot of time being raised as heterosexual. We therefore know a hell of a lot more about being straight than straights know about being gay. We needed the training to effectively "pass." Consequently we see the culture with a dual vision, and our particular "aliveness" to the double sense in which some things can be taken overqualifies us for camp expression.

Seeing through the travesty of the masculine role model is one reason for this gift. Only then is it possible to view Victor Mature as camp. People like Jayne Mansfield and her muscleman husband, Mickey Hargitay, stretched their sexual images so far out of proportion it was impossible not to smile.

Gay humor, however, springs from *all* our experiences as gay people. While our blanket oppression has given us plenty of fuel for tough wit, we have also been shaped by other forces. Gay humor is Lily Tomlin noting that "in the fifties nobody was gay, only shy." Certainly not camp, it uses our situation in order to comment on who we are. Gay humor is a nine-year-old "gay" Little Leaguer in Paramount's *The Bad News Bears* knowing instinctively how to mix a perfect martini. This type of humor may be used politically because it forces the issue of our visibility in nonstereotyped terms, poking fun at the myths instead of reinforcing them.

Camp, however, because it deals only frivolously with the roles we've been assigned and entails no criticism of them, is totally apolitical. Even conscious "camping" cannot be used politically, because that would mean opening the ranks to the masses to achieve a wide understanding and destroy the sensibility. Usually when this happens, the sensibility becomes a marketable "idea" functioning in an entirely different sense.

Consider Bette Midler about four years ago at the Continental Baths. She wears a pink towel as a turban, decorated with "fifteen cents worth of fake cherries." Her hand is on her hip:

"Well, let's see. What has been happening since I was here last? I ran into Martha Raye on the street, you'll all be delighted to know. You all remember Miss Raye. She was wearing a large button on her chest that said, 'Joan Crawford is a heterosexual.' But I tell you, honey, Miss Raye looked terrible. She'd just gotten beaten up. She was mugged by a Viet-Cong in the Christopher Street tearoom."

Midler was not being camp, she was "camping," and in order

to do that she had to poke fun at some otherwise "serious" things. Her monologue functioned as camp, too, as long as it stayed between the walls of the baths. As soon as she broke out and became a star, that material would have been incomprehensible to a mass audience except as vaguely vulgar attempts at humor. Camp protects itself.

One of the things Bruce Rodgers says about camp in *The Queens' Vernacular* is that although camp enjoyed a general "discovery" in the late sixties, it firmly remains a form of homosexual slang. I think the reason for that is at least partially the nonpolitical nature of camp. Remember, Carmen Miranda never *said* anything. She simply was what she was. Bette Midler practices a form of calculated camp, packaged so that people will think she's bringing them the real "dish" from the inside. She is, in fact, nostalgia for camp, using the sensibility itself in earlier forms to give the illusion of extravagance. Walking onstage at a New York club, Midler would often crack, "You like this dress? I was walking down Fifty-seventh Street today and I ripped it off Ginger Rogers's back." That's not all she ripped off.

The result of this crusade to enlighten the famous "general public" we all keep hearing about is that the artifacts of the gay world are being assimilated into the mainstream of the culture with no facts being offered. Midler isn't the only one selling our own visions back to us. At least all she's doing is enjoying it along with us. The rest of the world is behaving like a fox at a chicken sale, trying to learn the lingo in time for the next barbecue. Anyone gets to be "queen for a day," no strings attached and no risks involved. In the guise of bisexual chic, the gay sensibility in fashion, art, theater, and design is being marketed right out from under us because we still haven't the courage to claim our own lives.

The disturbing thing about the trend is that it markets only phrases and images, not ideas. We now have "closet" opera fans and people "coming out" as vegetarians. We have funny "gay" characters on television with lots of laughs but no ideas. We have lambdas being sold by *After Dark* magazine, which proclaims them "the latest thing"; and Continental Baths towels being sold by Bloomingdale's to couples looking for a peek at real decadence.

The clash, of course, will come when our visibility in the culture increases enough to manifest our incredible diversity. As of now, gay awareness is still confined to major urban centers. Miss Thing is alive and well in rural America and camping up a storm. If, however, the essence of camp is its love of the unnatural, as Sontag says, the more "natural" gay people become vis-à-vis society, the less likely we are to use camp as a means of communication or to be seen as camp figures. With the surfacing of gay people, the need for a "code" will disappear. None of this will affect the properties or the practice of seeing things as camp. What *will* be affected, I think, is the long association between gay humor and camp which has become almost automatic.

Even now, people who shape their entire lives in terms of camp are finding it difficult to ignore the reality of how "gay" is being sold to middle America while the Supreme Court denies our rights. The classic fifties flaming queen with forced invective to match becomes a little like a Diane Arbus photo in light of recent events, and the act of "camping" for an audience is becoming just another slick, meaningless charade.

The best camp will remain affectionate and naive. After all, Dale Evans is still alive, and if that isn't enough, we have disaster movies; Charlton Heston; chess pieces carved out of marzipan and swans carved out of ice at bar mitzvahs; plaster statues of Venus de Milo; Los Angeles; and little telephone tables with a place for the directory. If all else fails, the next time Queen Elizabeth has a luncheon, watch it on television. She arrives from her upstairs bedroom and enters her own dining room with a smart little leather handbag hanging from her arm. That Queen is such a camp.

## Life-Styles

# Coping with Couplehood

### REX REECE

Lloyd and Eric came into my office, sat on the sofa, looked questioningly at each other and then at me.

"Where do we start?" Lloyd broke the ice. He was the older of the couple; I guessed thirty-five, based on his thinning blond hair and the increasing dimension of his waist.

"Sometimes it's hard to start talking about very personal things with a complete stranger, but often it helps just to jump right in and say what's on your mind. Then later we can fill in the background and feelings," I urged.

Eric followed my suggestion. "Well, we've been together for a year and it's been good, but now we're fighting so much that we're afraid it's not going to last. We want it to, and we were hoping you could help." Eric was taller, younger, darker. He looked like he'd win scholarships if he answered ads about male modeling schools.

"Yeah," Lloyd seconded, "I think we've tried everything and it doesn't seem to work. We're at a standstill, a block. It feels hopeless sometimes."

Both men were dressed in gay summer fashion. Lloyd had appeared in the basics—Adidas, jeans, and Lacoste; Eric presented a more extraordinary impression with his earth-colored earth sandals and bright canary jumpsuit. The yellow was reflected in the sparkle of his dark eyes and was almost jarring in contrast to his glossy black curls and carefully trimmed mustache.

After a few moments more of general introductory interaction, I suggested that one of them wait in another room while I

*The Advocate,* October 19, 1977, pp. 31–32. Reprinted by permission of the author.

spoke privately with the other. Eric chose to leave, and I continued the interview alone with Lloyd.

Lloyd's gestures quickened, his voice edged upwards, and his hesitance seemed to fade somewhat with Eric out of the room.

"I know you're not supposed to find a lover at the baths," he reasoned as his body strained forward in the direction of his outstretched hand. "Believe me, I've been around long enough to know that. At least, none of my friends ever met each other there." He paused momentarily, then added quickly, "But *we* did." He spoke emphatically, almost defensively, as if he felt that having met at the baths was one strike against the survival of their relationship.

"It was one of those slow times, you know, during the day. I used to go a lot in the daytime," he continued parenthetically. "I never did like those hot, crowded nights when the air is heavy with the smell of sex and poppers." His palm caressed his cheek. "I had gone there out of being sort of down—I had made a goof at work that day. So I came home to take a shower and forget. After the shower I realized I had the crabs. I thought it was just the summer heat, you know?

"So I went to the baths, to forget, to relax. Part of me didn't want to make it with anybody, because I had just washed with A-200. I wasn't sure how well it worked or how long it took, and I didn't want to chance giving the crabs to anyone. They're a real pest, you know, the little buggers." He could chuckle momentarily. "But I decided to take the risk.

"To tell you the truth, I guess I was, as usual, hoping that '*he*,' you know, the 'right one' would be there and would fall madly in love with me." He punctuated this last sentence with a cynical guffaw; its unexpected loudness startled us both.

Fond recollections took command of his body movements. He slumped against the sofa, grinned, let his shoulders fall; his gaze fell toward his left hand as its fingers parted the sunbleached thick blond softness on his other wrist.

"I know you're not going to believe this—it sounds as corny as 'Kansas in August'—but we saw each other and that was it. We, or I at least, never saw another person the rest of the evening."

He sat quietly for a couple of minutes, then connected with

my eyes again. "It was really great those first few days, even for weeks, I guess. We saw a lot of each other for a couple of months, and after talking about it a lot, we decided Eric should move into my apartment. I had a lot of furniture and stuff; I was close to work and Eric had to drive around a lot to different parts of town anyway. So he moved in with me."

"And sex?" I asked. His face lit up again with a broad smile of spontaneous warmth. I could understand Eric's loving this man. "Well, I've never felt better, more free, more able to be myself in bed than when I'm with Eric. That's how I felt with him—free. You know, we didn't do anything really trippy, but I felt *good* with him. Most times I just liked being close to him, touching him, holding him. We didn't always have to be doing anything."

His face hardened, and his eyes left mine. "But it didn't last. After a couple of months' living together, we started nagging each other and drifting apart. Eric started going to bed with other guys; I was jealous, and we started fighting about that and most everything else." Here he stopped, breathed deeply, and tried to reverse the downward spiral of his words. He wasn't successful. "Why didn't it last? Why doesn't the feeling ever last?"

During this first session, Lloyd told me how things started going wrong. At first he had been very turned on by Eric's classic good looks and felt a real ego boost when he went out with Eric. He was proud to be seen with such a "hot number." But he found himself increasingly threatened by this same beauty; he felt a nagging insecurity because of the attention Eric received from other men. He wondered if he was good enough to hold onto Eric.

Lloyd felt competitive with Eric on several other levels. The kitchen belonged to Eric. Their friends gave Eric many strokes for performing so well with the soups and spoons. And Eric was much more the star when other people were around. He was comfortable with many different kinds of people and was often the center of attention, with his quick humor and tales of past adventures. Lloyd frequently felt ignored and jealous.

His arms unfolded in an expansive gesture of incomprehension. "We fight over the stupidest things," he continued, "like how the furniture should be arranged, the capital city of Nigeria, who should empty the garbage, and who should supervise the guy who comes in to clean the apartment on Mondays. They're trivial issues, but they seem terribly important when we fight about them."

Before the end of this first session, Lloyd had given a familiar and despairing recital. "I've been in many relationships that don't last very long. I've done enough of the bar, bath, and park trip. I'm tired of that; it doesn't give me what I want. I'm tired of the superficial one-night stands or quickies here and there. They all just leave me guilty and empty until the hornies strike again." Here he was fairly spitting out the words, almost out of breath. He paused, and I felt an expectation that's become familiar in my counseling experience—a feeling that the next point is the key issue for the speaker.

"Besides, the body's going, and I don't want to be alone when I'm up there in years."

He didn't stop there but continued with disparaging and self-accusatory questions. "Are gay men really so confused, insincere, and tacky that we can't make a relationship last? Do you think I have it in me to be able to love someone? Did I miss out on something? *What's wrong with me?*"

As Lloyd left the office, he sighed and asked—this time with a note of both hope and hopelessness in his voice—"Can we keep it together? Do you think you can help?"

"I want to. Together we'll work on it, we'll see what we can do." I did want to help; I hoped I would be able, but I hesitated to offer any guarantees.

Eric had a somewhat different perspective on their relationship, past and present. "I was doubtful from the first. I've been in and out of numerous affairs and short-lived relationships. I guess I'm just one of those people who find it hard to make a commitment." There was a sense of resignation and defeat in his tone. His hand grasped the arm of my sofa so hard that the whiteness stood out sharply against his tanned skin. The stiff fingers of his other hand pushed rhythmically up and down his left thigh. His voice was deep, his left leg bent and crossed over the right knee at the ankle. His posture, position, manner, and movements presented a comfortable picture of masculinity. He was a "natural man," with no pretense, no studied, self-conscious attempt at proper role-playing.

Eric listed his complaints. "Lloyd continues to ignore my feelings and desires—about everything from what movie to see to when and how to have sex. He's really selfish, but he won't listen when I try to talk with him about it. He just accuses me of the same fault. For example, he knows I like to eat out a lot, but he never suggests it, even on special occasions. I also like to cuddle a lot, but he never seems to initiate that. I should think that if he really cared for me, he would do some of the things I like sometimes. *He knows how I feel.*"

Here Eric changed his position, relaxed more, and took a deep breath before continuing his recital of grievances. "And he never listens to me. I try to talk about how I feel about things sometimes—I guess I'm the sensitive one—but he never really seems interested. All he wants to talk about is the bank. So I go see my friend Tony sometimes and we talk about things we have in common, things that Lloyd doesn't seem to care about. Then he gets jealous because I spend so much time away or because he's afraid I'm out having sex with other people. And sometimes I do. Not with Tony—he's too good a friend—but sometimes I make it with other guys."

His momentum continued to build; it was as if he'd been waiting to unburden himself. "And I feel guilty as hell about that. You can't just go hopping from person to person all the time if you're in love with one guy, can you? And it makes Lloyd so scared and mad and jealous. I try to tell him that those people don't matter, but he can't believe it.

"What do other people do? Can I learn to limit my sexual interest only to Lloyd?" He didn't wait for a response, but continued. "It's kind of depressing to think that I may be stuck forever with some sexual routine that's not very exciting."

He had turned sideways and was looking out the window during this release. Now he turned to me. His body was facing me directly, open to what I had to offer. "But I want to work it out." He repeated, "I want to work it out; I don't want to go out to the sex market again."

There was fear in his voice now. For a moment he was lost in thought, as if he were examining his reflected profile; then he startled himself back to the interaction with me. "But perhaps the worst feeling I have with him is that I am inferior." This confession he made with conviction. "Look, he's got a good job, managing a whole department, and still on the way up. And me, I'm still struggling, trying to find out if I can write. I get so depressed sometimes, wondering if I'll ever make it, frustrated because of the repeated rejections and angry because I have to smile and pretend to be enjoying myself as I talk to all those people who are judging my material. Lloyd is sane, secure, and smart. I feel like a neurotic scatterbrain sometimes by comparison. I know that I criticize and yell at him sometimes, but I do it partially because I feel so inadequate."

By now the hand that had been caressing his thigh was clasped tightly into a fist and was lightly pounding the pillow. There was a slight yet perceptible quiver in his chin, and his eyes seemed more moist and sparkly than before. He punched the cushion once again, swallowed, and his facial expression changed to grim determination. "I want to make this one last. Tell me what to do."

The frustrations and confusion expressed in this first counseling session with Lloyd and Eric represent only a few of what I believe are often serious barriers to the development of committed gay male relationships. Our culture has taught us much about being men and being gay. We've been conditioned in many ways that create conflicts in our love relationships. Recognizing these conventional problems—the existence of competition, the withholding of feelings of need and the conflicting expectations about sexual behavior—can help couples like Lloyd and Eric maintain satisfying relationships. Let's look more closely at these three barriers.

Men are supposed to win. Eric sometimes yelled at Lloyd because he felt inferior; he couldn't win. Lloyd was too "sane, secure, and smart." Lloyd reported that they "fought over the stupidest things." It seems that some of us must win, no matter how insignificant the issue. Our bodies were male when we were born, and as children we could not avoid the demands that we act like men. "Go out there and show them how it's done";

"Losers are sissies"; "It's a dog-eat-dog world"; "Don't let him take your toy away"; and "Don't settle for anything less than being number one." All these and many similar messages told us how to behave if we wanted to be loved, worthwhile, and appropriate—men. Remember for a moment the praise that came as a result of winning, from being the strongest, the first, the fastest, the brightest, the biggest, the best.

As a corollary to the exhortations to compete, to win, not to give in, we were taught to believe that softness, tenderness, acknowledgment of weaknesses and needs, and asking rather than demanding would make us lose, especially when we were in competition with other men. Sometimes we intensified these competitive values and fears of vulnerability. We couldn't accept early realizations that our feelings were somehow different from the feelings men around us seemed to express. Some of us didn't want to compete with other boys, but wanted to hold them, to be tender with them, so we overreacted to this unacceptable feeling by becoming even more competitive and distant. That indoctrination is not easy to forget, even when we later accept that it's good to love another man, physically and with feeling.

Eric *assumed* that Lloyd knew how he felt and was angry that Lloyd did not respond to these hidden feelings. He also feared letting Lloyd know he felt inadequate, afraid that Lloyd would then assert his supposed superiority or would reject Eric for his unmanly weaknesses. After all, we are attracted to *men,* and men are supposedly strong. Eric was trapped—he couldn't expose himself because he would feel awful about himself if he was not somehow stronger than Lloyd—he needed to win. How can two men who both need to be on top ever work it out?

A third broad area that creates barriers between men who want to stay together is sex. Again, as boys, many of us were taught that men are supposed to be sexually active, experienced, ready, and able. Can you remember exaggerating about your sexual experiences, especially during the teenage years or early twenties? There's also a myth that men are always horny, that men are all bubbling cauldrons of hot passion ready to explode any time in almost any circumstance. Unfortunately, many of us have bought this misconception.

The barriers to loving relationships become greater when you add some of the stereotypes and expectations about being gay. Everyone knows that all gay men do is have sex, right? If we don't, can't, or aren't interested, we begin to wonder what's wrong. Even if we accept that we can get by without so much sex, we still struggle to present what we think other men expect. In other words, "If I want him to like me, I have to be good in bed, I have to do what he wants sexually—I have to prove I'm a man in bed."

Lloyd feared that his relatively undramatic sexual needs and performances had become boring; Eric, in turn, had come to believe that sex must be continually new and innovative. He'd confused the need for closeness and acceptance with the need for sex. He was afraid to ask for the closeness, but because of an unfulfilled need, he demanded sexual attention from Lloyd. Lloyd felt the pressure and came to feel inadequate in satisfying Eric's desires. When Eric felt frustrated at Lloyd's lack of interest and attention, he sought the fulfillment of these needs in exciting sex with new people. He had great difficulty in expressing these needs directly and resented Lloyd's not responding without a request. But then he felt guilty about making it with other people because he knew Lloyd wanted a monogamous sexual relationship.

Because of the training many of us received as we grew up as well as the continuing values that surround us, we are often confronted with a sort of no-win situation when we attempt to become involved in loving relationships. Lloyd and Eric are two people who were taught that we should always win, we should never let anyone better us, we should take control and always be strong. But one of the ingredients of ongoing love and intimacy seems to be an ability to be vulnerable, to let one's weaknesses show and let the potential lover see the real thing. Many of us have a difficult time taking the risk. We've been taught well that if we let down our guard, another man will take advantage of our openness.

This catch-22, no-win, Scylla and Charybdis situation also applies to the conventional wisdom many of us accept about the relationship between love and sex and marriage. Many of us assumed we would grow up, fall in love, and get married. After all, that's what adults seemed to do, or want to do at least. Since many of us were told that sex, marriage, and love go together, many gay men learned to value a committed, monogamous relationship.

But we also got a contradictory message. Remember: Men are supposed to be sexually experienced and active. Add to that expectation the stereotype that gay men are supposed to have lots of sex with lots of different people, and we have a man being pulled in two different directions. On the one hand, to be happy and continue a relationship, a man must be sexually and lovingly monogamous. To fill the *gay male* role expectation, however, he must be sexually involved with different people, often, and good at it.

Many assumptions must be questioned by couples like Lloyd and Eric. This process can begin the realization that they each have choices about how their relationship can fit their unique needs. After watching them interact for several sessions, learning more of their history, and nourishing the relationship among the three of us, I approached some of these questions with both of them.

"Eric, what's the terrible thing that's likely to happen if Lloyd really becomes aware of how inferior you feel?" I asked this question during our eighth session together.

Lloyd smiled nervously while his index finger rapidly massaged his lower lip. Eric hesitated; he was at the edge of something, ready to see a familiar situation with new eyes. "I'm afraid." He spoke quietly, hesitated again, and allowed his glance to catch Lloyd's eyes, seeking reassurance and encouragement to go on.

"Sometimes it helps, Eric, if you can say what you're feeling right now." I gave additional encouragement.

"I want to know that Lloyd . . ." He looked from me to Lloyd and took one of Lloyd's hands between his two, squeezing gently as he spoke. "I'm afraid you won't respect me if you see my need for you. Compared to you I feel young and dumb and incompetent and I'm afraid that if you knew that, you'll go look for somebody stronger." After this rush of words, Eric dropped his head, waiting, not able to look at Lloyd's face.

Lloyd pulled his hand from between Eric's and tenderly placed it on one of Eric's cheeks. Then he tilted his face upwards so they could look directly and closely at each other. A tear on Eric's cheek quickly tumbled to his chin. Lloyd's voice was suddenly broken and unsure.

"Do you know how many times I've wanted to say the same to you? How many times I've felt unable to please you sexually? How much I feel I've let you down?" The questions continued as their arms enclosed each other.

In counseling couples like Eric and Lloyd, one of the things I try to do is help them become aware of the "role expectation messages" they've received about masculinity, sex, and relationship. I try to emphasize the messages that surround all of us as gay men, both in our larger culture and our own gay culture today. In understanding that these roles are arbitrary, many gay men can begin to move beyond attitudes, behaviors, and feelings that are limiting to the formation and continuation of loving relationships. We try to discover through an examination of values, expectations, and anxieties what kind of working relationship will be most suitable for the particular individuals in a couple. In other words, we work to get beyond the old messages as much as possible and discover what it is that these particular people need, want, or expect from each other in terms of sex, power, control, dependency, and roles.

After a few more sessions, we were ready to work at redefining the relationship according to Lloyd's and Eric's specific and individual needs.

"Lloyd, now that you accept that Eric's sexual activities with others aren't a reflection of your inadequacies, can you describe your feelings about his going out?"

By now, they had both learned that they were to talk with each other rather than through me. Lloyd looked at Eric; Eric turned toward Lloyd.

"I'm willing to allow your sexual contact with others," he vowed. "I'll probably continue to feel jealous sometimes, and I guess you'll just have to live with how that makes me behave." He paused and seemed to search in his thoughts and feelings for anything else he wanted to say. "I want to continue to tell you how I feel, but I know I won't be able. Sometimes I'll need your help, your reassurance, your encouragement."

With such couples, I work on actively integrating new ways of relating that will increase the likelihood of their individual interdependency needs being met. We achieve some of this changed behavior through role-playing and various skill-training exercises directed at opening up communication. We rehearse statements that begin "I want . . . ," "or I feel . . . ," or "When you do that, I feel . . ." Couples go home with instructions for experiences that are directed toward developing the ability to express tenderness and vulnerability, for making requests, for losing, but losing gracefully

Acknowledging that we sometimes interact in unsatisfactory ways because of our early conditioning helps take away feelings of inadequacy and supplies energy for more self-direction. No longer do we hear: "What's wrong with me?" Instead, it's: "I do have some control, some choice over how I will relate with this person." Practicing new ways to express ourselves, awkward though it may be, gives us the tools for getting more of what we want with each other and sometimes, of course, without each other.

There are conditions in our culture that make it difficult for gay men to "get it together." Many of them have to do with sex-role expectations or with self-fulfilling prophecies resulting from stereotypes about being a gay man. But because we are gay, there are also more opportunities for self-direction and definition in the way we interrelate. We *can* find our way out of the locked-in, expected patterns of interaction and discover new and more individually satisfying ways of relating to each other. We *can* develop our own definitions of relationship, through struggle and caring. And for some of us, this may evolve into a choice not to be in a committed one-to-one relationship at all, now or in the future.

# Women Among Men: Females in the Male Homosexual Community

CAROL A. B. WARREN

## INTRODUCTION

There are many types and contexts of relationship between people in general and between men and women in our society. This report is concerned with one particular *context:* the relationship between gay males in a secret urban gay community and the few lesbian and heterosexual women who are part of that community.* The *types* of relationships in which the men and women are engaged were, in Simmel's (1950) terminology, predominantly *sociable,* but also *sexual, intimate,* and *functional.*†

For Simmel, sociable relationships are characterized both negatively and positively: negatively by the absence of intimacy and the marketplace, and positively by the interactive qualities of lightness, frivolity, and play. The basis of sociable relationships is lighthearted interaction between all the parties present; thus intimacy is excluded from sociability both because it is not light and because it involves two persons in an intense we-

---

* For the purpose of this study, *interaction* refers to actual, concrete occasions of face-to-face interaction, while *relationship* denotes the repetition of such interaction between significant others over time.

† The discussion of sociable, intimate, and functional types of relationships is taken from Simmel (1950:40–57). The terms *sociable* and *intimate* are retained, but I have substituted *functional* or *useful* for his concept of the marketplace relationship.

---

*Archives of Sexual Behavior* 5, no. 2 (1976): 157–69. Copyright © 1976 Plenum Publishing Corporation. Reprinted by permission of the publisher and author.

relationship which excludes the others present. Sociable relations, whose main preoccupation is conversation, are an end in themselves, and not a means to some other end such as self-fulfillment, emotional sharing with another, or marketplace and monetary transactions whose goals transcend the immediate present.

The males in the secret gay community under observation (Warren, 1974) were involved with each other and with the females in social relationships which continued over time and which were characterized on each interactive occasion by light-hearted conversation, conviviality, and the spirit of fun, almost always oiled by the free flow of alcoholic beverages. Each interactive unit was transitory and spontaneous, but the members were bound by stringent rules of etiquette and propriety over time into relationships of obligation which belied the appearance of spontaneity and evanescence. I have discussed the nature of the relationships of obligation elsewhere (Warren, 1974): briefly, their main feature is the reciprocal obligation to provide occasions of sociability such as cocktail parties and dinner parties, in which the host is obligated to provide alcoholic beverages, the guests are obliged to provide sociable talk, and both are obligated to exchange roles sequentially over time.

Although the sociable relationships between the males often had sexual implications, those between the males and the females generally did not (see below). The males' sociable-sexual implications took the form of what Simmel calls "coquetry," or the play form of eroticism, rather than the serious search for intimacy that characterized other interactive settings for some of the males, or the equally serious cruising for casual "trade" that occurred in the barroom type of sociation.* A more long-term and domestic form of sexuality did play a part in the sociable arrangements, however, since many of the participants (both males and lesbians) lived in domestic sexual partnerships with same-sex members, and much of the socializing was done in couples.

In general, as Simmel points out, sociable interaction is most

---

* The term *trade* refers to casual, nonintimate sex of a businesslike nature.

successful when it takes place between people who are equal on some fundamental criterion such as social class or race, but who are temperamentally, cosmetically, and personally diverse. In the gay community, equality was premised on comembership in the male gay world, but this barrier could be transcended if the diversity and liveliness brought to sociability compensated for membership in other worlds. Because of the nature of sociability itself, gay and straight females, and even married couples and heterosexual males, could gain access to gay sociable relations:

> The fact is that whatever the participants in the gathering may possess in terms of objective attributes—attributes that are centered outside the particular gathering in question—must not enter it. . . . At most they may perform the role of mere nuances of that immaterial character with which reality alone, in general, is allowed to enter the social work of art called sociability [Simmel, 1950:46].

Sociable, intimate, and sexual interactions formed the nexus of relationships within the male gay world, and females entered into all three aspects. In this analysis, sexual and intimate interactions between females and gay males are a subsidiary theme. Sociable interaction is the major focus: that evanescent but serious play of adults at rest.

### THE LITERATURE

The literature on homosexuality has dealt very little with the role of women in the male gay world. There is a body of sociopsychiatric literature, well represented by Bergler (1959), in which homosexuality is presented as a "sickness" and the major tasks of experts are presented as the uncovering of its epidemiology, etiology, and cure. In this type of literature, women appear in the male gay experience generally as Mother, and always as negative. Put another way, the cause of homosexuality is presented as a fear and negative sexual avoidance of women engendered by Oedipal conflicts, rather than as a positive sexual liking for males which can occur independently of sexual activity with females.

A second set of sociological literature consists of qualitative or ethnographic studies of secret gay male communities (Hooker, 1963, 1965; Leznoff and Westley, 1967; Magee, 1966; Schofield, 1965; Warren, 1974). In these studies, descriptions of the existence and role of female members in the gay male circles are scarce, since the main focus is on the males themselves.

A recent set of literature, dealing with the overt rather than the secret gay community, presents a quite different view of females in the male gay community than that presented here. Humphreys (1971, 1972) in particular has documented the progress of overt, politically activist gay groups who confront rather than evade their stigma, ranging from groups which affiliate with the Third World to those which seek only gay liberation, and from groups which are all male to groups which are all female, with every variation in between.* These overt groups differ from the secret communities in more ways than this report could specify; some of the more important differences, however, include the purpose of group interaction and types of male-female relationships. Since these are the twin topics of this research, I will say briefly of the former that, beyond the search for sex, the major preoccupation of the overt groups is the struggle for political rights, while the major preoccupation of the secret groups is sociability. With respect to the latter, I can only suggest that the reader compare this study with those of Humphreys (1971, 1972), and comment that overtly involved women in gay groups tend to affiliate strongly with the women's liberation movement, while such affiliation on the part of the women studied here is, to say the least, muted.

### THE STUDY

This study represents a preliminary theoretical formulation of the role of women in the secret male gay community. It is exploratory rather than definitive in nature, because it is based on serendipitous encounters with women in the male gay world

---

* Despite the recent emphasis in the sociological and popular literature on the overt gay community, the secret one is still there. As of this writing, the major portion of the gay world has not risked coming "out of the closet."

during an ethnographic study of that world, and not on any representative sampling design. The setting for this analysis and the larger study of which it is a part (Warren 1974) was a Southern California city of approximately 700,000 population during 1968–1973. The data were gathered in a series of overlapping cliques of gay males who kept their homosexuality secret from most family and work audiences. Despite the changes in attitude purported to have taken place in society with regard to the stigma attached to homosexuality, these groups remained secret because of a lively sense of stigma and threat. The main fears verbalized by the members were occupational stigmatization—since most were in business or professional occupations—or being cast outside the pale of their families of origin.

The actual membership of the cliques fluctuated somewhat during the research period due to geographical, sexual, and social mobility; the maximum number of males I was acquainted with during the time period was well over one hundred, while the maximum of females was fifteen—which gives some indication of the ratio of males to females in the community. The males in the cliques knew one another, in the main, entirely outside of heterosexual context of work, the family, and straight friendships, and the same was true of the female gay members. All the female gays had access to lesbian communities, but all preferred membership in gay male groups. In contrast, some of the female heterosexual members had made their initial contact with one or two particular males in work or other nongay contexts. While most of the gay female's clique membership was multiple, like the men's, the heterosexual women tended to remain friends only with their initial contact or with one particular clique. Both men and women were mostly white, ranged in age from the mid-twenties to the mid-fifties, and were of a conservative middle-class life-style.

The method employed for the larger study of gay community was field research, supplemented by tape-recorded interviews of many of the members. The methodology was informed by the phenomenological or *verstehen* approach, by which I sought to understand the world as the members understood it, rather than as my presuppositions structured it. For this particular analysis, I concentrated on the vocabularies of motive (Mills, 1940) or accounts (Lyman and Scott, 1970) given by both male and female members of the presence of females in the male gay community, as well as observation and description of the types of sociable and other interaction within which these vocabularies of motive found expression.

## The Male Perspective

There were three types of accounts given by the men for the presence of the women in their community: the decorative, the surrogate, and the functional. In turn, the functionality of females within the male community was either within the community itself or in situations of passing as straight outside the gay community.

The decorative account of female membership refers back to the Simmelian analysis of sociability, in which the participants are expected to lend variety, distinctiveness, and entertainment to the proceedings, both in conversational brilliance and in presentation of self. On gay occasions of sociability, females—especially those willing to dress in flashy and traditionally "feminine" style—lent visual diversity to the interaction:

BARTENDER (in male gay bar, to two females): Why don't you come back here soon? You add some glamour to the place and it certainly needs it.

Related to the decorative aspect, some males expressed a desire to experience female cosmetic presentations of self through the females who attended occasions of sociability. In this sense, the females served as *surrogates* for otherwise unexpressed impulses, or vehicles through which they could be expressed:

Gilda and Kim entered the party, and immediately Jose and Emerson grabbed their earrings, put them on themselves, and paraded up and down the room, "modeling."

I went to a party quite plainly dressed, and the next day Elliott gave me a lecture on what he would have worn had he been given the marvelous opportunity that I, as a woman, had been given, to wear "fantastic clothes and lots of makeup."

The decorative and surrogate role of women in the male gay community is probably a factor in the selection by such male groups of traditionally "feminine" women, and, further, the "feminizing" of new female members entering the group:

> THOMAS: I can't stand bulldykes . . .
> INTERVIEWER: You mean lesbians?
> THOMAS: No, you know, bulldykes—truck drivers—I like a woman to be a woman, whether she's gay or straight.

There were two types of *function* which the women performed for the men in this secret male community: functions within the community and functions in relation to the outside world. Within the gay community, the presence of women functioned for the men as a means of social control by which certain outcomes to sociability occasions could be prevented, particularly orgies and other types of wild behavior:

> ALAIN: I like to have girls at parties . . . which is the same reason I like to have the guys wear suits and ties . . . it keeps them from getting too carried away, from camping and carrying on too much.

On other occasions, the women were used by the men in contexts outside the gay community, connected with family and work. In this role, the women assisted the men in the preservation of secrecy by helping them to construct a straight front:

> Alexis asked me to accompany him to his company dinner, which, he said he had not attended in five years. When I asked why, he answered: "You know I'm gay and you won't expect anything afterwards. Take a girl who thinks you're eligible, unattached, and a big stud into the bargain, and she won't leave you alone. Puts you in an awkward position."

The vocabularies of motive for using women in these ways were complex. The main stated motive for inviting women to sociable occasions was sociability itself, with functionality a secondary aspect—the same thing could often be accomplished just by getting the men to wear a coat and tie. But the motive for inviting women to social gatherings with family and workmates outside the gay community often transcended the realm of sociability altogether, and approximated Simmel's conception of a business relation, in which the interaction is a means to an end rather than an end in itself.

This functional relationship in relation to the straight world is based on the fact that society in general stigmatizes both male and female homosexuals, so that if they desire to keep their stigma hidden one of the best ways is to pretend to the status of a straight couple. The alternatives—to avoid straight socialization, to go alone, or to go with a same-sex lover—are less effective underpinnings for secrecy. Note that such a relationship works well only if the need is mutual: in fact, since the men faced more pressure to put on a straight front than the women, they sometimes found it difficult to persuade the gay women to cooperate.

The men were more likely to use the gay women than the "fag hags"* for stigma evasion, for a couple of reasons. One was that, in general, the gay women were more attractive and youthful than the female heterosexuals in the community, many of whom were unattractive in conventional terms, or of middle age, or both. Often the relationship between the gay men and fag hags, either apart from or together with the relationship of sociability, was a tradeoff of mothering for male attention. For the men, the main motive attributed to the fag hags' preference for the gay community is the attention they get there, although some assert that the women are latent homosexuals.

OLIVER: These women who hang around the gay men, they are either divorced and have children and the straight guys don't want them, or they are ugly or fat or something.

The other side of the bargain is the "understanding female companionship" the women give the men, often shading into

---

*Fag hag* (in different regions the term may be *fruit fly* or *faggotina*) is the male gay jargon for a female heterosexual who associates with the male gay community.

complete mothering. This means that some fag hags and gay men have the close, friendly type of relationship that Simmel calls intimacy. Some fag hags never extended this initial intimacy with one or two of the men into other sociability relations, while others moved from initial friendships into sociability cliques. However, gay men are more apt to allow gay than straight women to enter their sociability cliques, for a number of reasons including simple antiheterosexual prejudice, fear of the violation of secrecy, the suspicion of the fag hags' sociable motives and an imputation of sexual ones, and a preference for conventionally attractive women.

## The Females and the Female Perspective

Since the females within the gay male cliques were so few, I was able to get to know them all at least to a limited degree. There were eight lesbians and four heterosexual women within the groups, most of them for the entire 1968–1973 time period.

Like some of the men, a few of the women rarely called their membership in the male gay community into question, but most had vocabularies of motive to account for it. For the lesbians, these accounts explained why they preferred the male gay community to the female one; for the heterosexuals, why they preferred the company of gay men to that of straight.

Four types of accounts were given by the lesbians for their preference: the greater sociability of gay males than of most lesbians, a liking for traditionally "feminine" women, the safety factor, and functional reasons.

Most of the women asserted that the gay men were more accomplished at sociability than the women in the lesbian community, partly because they were more likely to adopt upper middle class type life-styles, and partly because they did not engage the women in the type of intrigue, jealousy, and bitchiness said to be common in the lesbian community:

KIM: Girls get so bitchy and jealous, it's pleasanter to be around the guys. And they treat you like a lady—better than any straight guy I have met. They have some *savior faire*.

This comment indicates one of the aspects of sociability which the women seemed to appreciate most: traditional male chivalrous attentions. Again, this was set within the context of sociability: These male attentions were of a light and playful form, and an end in themselves rather than a serious prelude to some future of sexual seduction.

These accounts remain within the arena of sociability, while the other three types of motives have aspects which transcend the sociable. In the first place, all the lesbians "put down" masculine or tailored lesbians, stating a preference for traditionally feminine women—a resource they saw as not available in the lesbian community. In this sense, they used the male community as a sexual hunting ground:

VIVA: I can't stand those bulldyke types.

KIM: If you run with the gay girls' group, you have to be rough and tough and look butch or they put you down.

LAUREN: The girls in the girls' bars are so fat and ugly. I would have been a long time in girls' bars before I met someone like Kim.

A second way in which the women used the male gay community was as a "safe" gay place in which to interact without the threat to stable sexual relationships of constant exposure to other women:

GILDA: It's a lot safer being around men than around a lot of cute girls—if there were any. Best to keep away from them and go with the guys if you want to keep your own relationship.

This comment is in line with Simon and Gagnon's (1967) notes about the lesbian community:

The population from which the individual lesbian is likely to select her friends is the same population from which she is likely to select her lovers and sexual partners. As a result, most discussions of friendships were filled with a sense of anticipated impermanence. The fact that friends are often ex-lovers or recent rivals appears to foster an ultimate reserve, or, in some extreme cases, a constant mistrust [p. 237].

Although some of the gay women in the same sociability

cliques in the male community were ex-lovers, all *new* partners of members during the research process were strangers to the group. It may be that in this instance the females simply followed the pattern of the males rather than of the type of lesbian community described by Simon and Gagnon. In the male community, an incestlike taboo on casual sex with co-clique members was combined with the constant interaction of ex-lovers (after a suitable mourning period) in an almost brotherly type of relationship. The women followed the same two patterns. The gay males agreed with the safety aspect of the females' accounts of their membership:

KENNETH: The girls who just go around with the guys are so much smarter—girls tend to have so much trouble if they get together, and that way they stay out of it.

Like the men, some of the women used males in the construction of straight fronts in straight settings, although they apparently felt less pressure to do so. While the men's front-construction was most often in the area of work, the women's was more often in the area of family, although both were noted:

Gilda took Daniel to her school play, where, as a drama teacher, she felt she should show up, and with a date.

Kim often sent photos of herself and a gay man, dressed up and arms entwined, to her parents back East. She figured, she said, that they would think she was going with some guy.

The major account given by the *heterosexual females* for their involvement in the gay rather than the straight world was that homosexual males were preferable as social companions to heterosexual males:

NOELLE: I just like the gay men better. When you're getting older, they are the only men who will really appreciate you, be warm to you.

MILDRED: The gay men make me feel more like a woman than the straight men, who just grab at you and then go watch TV.

INTERVIEWER: Have you ever had sex with one of the gay guys?

MILDRED: Oh yes, occasionally, but I'd never say anything in front of the group, or indicate anything to anyone.

INTERVIEWER: Do you have a straight sex life?

MILDRED: Yes, but I keep that separate and I don't get too close to the straight men because I know I'll always be disappointed.

## At Close Quarters: Intimate and Sexual Relationships

As Simmel sees it, intimacy is a type of relationship in which interaction is bounded by few of the role constraints of everyday life, and its goal is to communicate one's "true self" to another. This type of friendship tended to be more common between the men and the heterosexual women than between the men and the lesbians.* Sexual relationships may be the accompaniment of intimacy, or they may be at quite the opposite pole—a business-like arrangement between prostitute and client, or cruiser and pickup. While friendship is a psychic intimacy, this section is concerned more with relationships of physical proximity between women and gay men, as wives, lovers, and roommates—with intimacy at close quarters.

The data on such intimate relationships are rare, perhaps because such relationships are rare. In my several years of research I encountered many instances of the sociable and functional types of relationship, but heard of physically intimate and sexual ones only at second hand. Most of these relationships evolved from earlier, purely sociable types of interaction.

Aside from the purely psychic intimacy of friendship, some gay men and women were intimate as roommates as well as friends, without any sexual involvement with one another:

Christopher has a lesbian roommate, with whom he claims to have lived in asexual but intimate harmony for seven years.

While they were college students, Kim and Jason roomed together briefly, until Kim met Lauren.

As opposed to true intimacy, which, like sociability, has no ends

---

* The probable reason for this friendship preference is that so many of the lesbians were engaged in stable or unstable sexual relationships which occupied much of their emotional life, while most of the fag hags were emotionally alone.

beyond itself, some of the men and women lived in liaisons designed for stigma evasion, as husbands and wives or couples. The stigma-evading liaison, of course, is just a longer-term and more committed type of functionality than the situated occasions described above.

Alex had two friends in Desert City, both prominent socialites in that small town, who were gay and had lesbian "front" wives. The two couples lived next door, ostensibly as cross-sex but actually as same-sex couples, with their houses connected by a secret passageway so they could secretly rearrange themselves when called upon by family or fellow citizens. I met the two men about a year after Alex told me this story, and they modified it for me considerably. One of the cross-sex couples was married and they were socialites; the other couple was not married (the woman had just entered the picture). It was indeed a "front marriage" without hetero*sexual* relationships, for family and business-social reasons, and the houses and passageway existed. However, the unmarried woman was jealous of the time the married pair spent socializing together, although the unmarried man claimed he didn't care.

In these situations, the marriage is contracted without the presumption of sexual activity between the gay man and gay woman, and for the purpose of remaining secretly gay. However, such a marriage may also be used for migration from the gay world:

Frank told me about two gay friends of his (a male and a female) who decided the gay life was terrible. So they got married and had children and, according to Frank, have stayed away from homo*sexual* and homo*sociable* involvements for ten years. (Frank is a *friend.)*

Finally, the marriage may be contracted on the asexual presumption for stigma evasion purposes, but this contract is later broken:

Penny (a masculine lesbian from the lesbian community) said she had married a gay guy for companionship in a "front marriage" and it had worked out badly. He used to come home drunk sometimes after unsuccessful searches for male sexual partners, and make sexual advances to her, in defiance of all previously agreed-upon proprieties. They got a divorce.

Of course, gay men get involved in sexual and intimate relationships with straight women, too; the friendship type of intimacy has already been discussed. Other gay men marry heterosexual women, for a variety of motives and in a variety of styles: Some wives never know about their husbands' sexual orientation, some know but never mention it, while still others interact as part of the gay community:*

One night at the Alamo I observed a pretty woman clinging to the arm of a gay guy I had seen a few times there before, alone. When I asked who she was, Dirk explained that she was a "straight" girl who had been going with the guy for over a year, and "took all sorts of shit from him, like banging away with some trick in the next bedroom."
But she was really in love with him so she "understood"—and they were getting married next month at another gay bar.

One of a pair of homosexual brothers, after a lifetime involvement in the gay community, got married and produced a child. The wife is reputed to "know," but they rarely interact with the gay community and it is never mentioned. (A year before the marriage I observed the man and a lesbian in one of the gay bars drunkenly announcing that they were going to get married and convert each other.)

The most interesting aspect of these marital or sexual types of relationships is the universal presumption among members of the gay community that "they won't work." Among those who have attempted intimate-physical or sexual relationships, and among those who have not, there is an insistence that "it is doomed to failure." One major reason for this presumption is the ideology that homosexuality, or gayness, is part of the *essential self* of the gay person and thus can never be changed (see also Warren, 1974):

INTERVIEWER: Why do you say a gay front marriage will never work?

---

* See Ross (1971) for a discussion of married homosexuals and Cory (1951) for a personal reminiscence.

BARTENDER: If you marry, or even if you just live together as roommates, you get emotionally fond of each other—right? And things don't always go right in your gay affairs, right? So one night when the moon is full and you've had a few drinks, you decide to express that fondness and intimacy and you get in bed together. So on that basis, which is human nature, it would never work.

INTERVIEWER: Why would the jumping in bed make it "not work"?

BARTENDER: Because you are both basically gay, that's why.

A second major reason for the presumption of failure in gay front marriage and roommate arrangements is the constant possibility of one or the other person finding a long-term or serious sexual partner, with the attendant jealousies and disruptions:

ROBERTO: Guys and girls trying to be roommates—there's always trouble, like one of them finds someone else and the other person feels jealous, feels shut out, even if it's not a sexual relationship, and more so if it is. Or one person is not home when the other is lonely, or they get in each other's way when they want to have lovers in. . . .

KIM: When I roomed with Jason for a while it was great until I met Lauren, then he got jealous and left notes around the house saying he was lonely and I felt guilty because he is my best friend, and he really put Lauren down whenever he could.

Finally, the men and women reported dissensus about various matters of life-style:

JOE: I let Annie and Losetta stay with me some months while they were looking for jobs and it really bothered me after a while—they were so sloppy, and I couldn't bear the thought of the disgusting things they might leave in the bathroom.


## CONCLUSION

These data on women in the male gay world serve to flesh out Simmel's formal sociological analysis of the sociability relation in society, particularly in its aspect of transcending and toying with the harsh realities of everyday life. In such a play world, even those who do not share in relevant class or caste statuses (in this case maleness and gayness), if they are adept at play, can find a place.

From sociable relations can develop intimacies of friendship, and sexual relations of varying degrees of intimacy, between gay males and both heterosexual and gay women. In addition, out of intimate friendships between gay males and heterosexuals in other settings, heterosexual women with unsatisfying heterosexual lives can move into gay sociability settings.

Finally, these findings illuminate a variety of adaptations to stigma in our society. In a society which stigmatizes older, divorced heterosexual women, these women may form relationships with other categories of the stigmatized—in this case the secret gays. Similarly, the formation of relationships between gay men and women in our society serves to mitigate public stigma, under the option of secret rather than overt homosexuality, in the case of "passing as straight."

## REFERENCES

BERGLER, EDMUND. *One Thousand Homosexuals*. Paterson, N.J.: Pageant Books, 1959.

CORY, DONALD W. *The Homosexual in America*. New York: Greenberg, 1951.

HOOKER, EVELYN. "Male Homosexuality." In N. L. Farberow, ed., *Taboo Topics*. New York: Atherton Press, 1963.

———. "Male Homosexuals and Their 'Worlds.' " In Judd Marmor, ed., *Sexual Inversion: The Multiple Roots of Homosexuality*. New York: Basic Books, 1965.

HUMPHREYS, LAUD. "New Styles in Homosexual Manliness." *Trans-Action*, March–April, 1971, pp. 38–46, 64–65.

———. *Out of the Closets: The Sociology of Homosexual Liberation*. Englewood Cliffs, N.J.: Prentice-Hall, 1972.

LEZNOFF, M., and W. WESTLEY. "The Homosexual Community." In John H. Gagnon and William Simon, eds., *Sexual Deviance*. New York: Harper & Row, 1967.

LYMAN, STANFORD M., and MARVIN B. SCOTT. *A Sociology of the Absurd.* New York: Appleton-Century-Crofts, 1970.

MAGEE, B. *One in Twenty,* New York: Stein and Day, 1966.

MILLS, C. WRIGHT. "Situated Actions and Vocabularies of Motive." *American Sociological Review* 5 (1940): 904–13.

ROSS, H. LAURENCE. "Modes of Adjustment of Married Homosexuals." *Social Problems* 18 (1971): 385–93.

SCHOFIELD, MICHAEL. *Sociological Aspects of Homosexuality.* Boston: Little, Brown, 1965.

SIMMEL, GEORG. *The Sociology of Georg Simmel.* Kurt Wolff, ed./trans. New York: Free Press, 1950.

SIMON, WILLIAM, and JOHN H. GAGNON. "The Lesbians: A Preliminary Overview." In John H. Gagnon and William Simon, eds., *Sexual Deviance.* New York: Harper & Row, 1967.

WARREN, CAROL A. B. *Identity and Community in the Gay World.* New York: Wiley, 1974.

# Unpromised Paternity:
# The Life-Styles of Gay Fathers

BRIAN MILLER

## INTRODUCTION

Our society does not promise equal opportunity to gay people. Most of all it does not promise the opportunity of child rearing to gay men. It is sometimes assumed that gays have infantile development themselves, or they molest and pervert children entrusted to their care. Consequently, many people are surprised to learn there are gay fathers with healthy children, fathers who have achieved their unpromised paternity. Over the past several years, I have conducted an exploratory investigation of the phenomenon of gay fatherhood (Miller, 1978a, b, c, d). This paper describes the life-styles of gay fathers in an attempt to answer how these men integrate the seemingly contradictory statuses of homosexual and father.

## NUMBER OF GAY FATHERS

The scarcity of sociological literature on gay fathers reflects society's general lack of awareness about this phenomenon. Some work has been completed on lesbian mothers (Kirkpatrick *et al.,* 1976; Pagelow, 1978), but gay fathers are only hinted at in sociological literature, not discussed in their own right. Schofield (1965), in a British study of homosexual patients and prisoners, finds 20 percent to be heterosexually married. Ross

A version of this paper was presented at the American Sociological Association annual meetings in San Francisco, September 1978.

Thanks are extended to Professor Gordon Hirabayashi, University of Alberta, and Professor Laud Humphreys, Pitzer College, for their helpful comments on this paper.

(1971) cites a review of gay studies that indicates that from 8 to 25 percent of the male homosexuals interviewed have wives. Weinberg and Williams (1974) find 13.3 percent of their American sample of gay bar patrons have experienced heterosexual marriage.

The first sensitive discussions of gay fatherhood have come, not from academia, but from anecdotal accounts: Sindt, 1974; Mager, 1975; Shilts, 1975; Brown, 1976; Klaich, 1976; Babuscio, 1977; Clark, 1977; Gengle, 1977; Lynch, 1978. Their insights have replaced older, pathology-oriented, psychoanalytic case studies of married gays: Allan, 1957; Bieber, 1969; Imielinski, 1969. However, sociological investigations of gay fathers remain neglected; hence, the present study.

## FINDING GAY FATHERS

Tape-recorded depth interviews were conducted with forty men who rate themselves as homosexual on one of the sexual scales employed, and who have a regular interaction with and legal responsibility for one or more children. They were contacted by means of multiple-source snowball samples, each respondent being asked to suggest other potential interviewees. The fathers display a wide range of living and custody arrangements: living with wife and children, living away from wife but with children, visiting rights to children, adoptive gay father, split custody ("one for you and one for me"), divided custody (child spends part of the year with mother and part with father). Their residences span across the United States and Canada: San Diego, Columbus, Washington, Ottawa, Vancouver, and a number of other communities. Socioeconomic backgrounds range from working class to lower-upper class including, among others, such occupations as file clerk, lawyer, short-order cook, banker, professor.

The semistructured interview probed for information concerning the father's family of orientation, family of procreation, and relationships with spouse, children, employer, gay and straight friends. Additional details and inferences about life-style were recorded, where possible, by interviewing in the father's residence, and by interviewing friends and relatives.

Each father was asked to indicate, using the Kinsey seven-point sexual orientation scale, the orientation of his sexual behavior over his lifetime and at present, and the orientation of his sexual fantasy over his lifetime and at present. No subject ranks himself consistently on all four scales, but all men rate predominantly homosexual in the present mix of their homosexual to heterosexual responses.

This study is exploratory and, consequently, its conclusions are tentative. The complexity of the issues involved necessitates that findings be considered suggestive, rather than definitive.

## VARIANT LIFE-STYLES

Descriptions of the fathers' life-styles are organized into a typology (see Figure 1) whose two variables are living arrangement and social and occupational resources, two of the most important criteria for increasing personal freedom to move in the gay world. Living arrangement was determined by whether or not the father was living with his wife. Social and occupational resources were determined by an index that incorporated measures of the following: occupational autonomy, occupational acceptance of homosexuality, access to a community of gay institutions, and education skills.

The typology forms four cells, each describing a particular father's life-style: trade father, homosexual father, gay father, and publicly gay father. Details follow on their relationships with spouse, children, gay and straight friends, and how the men cope with each role. Special attention is given to how these men structure their lives in order to solve the seemingly anomalous union of homosexuality with fatherhood.

RESOURCES

| LIVING ARRANGEMENT | Low Social And Occupational Resources | High Social And Occupational Resources |
|---|---|---|
| Living with Wife | Trade Fathers (N = 8) | Homosexual Fathers (N = 9) |
| Living Apart from Wife | Gay Fathers (N = 10) | Publicly Gay Fathers (N = 13) |

Figure 1
Typology of Fathers Participating in Homosexual Behavior by Living Arrangement and Resources

## Trade Fathers

"Trade" refers to a man who engages in furtive sexual behavior with men, but who is reluctant to accept this behavior as anything more than a genital urge (Humphreys, 1975). In spite of his behavior, he thinks of himself as heterosexual and maintains the outward appearance of a conventional working- to middle-class suburban father. Isolation from the gay community combines with engulfment in a heterosexual role to burden him with the only-one-in-the-world feeling. Wives, children, and associates are ostensibly unaware of his extramarital sexual behavior. Elaborate rendezvous strategies and facades aid in separating his heterosexual and homosexual worlds.

The trade father, to protect his discreditable heterosexual identity, must restrict his extramarital sex to clandestine, impersonal encounters in tearooms, parks, highway rest stops, with hitchhikers or male hustlers. Afraid of discovery, he cannot meet gay people in sociable gay contexts such as bars and clubs. All trade fathers in this sample say they have difficulty finding enough gay partners and free time to satisfy their homoerotic desires. Concocting legitimate-sounding opportunities to get away from the family is difficult. One father discovered he could take extended Saturday grocery-buying trips as a cover to search for sex, a tactic that prompted his waiting family to nickname him "The Hong Kong Shopper."

Accounts given by trade fathers to explain their behavior and to minimize its significance include:

My wife won't give the sex I want.

Going down on guys isn't real [gay] sex 'cause I never do kissing stuff.

Chicks cost money and hassle the marriage; fooling with guys is free and easy.

Premarital homosexual behavior was often disavowed with "Christ, was I drunk last night!"

Trade fathers see themselves as "not really homosexual." They find it difficult to reconcile their masculine self-image with the popular image of gays as hatefully effeminate. They cannot simultaneously see themselves as worthwhile persons and as homosexuals. The most they can acknowledge is that they often get together with other men to ejaculate and that they fantasize about men during sex with their wives.

In spite of trade fathers' accounts, all say they experience a great deal of guilt about leading double lives. Many have sought counseling. They view alternatives to marriage as severely limited. For example, none sees the gay world as a viable option. Frequently, they describe it as "superficial," "bitchy," "unstable," "full of violence." Given their limited exposure to only the impersonal homosexual underground, not to loving gay relationships, their negative perception is somewhat justified. Humphreys' studies of homosexual victims of homicide (1976) and of tearoom arrests (1975), for example, reveal most of these men are trade fathers. As long as they remain marginal to the gay world, their ability to achieve safe, fulfilling, homosexual relationships remains minimal.

Trade fathers find it difficult to talk about their children.

They express guilt that their work and sex schedules do not allow them to spend as much time with their children as they would like. They report considerable conflict with wives, who object to their disproportionate time spent away from home and neglect of parental duties. Nevertheless, most trade fathers say the children are the main reason for remaining with the wife:

I know it sounds terrible, but my kids are the major drawing card.

I think they like me more than their mother. I couldn't leave them forever.

## Homosexual Fathers

"Homosexual" refers to a man who engages in sexual behavior with men and whose self-identity, but not public identity, is consistent with it. Such a man is marginal to the gay community since he, like the trade father, has a heterosexual public identity and a conventional, heterosexual family life-style. Although the homosexual father is just as closeted as the trade father to his wife and friends, he is much more comfortable with his homoerotic behavior and is more likely to admit his sexual orientation to other homosexuals.

The homosexual father, compared with the trade father, has higher social and occupational resources. This provides him the means for an expanded repertoire of sexual outlets. Call boys or a separate apartment for tricking provides relatively safe sexual facilities. Here, homosexual fathers are less likely to encounter entrapment, police, or queer bashers. Gay bars and baths are somewhat inaccessible since they often start too late, and homosexual fathers cannot regularly find excuses for extended night absences. Some alternatively resort to lunch-hour or presupper "quickies" at the baths.

Homosexual fathers expend great amounts of energy in keeping their two worlds separate. Respondents report constructing fake identities, names, employment, addresses, to prevent possible tailing by sexual partners. Cover stories are manufactured for wives, co-workers, and friends. Some men have secret post office boxes or separate office phones reserved for clandestine, gay-related business. Some have hidden gay magazines; others have address-book codes so gay activities can be secretly recorded.

In spite of these measures, homosexual fathers report many facade-cracking incidents: transferring body lice and VD from a hustler to the wife; being caught on the street with a gay friend whose presence cannot be explained; blurting out praise for an event, then remembering it was attended with a gay friend, not the wife.

Homosexual fathers who travel as part of their business or have loosely structured working hours enjoy relative freedom. Absences and incidents can be more easily covered:

I don't know what I'd do without convention trips. They're the only opportunity when I have time to make real love to a guy. Otherwise, it's just fast tricking. Questions from home aren't easy to field.

A minority of homosexual fathers are able to mix their hetero- and homosexual worlds, notably those who circulate in the fields of the arts and academia. Their marriages reflect their perception that an outward heterosexual identity is essential if they are to maintain their public's loyalty and professional credibility. Their circle is that of the relatively wealthy and tolerant where the epitaph "perversion" is replaced by the more neutral "eccentricity," and variant behavior is accepted as long as you are discreet and "don't rub you wife's nose in it." Several of these men socialize openly with their lovers, whom wives and others ostensibly know as merely work assistants or friends-of-the-family. This adjustment, however, is tenuous:

I hope my wife and lover don't get too close 'cause some of my stories don't add up. They both give me flack 'cause each of them wants more of my time. I'm not sure what friends and office people think of my comings and goings. Parties are the scariest. I pray people stay sober and polite enough to keep suspicions to themselves.

One relatively affluent respondent living in an alternative-lifestyle, extended-family setting claims success at openly integrating his hetero- and homosexual worlds, but this is the only case sampled where such a mix appears comfortable.

The guilt most homosexual fathers experience is reflected in what might be called a Santa Claus syndrome. They shower their wives, children, and, sometimes, gay partners with excessive gifts to assuage their feelings that they have done a terrible thing to these people by being a homosexual father. This practice has many of these men in extreme debt. They use their credit cards to manage guilt, and explain family overindulgence with "It's the least I can do for having ruined their chance to grow up in a normal home." Like the trade father, the homosexual father regrets that performance of his breadwinner, husband, and homosexual roles leave little time for his father role. This partially accounts for his remaining with the family: "I'd leave this marriage tomorrow, only I haven't seen enough of my kids' growth and I don't know them yet." Other reasons for staying include perceived lack of a viable alternative, perceived social stigma, and decreased standard of living necessitated by a divorce.

## Gay Fathers

"Gay" refers to a man who engages in homosexual behavior, whose self-identity and, to a limited extent, public identity reflect acceptance, not denial, of the validity of his behavior. Since the gay father is generally not living with his wife or children, his life-style approximates that of the gay single. He is well acquainted with such social aspects of the gay world as bars and private parties.

Upon leaving their wives, gay fathers in this sample enhanced their self-image. They became more physically fit, built up their bodies, and adopted more flattering clothing and hair styles. Many report the elimination of nervous and psychosomatic discomforts such as ulcers, excessive fatigue, and headaches. The better care they take of themselves was expressed by one who said, "Being in the gay world, away from my hopeless marriage, gives me more reasons to live."

Gay fathers' relationships with other gays approximate either serial monogamy or open unions where sexual freedom is mutually maximized. Nonsexual relationships with gay friends assume considerable importance in the definition of self. Extensive socializing and modestly priced but conspicuous consumption are central traits of the gay father's life-style.

Institutions in the gay world for impersonal sex are patronized relatively *in*frequently by gay fathers. They prefer meeting other gays in contexts that are not only sexual but social: gay gyms and sports clubs, bars, churches and synagogues, residential areas, medical and counseling clinics, shops and theaters, gay political and charity clubs, chartered vacations, gay barbershops and bookstores, and gay special-interest organizations such as those for antique collectors and motorcyclists.

Gay fathers, rather than residing with their children, have arranged regular visiting schedules with them. They do not have the financial resources either to persuade their wives to relinquish the children or to hire surrogate care for them while devoting needed time to their careers. All the gay father's significant others, except his children and employer, tend to know he is gay. In the absence of family discussion on the topic, perceptive children may still have suspicions. One man who thought he was discreet was startled when his twelve-year-old daughter asked: "How come the men you sleep with are better looking than the men Mommy sleeps with?" Other fathers felt their older children "must suspect," but were apprehensive about open acknowledgment.

Secrecy about being gay exists with children and employers since the gay father's relatively low social and occupational resources do not allow him to fight back should his gayness an issue in the community. His wife might deny him child-visiting privileges and his employer might dismiss him. Successful legal appeal for gay fathers in such matters is rare (Boggan et al., 1975), a condition these men perceive as legally sanctioned blackmail. Contrary to expectation that only hoodlums blackmail gays, virtually all the blackmail reported by the respondents was initiated by spouses. One respondent said his wife threatened: "If you don't do everything my way, I'll expose your gayness to the court; then you'll never see your job or kids again." Some wives moved with the children to distant cities in order to make frequent father visits impossible. Men who are able to terminate marriages without their spouse's discovering their gayness avoid this problem. However, fear of subsequent exposure and loss of children through a new court order remains and forces some gay fathers with low social and occupational resources to stay partially closeted even after marital dissolution.

## Publicly Gay Fathers

"Publicly gay" refers to a man who not only engages in homosexual behavior and has a self-identity reflective of that behavior, but who proudly acknowledges his life-style even if such candor entails abuse. Publicly gay fathers comprise the largest section of the sample, primarily because such men are open about their gayness and easy to contact. Although they come from the full range of economic backgrounds, they rank high on our index of social and occupational resources. Some are employed by tolerant bosses; some are full-time gay activists; others are self-employed, often in businesses that have large gay clienteles.

Publicly gay fathers organize their symbolic world, to a great extent, around gay culture. Much of their leisure, if not occupation, is spent in gay-related pursuits. Their outlook characterizes them as "born-again gays." They have experienced the trauma of bitterly unhappy marriages, the struggle of achieving a gay identity, and now feel they finally have arrived at a satisfactory adjustment:

I tried everything to prove I wasn't gay. I joined the army, grew a beard, got psychoanalyzed, had sex with umpteen women, got married, and became a father. It worked for a while, but I still felt unfinished. Now that I'm openly gay, the wholeness is here.

A number of publicly gay fathers have full-time custody of their children and are living with a lover. Two respondents have never married, but managed to adopt children through marginally legitimate channels. Since these men have avoided the pain of heterosexual marriage and divorce, their histories are the most positive.

In all cases, the children are aware of their father's sexuality. Children interviewed said:

I'm glad Dad came out to me; it makes him more human.

I feel freer to discuss my sexual feelings with him now. He understands both sides.

Problems with child rearing are not foreign to publicly gay fathers, but they appear to be no more than those reported by single, heterosexual fathers with custody (Hetherington et al., 1976; Mendes, 1976; Orthner et al., 1976; Victor and Winkler, 1977). Interestingly, publicly gay fathers are least likely of all the respondents to favor discipline involving corporal punishment.

At the time of the interview, no respondent belonged to a self-help organization such as Gay Fathers Unlimited, but several have since joined similar groups. Here they find a medium in which to share their special concerns. Publicly gay fathers who live with their children and lover are more sedentary and more apt to have a close circle of gay friends, rather than being at the center of gay social institutions like the gay fathers. Most of the men waged difficult battles to obtain custody of their children and express concomitantly high commitment to spending considerable time with them.

## DISCUSSION

The general tendency is for trade fathers to come out and move toward becoming publicly gay fathers. Some are blocked in this movement by their inability to leave their wife and by inadequate resources.

This study has two major findings. First, while gayness is incompatible with traditional marriages, gayness is compatible with fathering. With one exception, all respondents report discordant relationships with wives. Highly compartmentalized life-styles and deceit often repress open marital conflict, but unresolved tension characterizes such unions. By contrast, men who leave their spouse and enter the gay world report gay relationships to be more harmonious than marital relationships. They also report fathering to be more important and more fulfilling now that they are away from their marriage.

Second, gay fathers who come out perceive much less discrimination from family, friends, and co-workers than the closeted ones anticipate. Certainly wives are upset by their husband's revelation, but gay fathers are often surprised by the positive responses of their children and parents.

Many fathers remain closeted fearing their gay life-style will result in their children's encountering homophobia. While this is possible, openly gay fathers can also give their children the resources to defeat such bigotry, as the following statements suggest:

My ten-year-old son asked me what to do about a playmate who said, "Your old man is a queer and you're going to be one too." After we discussed the issue, he told his playmate, "So what."

The school board was debating whether homosexuality should be discussed in family-life classes. [My sixteen-year-old daughter who is on the Student Council] asked me my position. Then she went before the board and told them, "Why not teach about homosexuals? For ten years I've known my dad is one, and it hasn't hurt me or our relationship." I think she blew their minds.

Some people worry that the gay father's children will be molested by his gay friends or that the children, especially boys, will "catch" homosexuality by being near gays. Evidence from this study indicates such fears are not warranted.

Future prospects for gay fathers hinge largely on the success of the gay liberation movement. Movement victories will allow existing gay fathers to come out and also permit more adoptions by gay singles. As viable alternatives for fathering are made available within the gay world, fewer gays are likely to get involved in heterosexual marriages. Gay men, unwilling to become fathers in the conventional way, have for years successfully contributed to child rearing as surrogate parents: teachers, day-care personnel, scout leaders, ministers, policemen, guidance counselors, coaches, and pediatricians. Now movement victories may allow a proliferation of gay-family life-styles so that gay men may openly achieve their unpromised paternity and demonstrate what promising parents they can be.

## REFERENCES

ALLEN, C. "When homosexuals marry," *Sexology* (February 1957): 416–20.

BABUSCIO, J. *We Speak for Ourselves*. Philadelphia: Fortress, 1977.

BIEBER, I. "The married male homosexual." *Medical Aspects of Human Sexuality 3* (1969): 76–84.

BOGGAN, E. CARRINGTON, MARILYN G. HAFT, CHARLES LISTER, and JOHN P. RUPP. "The Gay Family." In E. Carrington Boggan et al., *The Rights of Gay People*. New York: Avon Books, 1975.

BROWN, H. "Married homosexuals," in H. Brown, *Familiar Faces, Hidden Lives*. New York: Harcourt Brace Jovanovich, 1976.

CLARK, D. "Husbands and wives; daughters and sons," in D. Clark, *Loving Someone Gay*. Millbrae, Calif.: Celestial Arts, 1977.

GENGLE, D. "All in the gay family," *The Advocate* 224 (September 1977): 33–36.

HETHERINGTON, E. MAVIS, MARTHA COX, and ROGER COX. "Divorced Fathers." *The Family Coordinator* 25 (October 1976): 417–28.

HUMPHREYS, LAUD. *Tearoom Trade: Impersonal Sex in Public Places*. Enlarged ed. Chicago: Aldine, 1975.

———. "The Case of the Gay Corpse: Homosexual Victims of Homicide." Paper presented at American Society of Criminology Meetings, Tucson, Arizona, November 1976.

IMIELINSKI, K. "Homosexuality in Males with Particular Reference to Marriage," *Psychotherapy and Psychosomatics* 17 (1969): 126–32.

KIRKPATRICK, M., R. ROY, and K. SMITH "A New Look at Lesbian Mothers," *Human Behavior* 5 (August 1976): 60–61.

KLAICH, D. "Parents Who Are Gay," *New Times* (July 1976): 34–42.

LYNCH, M. "Forgotten Fathers," *The Body Politic* 42 (April 1978): 1, 10–12.

MAGER, D. "Faggot Father." in K. Jay and A. Young, eds., *After You're Out*. New York: Gage, 1975.

MENDES, HELEN A. "Single Fathers." *The Family Coordinator* 25 (1976): 439–44.

MILLER, BRIAN. "Methodological Considerations in Researching a Disvalued Minority." Paper presented at the Gender Identity Meeting, UCLA Neuropsychiatric Center, Los Angeles, January 1978a.

———. "Coping Patterns and Identity of Atypical Fathers." Paper presented at the Canadian Sociology and Anthropology Association Meetings, London, Canada, May 1978b.

———. "Adult Sexual Resocialization: Adjustments Toward a Stigmatized Identity." In *Alternative Lifestyles* 1, no. 2 (May 1978c).

———. "Stigma Contamination: Attitudes and Adjustments of Women Married to Gay Men." Paper presented at the Canadian Psychological Association Meetings, Ottawa, June 1978d.

PAGELOW, M. D. "Lesbian and Straight mothers," in K. Henry, ed., *Social Problems*. Glenview, Ill.: Scott, Foresman, 1978

ROSS, H. L. "Modes of Adjustment of Married Homosexuals," *Social Problems* 18 (Winter 1978): 385–93.

SCHOFIELD, M. *Sociological Aspects of Homosexuality*. London: Longmans, 1965.

SHILTS, R. "Gay People Make Babies Too," *The Advocate* 175 (October 1975): 25.

ORTHNER, DENNIS K., TERRY BROWN, and DENNIS FERGUSON. "Single-Parent Fatherhood: An Emerging Family Life-style." *The Family Coordinator* 25 (1976): 429–37.

WEINBERG, M., and C. WILLIAMS. *Male Homosexuals: Their Problems and Adaptations*. New York: Oxford University Press, 1974.

VICTOR, IRA, and WIN ANN WINKLER. *Fathers and Custody*. New York: Hawthorn, 1977.

# The Aging Male Homosexual: Myth and Reality

## JIM KELLY

This article discusses some of the findings of a recent study of 241 gay* men between the ages of sixteen and seventy-nine† in the Los Angeles metropolitan area. While the original study examined the attitudes, stereotypes, and characteristics of these men in reference to aging, focus here is on the characteristics which older‡ gay men in the study group have in comparison to specific popular myths and on the problems encountered by these men.

Data were collected through questionnaire, interview, and participant observation techniques over a two-year period (1973–1974). As there are no accurate accounts of the racial, age, or socioeconomic parameters of the American gay subgroup, probability sampling techniques were virtually impossible

*The Gerontologist* 17, no. 4 (August 1977). Copyright © 1976 by the Gerontological Society. Reprinted by permission of the publisher and author.

* "Gay" is the widely preferred subculture term for those who engage primarily in homosexual relations. Judd Marmor's (1965) interpretation of the term "homosexual" appears to be one of the most definitive: "One who is motivated in adult life by a definite preferential erotic attraction to members of the same sex and who usually (but not necessarily) engages in overt sexual relations with them."

† The highest concentration of individuals is in the 20- to 34-year age range for the large questionnaire group; the age range for this group is 60 years, with a mean age of 33 years. In the interview groups the age distribution is purposively bimodal, with seven scores in the 20–24 bracket and eight in the 65–79 age interval. The rest of the frequencies for the interviewers tend to be distributed more evenly, although no interviewees were in their 50s.

‡Except when used in a context such as "men older than twenty-five," the term "older" is defined by the majority responses of the men themselves. Most saw fifty as the end of the middle age and the beginning of old age.

to employ. This study must, therefore, be considered an exploratory account; its findings are not meant to be generalizable to all
aging gay men.*   Almost all studies of noninstitutionalized gay
men have used gay organizations (Hooker, 1956; Evans, 1969),
gay bars (Myrick, 1974), friendship networks (Loney, 1972), or
a combination of these (Saghir and Robins, 1973; Weinberg and
Williams, 1974). However, the scientific value and importance
of research which limits its vantage point to small enclaves of the
gay world is now being questioned by both scientists and gay
people.

This study used a period of participant observation in the Los
Angeles gay community to discover alternative sample sources.
In order to allow for the widest range of respondent characteristics, it was decided to avoid the sampling of bars, baths, and
similar establishments which charge fees and which are generally recognized, in the gay community, as primarily "sexual
hunting grounds." It was thought, on the basis of participant
observation, that sampling these places might systematically
exclude the very poor, and perhaps also some persons in settled
gay liaisons and some older persons.

Continued observations led to the selection of a popular gay
beach and the Los Angeles Metropolitan Community Church
(mother church) congregation as major sample sources, along
with advertisements in several gay-oriented newspapers, and the
use of friendship networks.

One hundred ninety-three questionnaires and forty-eight interviews were analyzed. Thirty of the men stated they were over
age 65; seven in the older group refused to divulge their age; and
six were over 75 (all interview material quoted in this article
comes from conversations with men over age 65).

During data collection trust and confidence were established
primarily through viewing the gay men involved as experts with
experience in "living in a certain milieu." Study participants

---

*Because significant differences may exist between gay men's and wom-
en's communities, only gay males are included in this analysis. Review of
several articles (Simon and Gagnon, 1967; Saghir, 1969; Saghir and Robins,
1973) indicates that "many of the sexual behaviors of adult homosexual men
differ from those of adult homosexual women" (Saghir, 1969).

were viewed not simply as research "objects" but as valuable informants helping the researcher to become aware of the characteristics and types of attitudes extant in their community.

## STEREOTYPES

The old in general are often stereotyped. A number of myths, stigmas, negative societal beliefs, and definitions tend to be attached to older persons. However, while the elderly have been generalized to be "politically conservative," "senile," "fanatically religious," and "incapable of sexual activity or interest" (Bengtson, 1973), older gay men have repeatedly been singled out as particularly pathetic figures. Stereotyping, in fact, is not uncommon in supposedly scientific literature. Allen (1961) writes in *The Third Sex:* "The aging homosexual tends to become distinctly odd. . . ."

Stearn (1961) elaborates on the "oddities of older gays" in *The Sixth Man,* where he represents the unaffluent older gay as living "in the Bowery, seeking oblivion in handouts and cheap wine" and "regress[ing] to a point where he preys on small children." Newton in her 1972 research defines gay men as "old" at thirty.

Even within the gay subculture the older man is often stigmatized. The "faggot's faggot" was the phrase chosen by a columnist (Kochera, 1973) in the *Pittsburgh Gay News* in an article deploring the Pittsburgh subculture's stigmatization of older gays. Just as gay people in general form a predominantly "secret" society within the large society, columnist Kochera describes these groups as symbolically stigmatized "unseen victims of ignorance and oppression" about which a hazy folklore seems to exist.

In the "hazy folklore" there are myths and stereotypes and assumptions about the participation of older gay men in subculture activities, about their interpersonal association with other gay men, about their self-identifications as gay people, and about their sexuality.

This is one composite stereotype of the supposed characteristics and activities of the aging gay man. He no longer goes to bars, having lost his physical attractiveness and his sexual appeal to the young men he craves. He is oversexed, but his sex life is very unsatisfactory. He has been unable to form a lasting relationship with a sexual partner, and he is seldom active sexually anymore. When he does have sex it is usually in a "tearoom" (public toilet). He has disengaged from the gay world and his acquaintances in it. He is retreating further and further into the "closet"—fearful of disclosure of his "perversion." Most of his associations now are increasingly with heterosexuals. In a bizarre and deviant world centered around age, he is labeled "an old queen," as he has become quite effeminate.

The aging gay men in this study bear little resemblance to this stereotyped composite image of their socially inferred characteristics.

In contrast to the mythical man, the "composite" older man in the study group does not frequent tearooms but occasionally goes out to bars, particularly those that serve his peer group. Only 4 percent of the questionnaire sample and one interviewee mentioned having been in a tearoom in the past six months. Of the 4 percent participating in tearoom activity, over half (53.7 percent) were "younger," under age thirty-six. However, 63 percent of those between fifty-six and sixty-five described themselves as bargoers.

In the study group, the extent of the typical older man's participation in the gay world is low to moderate and based largely on his individual desires. Of the gay people who completed questionnaires for this project, most seem to feel that their level of participation in the gay world's round of activities is low (30 percent) to moderate (52 percent). However, no one over age sixty-five indicated that he had disengaged from activities in the gay world.

The composite older man in the study group says his concern about disclosure of his sexual orientation is related to his many years of working in a profession where known gays are not tolerated. Of the gay men over age thirty-six responding to the questionnaire, 63 percent expressed "high concern" over disclosure of sexual orientation. However, many respondents indicated that they were merely "concerned," and in some cases concerned *only* about *occupational* disclosure. One retired interviewee, for example, expressed relief:

> . . . Indifferent now, but I used to be concerned about it when I was in industry. I wouldn't want it disclosed. I don't want to be labeled.

The representative aging gay man studied his many gay friends and fewer heterosexual friends. The majority of the gay men studied here, of all ages, ranked their degree of social association with other gay people as "moderate" (44 percent to "high" (42 percent), with the overwhelming majority of interviewees (twenty-three) rating their association as "high." The youngest and oldest respondents were lower in the extent of their association with gays. However, few respondents indicated low association with gays to begin with, and percentages on the low association item are widely dispersed across the age categories. Association with heterosexuals was found to decrease dramatically with increasing age. While 42 percent of those under twenty-six ranked social association with heterosexuals high, the combined percentages of the oldest three age brackets equals only 36 percent.

The sex life of the older man in the Los Angeles study is, characteristically, quite satisfactory, and he desires sexual contact with adult men, especially those near his own age. He is not, however, currently involved in a gay liaison.* Of those in the 50–65 age bracket, 50 percent reported satisfactory sex lives; 83 percent of the respondents over age 65 report being sexually satisfied. Content analysis of interviews with older gays indicates that the majority of older interviewees are sexually interested and satisfied in relationships with, or are attracted toward, adult men—oftentimes men in their own age cohort. The number of persons involved in liaisons seems to increase with age, peaking with 59 percent of those forty-six to fifty-five years old being members of gay partnerships. After this apex, partnerships decrease to almost none. Two reasons for this decline often mentioned by older gays were the death of the loved one and the

---

* "Liaison" refers to an emotional and sexual relationship of one year's duration, or longer

rejection of the notion of having a single lifelong lover.

The typical older man in this study neither considers himself effeminate nor likes to define himself in terms of gay age labels, but he remembers the terms that were commonly applied to "older gays" when he was younger. Only twelve men over age thirty in the questionnaire and interview samples combined defined themselves with feminine self-identifications such as "closet queen," "nelly," etc.

## PROBLEMS FACED BY OLDER GAYS

While these gay men do not seem to fit the stereotypes which mark them as lonely, sexually frustrated, and unhappy, they are not without problems and potential problems.

Aging gays face the same problems of stigmatization of "age," loss of people emotionally important to them, and fear of institutionalization encountered by many older Americans:

I saw a guy, I know of a guy seventy-five, who keeps himself in good shape, you know. When you talk to him, you never think of talking to an old man. He is very sexy appearing and he doesn't talk and act like, quote, "old man," unquote. You know there is a certain stereotype we have in the whole of our society. You act as if you're a housewife, or you are this. So act in these things. Certain repertoire we sort of force on all the people that they got to act, got to move slow, they got to do a whole lot of crap, dress certainly, but they have to have certain attitudes; they can't be too vivacious [Interview].

I have no fear of growing old except that you face more loneliness than you do when you're young. I lost my lover when we looked forward to spending our retirement years together, going places, doing things together. Couldn't do it when we were working and then to have it all wiped away overnight. It left me with nobody and not much chance of finding anybody at this age. [Interview]

I hope that I don't end up going to a nursing home. I don't live too far from one now. I walk by there and I see some of these poor old devils, male and female, stuck there on chairs, etc. Nobody gives a damn. [Interview]

In addition to these problems of aging, older gays face unique discriminations related to the stigmatization of their sexual identity.

The discriminatory impact of many practices, laws, rules, and conventions seems to increase for the gay man as he ages. For example, several life insurance companies have allegedly refused to insure persons after uncovering evidence of their sexual orientation (Teal, 1971).

Also, while the emotional, economic, and physical security children can provide for aging parents is a common theme of heterosexual society, only very recently has the concept of gay adoptive parents gained an audience (Altman, 1971). Perhaps among the most chillingly tragic and painful discriminatory barriers gays may face are hospital visiting regulations:

A report in the *London Times* referred to a lesbian dying in a hospital who was only allowed visits from her immediate family, and her partner of twenty years was excluded (London West End Group, 1974).

When a lover dies, his gay companion faces possible legal discrimination. If no wills are involved, and there are no children from the marriage, the surviving spouse of a heterosexual couple can inherit the other's property automatically. When one party of a gay union dies without a will, however, his property goes to the deceased's family. Even if a will has been drawn up in which a gay person leaves all of his property to his lover, his family may contest and break the will on the grounds of "undue influence." Also, while a heterosexual spouse can inherit through the deceased partner, this right is not legally provided for the gay spouse. "A gay person cannot inherit his deceased lover's grandmother's estate under any circumstances" (Baker, in Teal, 1971).

Property ownership also can become a legal problem for the surviving spouse in a gay relationship:

In some states ... there is a form of ownership of property that is reserved solely to married couples. It's called "Tenancy by the Entirety." It guarantees that the property will go to the surviving spouse despite claims of creditors. Gay people can hold property in "joint Tenancy," i.e., co-owners, but creditors can get to the property and thus there is no guarantee the surviving "spouse" will end up with it [Baker, in Teal, 1971].

In addition, only the surviving spouse of a legal marriage can sue a third party for "wrongful death" through malpractice or other negligence. Therefore, this redress is not open to gay couples whose bonds are not legally binding (Baker, in Teal, 1971).

And when a lover dies, his gay companion may also be subjected to the personal, sometimes overt, sometimes subtle, prejudice of his loved one's family. Isherwood (1961) evokes the memory of such an experience in his aging gay protagonist, George:

> But how very strange to sit here . . . and remember that night when the long distance call came through from Ohio. An uncle of Jim's whom he'd never met—trying to be sympathetic, even admitting George's right to a small honorary share in the sacred family grief. . . .

## SOCIAL CHANGE

It seems obvious that there are laws to change and discriminatory institutional regulations to be challenged. Social situations and institutions, however, may be easier to change than individual prejudicial attitudes. It has been suggested, in fact (Altman, 1971), that the popular depiction of gays as pathetic and troubled fulfills an ethnocentric need among the liberal elements of current society:

> Most liberal opinion is horrified by persecution of homosexuals and supportive of abolishing the antihomosexual laws without really accepting homosexuality as a full and satisfying form of sexual and emotional behavior. Such tolerance of homosexuality can co-exist with considerable suspicion of and hostility toward it, and this hostility is reinforced in all sorts of ways within our society.

Hostility is reinforced by those psychotherapists who, according to Dr. Clarence A. Tripp, director of Psychological Research Associates, are "frightening the (gay) patient with the image of the aging, lonely homosexual" (Debate, 1971). Hostility is also reinforced by social science researchers who continue to fuel the myths about older gays. One very recent example of this is the British report *Campaign for Homosexual Equality* (London West End Group, 1974), which suggestively features this quotation on its cover:

Retired and retiring gay, bereft of mate of 31 years, fanatically sincere, needs an understanding pal desperately (over 21). London/Northarts. Box 12.

And hostility is reinforced too, by all those educators, scientists, and authors who continue to simply ignore "homosexuality" as a viable life-style for older people. This excerpt from the gerontological literature on sexuality is a classic example of this type of oversight:

. . . the widespread ignorance about sex and the high frequency in our society of excessive inhibition with respect to behavior that can lead to gratifying heterosexual relationships and the relief of sexual tensions make sexual problems one of the most common causes of helpless feelings among the aging [Goldfarb, in Berezin, 1969].

Although the research findings reported in this article are based on a nonprobability sample of one community, there seems to be *no further rationale* for the application of certain "blanket" stereotypes about aging gay men, as these men, as least, are living proof that such assertions are not always accurate. There is little evidence in this study to suggest that being gay causes problems in old age, but there is a great deal of evidence to suggest that societal stigma cause problems *for* aging gays. Only when society becomes aware of and accepts this important distinction can full acceptance and equality for older gay people become a real possibility.

## REFERENCES

ALLEN, CLIFFORD. "The Aging Homosexual." In Isadore Rubin, ed., *The Third Sex*. New York: New Book, 1961.

ALTMAN, DENNIS. *Homosexual Oppression and Liberation*. New York: Avon Books, 1971.

BENGTSON, VERN L. *The Social Psychology of Aging*. Indianapolis: Bobbs-Merrill, 1973.

BEREZIN, MARTIN A. "Sex and Old Age: A Review of the Literature." *Journal of Geriatric Psychiatry* 2 (1969): 131–49.

"Can Homosexuals Change with Psychotherapy?" Debate, in *Sexual Behavior* 42 (1971): 42–49.

EVANS, RAY B. "Childhood Parental Relationships of Homosexual Men." *Journal of Consulting and Clinical Psychology* 33 (1969):129–35.

HOOKER, EVELYN. "A Preliminary Analysis of Group Behavior of Homosexuals." *Journal of Psychology* 42 (1956): 217–25.

ISHERWOOD, CHRISTOPHER. *A Single Man.* London: Methuen, 1961.

KOCHERA, BRIAN. "The Faggot's Faggot . . . Gay Senior Citizens and Gay S & M." *Pittsburgh Gay News,* September 1, 1973, p. 6.

London West End Group. *Campaign for Homosexual Equality:* Monograph. London, 1974.

LONEY, JAN. "Background Factors, Sexual Experiences, and Attitudes Toward Treatment in Two 'Normal' Homosexual Samples." *Journal of Consulting and Clinical Psychology* 38 (1972): 57–65.

MARMOR, JUDD, ed. *Sexual Inversion: The Multiple Roots of Homosexuality.* New York: Basic Books, 1965.

MYRICK, FRED. "Attitudinal Difference Between Heterosexually and Homosexually Oriented Males and Between Covert and Overt Male Homosexuals." *Journal of Abnormal Psychology* 83 (1974): 81–86.

NEWTON, ESTHER. *Mother Camp: Female Impersonators in America.* Englewood Cliffs, N.J.: Prentice–Hall, 1972.

SAGHIR, MARCEL T. "Homosexuality" II: Sexual Behavior of the Male Homosexual." *Archives of General Psychiatry* 21 (1969): 219–29.

SAGHIR, MARCEL T., and ELI ROBINS. *Male and Female Homosexuality.* Baltimore: Williams & Wilkins, 1973.

SIMON, WILLIAM, and JOHN H. GAGNON. "Femininity in the Lesbian Community." *Social Problems* 15 (1967): 212–21.

STEARN, JESS. *The Sixth Man.* New York: Doubleday, 1961.

TEAL, DONN. *The Gay Militants.* New York: Stein & Day, 1971.

WEINBERG, MARTIN S., and COLIN J. WILLIAMS. *Male Homosexuals: Their Problems and Adaptations.* New York: Oxford University Press, 1974.

# Black and Gay

## JOHN VICTOR SOARES

Whether subtle or not, racism in the gay subculture is a reality that all black gay people deal with, unless—perhaps implausibly—they have insulated themselves with a closed circle of close friends. It is a recurrent reality for which coping mechanisms have been developed and are activated with such practiced efficiency that they are not infrequently subconscious. But they are not so consistently subconscious that racism is not commented on—at times with bitterness, at times with amusement, occasionally with indignation, but never with despair; for after all, black people are wont to deal with difficulty. It is their misfortune, their challenge, their inhumanely assigned task.

It would be unwarranted, given the facts, to assume that because gay people are members of a minority group themselves, they are free of the racism that pervades American society in general. Just as gay people have stationed themselves in the full range of professions and life-styles found throughout the nation, so also have they acquired attitudes and behavioral patterns— also found throughout the nation—which go to make up racism.

To those who have moved in both straight and gay circles, it does indeed appear that for every racially colored posture that is found in straight society, there is a corresponding one in gay society. For example, just as some straight black women have complained about black men who are eternally pursuing the pleasures of white flesh, so also have some black gay men complained about their black gay brothers who are fast on their way to becoming "snow queens" (if they aren't already there).

*The Advocate,* November 17, 1976. Copyright © 1976, Liberation Publications, Inc. Reprinted by permission of the publisher.

Carl (all names have been changed) is one black gay man who has gained (and earned) a reputation in Chicago for tricking with whites only, and this has not gone uncommented upon by one of the wags of Chicagoland: "You know Carl is colorblind—he can't see anything darker than white."

But on the other hand, there are black people who stick to black people. As one black San Franciscan known for his indelicate turns of phrase explains it, "I don't want no needle noses and razor lips. I get all the needles I need at the VD clinic, and the last time I saw a razor, it was trying to cut me!"

In spite of this, it must be remembered that racism is not necessarily a critical issue for black gay people in every situation. Obviously, there is a way to nullify it as far as gay-centered activities are concerned, and this way is through interaction in the black gay community. Of course, the extent to which such a community is available depends on the place one finds oneself.

Chances of finding an active and productive social life in the black gay community are far better in key cities with large black populations than in cities and areas sparsely populated by black people. Often, too, there may be an important black population in a certain area, but for various reasons black gay social life is not highly organized and intense as in such black gay supercenters as New York, Washington, D.C., Los Angeles, Atlanta, and Chicago. Although Detroit and St. Louis, for example, have sizable black populations, black gay social life simply does not muster up to the standards of sparkle, lavishness, and frequency of entertainment that are so observable in the supercenters.

Black gay social life in the supercenters is augmented by a selection of black bars and, in some cases, baths. There are predominantly black baths in New York and of late in San Francisco. In these gathering places, an undeniably stimulating selection of physical types and background profiles is presented for the patron's perusal. In an evening, Los Angeles Catch One alone will offer the full range of basic black—from the Levis-clad types serving up endless butch-allure to the slick, sparkling Hollywood types in slacks/print shirt ensembles to the superfly types, unequaled masters in the projection of sartorial dash and splendor.

In these settings, racism is largely a nonissue. If a black gay man can't convince his Ethiopian prince that a visit to his apartment is indispensable, he will simply have to review his act. A white patron, however, may find in some cases that his products are not in demand, but of course he knew beforehand the orientation of the market.

The integrated gay community, where blacks, whites, and others mingle, is where racism can become an issue, and its importance as an issue depends largely on where one lives. The integrated gay community offers a range of activities parallel to those in the black gay community, one difference being that there is a heavier emphasis on home entertainment in the black one. This is probably a holdover from the days of practically universal discrimination in public places. Since public entertainment was limited, black people heavily oriented their social life toward home entertainment.

This emphasis on home entertainment is but one small factor that goes into the making of the distinctive black culture. Many traits of black culture are distinctive, and some are more obvious and interesting than others. One trait that has been commented on by black gay people of a comparative turn of mind with multicultural experiences behind them is the relatively routine acceptance of gay family members. Some believe this is particularly true of black people of the working class or of a working-class background, but quite a bit less so with middle-class black families.

Black, middle-class families, notably the black "sociable" described by Nathan Hare in *The Black Anglo-Saxons* and by E. Franklin Frazier in his classic *The Black Bourgeoisie,* are so persistently monitoring their social standing that any family member departing from their peer group norm would experience a certain degree of ostracism. But for what appears to be the majority of working-class black people, gay lovers and steadies are accepted by or even into the family with a lack of flag waving and statement making that has been known to surprise even their middle-class black brothers.

There is indeed a complex of value and behavioral differences that separates middle-class black people from working-class black people. Sure, one can speak of an overall black culture, but even within it there are subcultures that are to be distinguished simply because they are real. The black community is no more classless or less diverse, regardless of what we might wish, than any other community of its size in the modern, industrialized world. This is a fact of which the average white person seems insufficiently aware.

The major complaint of black gay (and nongay) people of all class backgrounds, though, is that too many white people approach them not assuming they are members of any real black group but as though they were some mythical black characters created by the movie and social science industries, both known for the excessive attention they give unrealistically selected and misinterpreted aspects of the culture of poverty.

As with any other community, the members of the black community assume a wide range of roles. As far as gay roles in the black community are concerned, it is perhaps less than fortunate that the street sissy is the only one that is highly visible. This role is also institutionalized in that there is a preexisting role-model for those who would assume this role, and they are judged accordingly. It carries its own status, and rights and responsibilities pertaining to that status.

The street sissy typically excels in flamboyance and confrontation—and ass kicking. Hardly ever admired, he is always respected. But like all people who step into roles institutionalized by whatever culture, they most commonly find themselves trapped. One cannot be a street sissy part-time any more than one can be the baddest motherfucker on the block part-time. Neither does this institutionalized role allow for creative personal growth and development. It is a cultural prison that obscures endless possibilities for a homosexual life-style for adolescents who would love members of their own sex. Too many believe that it is the only gay role available to them because it is the only one they are fully aware of. Perhaps too many reject being gay as a real option because their cultural screen prevents them from seeing that *gay* is defined by sexual preferences only, and not any particular life-style.

To personalize a bit, let's say that you are black and you have

indeed emerged into gay life. What forms of racism will you find
and how will you go about dealing with them, particularly in
that most important endeavor—your pursuit of Mr. Him, The
One, Prince Dashing, and Sir Stud? (Pick one. You can't have
them all.)

First of all, although we all would probably like to do
something toward effecting social change, our daily goals must
be met within the context of the present. The patterns and
density, so to speak, of racism throughout the country are not
going to change overnight. Realizing this, you have to take stock
of your options and lay out your cards in a way that will
maximize possibilities for success in the general area of cruising.

Many of us have jobs that chain us to a particular location,
but whenever relocation is possible, thought should be given to
where possibilities can be maximized. If you are interested in
meeting other black people, the black gay supercenters are an
obvious choice. There is no point to remaining in Peoria if a
move to Atlanta, New York, Los Angeles, Chicago, or any other
locale with socially active black gay populations is possible. Even
if you are interested equally in black people, white people,
Eskimos, and Arabs, or primarily interested in white people or
some other nonblack group, it's always terribly convenient to
have an active black gay community as a backup when you tire
of bridging a culture gap, constantly dealing with racism or an
absence of variety. After all, the quest for variety is a primary
activity of too many people not to have something in its favor.

The black gay supercenters are not the only places where
lively black gay communities can be found. Some cities that
aren't major metropolises have very socially active black gay
groups simply because they have a core group of black gay
people (generally higher-income professionals) who have the
enthusiasm and the means to keep things lively. In those "mini-
centers" there is a regular, if not weekly, round of sumptuously
fun parties and get-togethers. San Diego is currently one of the
mini-centers. Mini-centers are particularly active on weekends
when well-known black entertainers are performing in town.

Cities having black colleges also offer rich possibilities. Black
gay communities in these cities tend to be very unpublic and

have their own distinctive style. Since these communities are very private-party oriented, unless you have friends there, you'll simply have to wait until you receive an invitation. In the meantime, smile a lot and listen closely for double-entendres in your conversations with nice men.

Black social fraternities at integrated colleges aren't quite like they are at black colleges. This is to say that the real personality of these fraternities is more clearly observable at the black colleges. The stereotype of the Alphas is that they are class- (and formerly color-) conscious and scholarly. The Kappa stereotype is that of the good-time jock. Of the Omegas (nicknamed "Cues"), it is said that they are many things, but always gorgeous. These stereotypes are repeated openly. What is whispered behind not firmly closed doors is that one of these three major fraternities attracts more gay people than the others. Your assignment: to verify the rumor.

There are too many black college towns to list, but some of the major ones are Nashville (Fisk, Tennessee A&I, and Meharry Medical College); Atlanta (Atlanta University and other schools, including Morehouse, Martin Luther King's alma mater and the leading college for black men; Atlanta is a supercenter, too, making it double-plus good); Hampton, Virginia (Hampton Institute); Baltimore (Morgan State); Baton Rouge (Louisiana State); and Washington, D.C. (Howard, the nation's leading predominantly black university; Washington, like Atlanta, gets the double star).

Some black gay people have sung the glories of being "the only one." This is one version of the theory of scarcity; the fewer there are, the more they are appreciated.

"Before I went to Spain the first time, I asked a good friend who is Spanish how I would like it. I was told that I'd be an *articulo de lujo* (luxury item) because there are so few black people in Spain." This is the comment of one well-traveled New Yorker.

Traditionally, the best place to be a luxury item has been Europe. Josephine Baker discovered this early on, and there has been a steady stream of black people across the Atlantic ever since. In a real sense, Europe remains the eternal alternative.

Even though there have been recent influxes of darker peoples from the ex-colonies who are daily confronted with perceptible increments in racism, American black people have for the most part retained their special place.

The major capitals all have their American black colonies—expatriate writers, jazz musicians, blues singers, inveterate good-time seekers, and summer tourists. They are all there, and so are circles of black American gay people.

But Paris reigns. For several years Les Deux Maggots, a cafe across the street from the eminently flammable Le Drugstore, served with distinction as an early evening convention site for a core group of black gay people and their Parisian fans. Perhaps it is no more. In these economically troubled times, zipping off to Paris for a current verification is easier said than done, but duly note that when one bistro falls from favor, another shall arise to take its place.

If you decide to seize your eternal alternative, you might as well do up the Eternal City. And don't forget the rest of Italy—the provinces count too. Meet a model in Milan. Inject yourself into the fine arts of Florence. Get to Germany. Go see Scandinavia. Find out precisely how a little bit of chocolate goes a long way in Europe.

If you want to be truly lionized, try eastern Europe. A celebrity in Paris is a superstar in Budapest. (Fun-wise, however, it's better to be just a celebrity in Paris than a superstar in Budapest.) Plan to be bored into vegetablehood in Britain unless you hook up with Australians or New Zealanders there; they may consume you with their enthusiasm.

While Europe and other options abroad are indisputably good vacation bets, you won't be interested in expatriating yourself if you're like most. Concentrating again on these fifty states, there are some important decisions to be made concerning where one lives.

While the South is getting better with respect to race relations, the South, aside from Atlanta and Houston, may be impenetrable if you aren't attuned to southern ways or don't have close contacts there. New Orleans, for example, has certainly improved since the late sixties, but, as many refugees who have relocated at points north will tell you, the city has yet a number of important steps to make in shedding itself of its antebellum ways.

A gaggle of social observers steadfastly claims that there is a new South, and there is to an extent. But it's important also to remember that there is an old North, which has for too long been smug vis-à-vis the South. Living north of the Mason-Dixon line, as we all know, is no certain solution to the problem of racism.

Of all northern cities, Chicago reigns as the repository preeminent of ethnic polarization and truly stupefying race hatred. While it certainly has more points of interest than Omaha and some pockets of racial harmony, New York, Los Angeles, San Francisco, Seattle, and a host of other cities have a distinctly more benign overall outlook on ethnic diversity.

Natives of Chicago seem to have internalized an activity program designed to avoid ugly experiences, but the unaware black newcomer should prepare her/himself for unpleasantries, particularly if (s)he strays from the main bars and bar areas: Regardless of what the chamber of commerce may tell you, there are still bars in Chicago (gay and nongay) that don't serve black people, and there are neighborhoods where the intervention of the Pope and the President are prerequisite for your obtaining an apartment.

These minor difficulties notwithstanding, once you are located in a given place (even Chicago), there are things that can be done to heighten your pleasure and increase your trick-out ratio. (Even if you seek a more lasting relationship, remember lovers were often once tricks.)

Axiom number one in the science of black cruising is: Don't waste a lot of time in "lily white" gathering places, unless you go for nonsexual reasons. Lily white gathering places are thus for a reason. If black people are successful in a place, word will spread and black people will be there in appreciable numbers. If a place has remained quite white, it is because it has a basically white theme with no black flourishes.

Now every axiom that is worth its salt has a few good old-fashioned exceptions. Axiom number one is not good for places where there is a tiny black population. When there are only a dozen blacks in town, they can't cover every watering hole. Related to places with tiny black populations are places like California, which have a relatively small black population. You will probably find any bar in California pleasant and reasonably productive if you fit in with its basic theme—leather, western, fru-fru fluffy sweater, etc. And then there's New York.

New York (like San Francisco) has so many gay establishments that tend to specialize heavily that a place may have a minuscule black patronage because few black people are into its specialty. When you are one of two or three black people in a place, a subtle message is being conveyed. People (black and nonblack) who are looking for black people, or at least willing to consider them, tend to collect at heavily integrated addresses.

If you are the type of person who is inclined to collect brief bios on your tricks, lovers, steadies, and regulars, you will find after a few years that the white ones all tend to come from certain places. The places they grew up in will, in the great majority of cases, be exactly the places in this country and abroad that are most hospitable to black peple. Don't be surprised, for example, if most white Americans you connect with are from these regions: (1) the north Midwest (Wisconsin, Minnesota, Iowa, and Michigan), (2) Pennsylvania Dutch country, (3) California, (4) the New York City area, and (5) Texas.

New York is cosmopolitan. California more than much of the rest of the country is laid-back and less into hassles, racial or otherwise. The north Midwest, especially Minnesota, has a small black population also. I don't really know about its population or how it got on the list, but I can count and I certainly know it belongs there. Texas is something of a puzzle, too. I don't really have any information on Texas that would explain why Texans are so consistently charming and accommodating (and such masters of the magic touch). You may be skeptical about this list, but be apprised that many black people have confirmed it.

"And what about white Southerners?" you may ask. "Is the first telltale syllable of a southern accent grounds for initiating a quarantine?" Most probably not. The consensus among many black gay veterans is that Southerners who have withdrawn themselves from their homeland are, in general, smashingly reconstructed.

Those who have remained at home, however, tend to be quite distant. In a predominantly white bar in the South, be prepared to be studiously ignored—as you would be in Miami, for example, which is overwhelmingly southern in spirit. (By the way, don't venture toward the outskirts of Miami or points farther inland; they can be as dangerous as deepest Mississippi for northern blacks not attuned to southern behavior.) Miami Beach is quite another story, though. Cross the bay from Miami and be prepared to enter New York's southern annex.

So much for the regional correlates of your future success among white people, for there are indeed other matters of concern. One of the syndromes of gay life that some find worrisome is the "snow queen" syndrome. Related to the snow queen syndrome is the "chocolate queen" syndrome. Both terms have widely used equivalents, but they are inadmissibly derogatory.

Snow queens specialize in people who are like snow, not people who are flaky necessarily, but those who are white. His opposite, the chocolate queen, eschews the lighter things in life and concentrates on the distant sons of Mother Africa, and he has been known to tap the African source itself. Snow queens and chocolate queens come in all colors and will be found in appropriate settings—snow queens where white people abound, chocolate queens where black people abound.

The difficult question concerning color-queenism is not whether it really exists; it does indeed, as a quick perusal of personal ads in gay publications will show. The question is: Who are the chocolate and snow queens and what is to be done about them, if anything?

One widely held opinion is that any people who would rule other groups of people out of certain aspects of their life on the basis of something so fundamentally trivial as skin color must certainly be sick. Others have rejected this opinion, saying that a color requirement in sex partners is to be likened to other requirements—muscularity requirements, weight and height requirements, endowment requirements, and so forth. We all have such requirements, they say.

Be that all as it may, many people simply don't take their preferences or requirements seriously. Most of us have gone out cruising for one type many times and quite happily gone home with almost the opposite, oblivious to our original program for the evening.

Still a third group maintains that color requirements are not so much sick as stupid: Why rule out anybody before you've even seen him? And why rule him out indeed. One white ex-snow queen from Chicago is now living in connubial bliss with a black lover in San Francisco. Most of his friends can't quite understand it, but he himself has alluded to the answer: Getting out of Chicago with its racism-polluted atmosphere and moving to a more benign California allowed him for the first time to deal with black people as people; the rest is history.

One self-proclaimed chocolate queen in Los Angeles praises daily the wonders of his black tricks, but white tricks can often be seen leaving his home. One self-avowed snow queen living in New York has an out-of-town lover who is black. When asked to explain his black lover, he responds, "Oh Bert. Well, he's special." One would presume as much if he is a lover for whom distance has been overcome.

The real problem, perhaps, with color-queenism is not so much whether it is a requirement or a preference, but what kinds of overall attitudes toward ethnic groups go along with it. Many black people have complained that white chocolate queens aren't really oriented toward black people as real people, but as stereotypes—as fantasy-fulfillment devices. Uncomfortably, many chocolate queens are forever seeking the "primitive black stud," for example, the perfect embodiment of raw sexuality without intellect.

Other black people have complained that white chocolate queens approach black people regularly because, having inferiority complexes, they don't feel themselves good enough for white people. The insulting implication is that black people, being inferior, will accept them. Another version of this complaint is that too many white people have turned to being chocolate queens only after they have become less desirable (or feel they have) because of age, homeliness, and/or general misuse.

One black gay man who came out at eighteen claims that at

the time he wouldn't look at a man under forty. Young men simply didn't turn him on. Most of the older men he connected with just happened to be white. All of this has dramatically changed. "Now I refuse to deal with any white men over thirty. I got tired of being treated like an object, people thinking I was a hustler or a thief." He also added that many specialized in black people, apparently believing that practically any young black person was available and for a bargain basement price. In spite of all the recriminations and complaints, though, it is a fact that some people have found satisfaction in interracial coupling. To put it briefly, as a black person emerging into gay life, you will face problems, but the problems you will face are certainly not qualitatively different from those you have faced and dealt with all your life. You are to a significant degree mobile; you can place yourself in those locales and among those people that are most positively disposed toward you as a person. You have an organized and active black gay community at your disposal. Its members enthusiastically await your first knock on their door and will willingly lay before you countless programs for action in dealing with issues going beyond those discussed. What is more, they will itemize the rewarding possibilities that you will explore as time goes on.

Importantly, you might bear in mind that many people believe that a shift in the foundation of the world will inevitably come, one which will witness a more just and harmonious relationship between peoples. "Now this shift in the foundation of the world," as James Baldwin has put it, "will not be instituted in an hour, but neither will it take 1,000 years."

# The Male Prostitute

## MARTIN HOFFMAN

Prostitution, like pornography, is a service provided primarily for males. The "gigolo," although he may be a sexual partner for his female client, seems to be employed as much and probably more for companionship and the personal relationship of an "escort" than for the strictly sexual services we associate with prostitution. Hence, the male prostitute serves a male clientele. Does that make one or both of them homosexual? The answer to this question is essential to understanding the motives and behavior of the "hustler."

In this article, I shall occasionally use such slang terms as "hustler" for prostitute, "score" for client or customer, "gay" for homosexual, and "straight" for heterosexual—because that is the jargon of the group I am discussing. Probably one of the greatest dangers that exists in studying deviant, "exotic" subcultures is that we tend to treat them as foreign, as wholly alien to our own existence, as *merely* objects of study. In so doing we often lose not only that larger sense of compassion we ought to feel for our fellow human creatures, but we also so distance ourselves from the objects of such inquiry that we are prone to make glaring mistakes in interpretation of the phenomena and gross overgeneralizations, which might have been avoided had we not tried to hold the subject matter as far away from the viewing eye as possible and thereby lost our ability to apply "common sense" to the problems we are asked to illuminate.

One of the most beautiful and compelling descriptions of the life of the male prostitute is John Rechy's novel *City of Night.* In brief, Rechy's novel, which I most strongly recommend to anyone who wants to understand the hustling scene, describes a young man's entry into that life and his myriad adventures in it.

*Sexual Behavior* 2 (August 1972): 16–21. Reprinted by permission of the author.

Rechy's hero thinks of himself as a hustler, though not as a homosexual. It is clear, however, that for him, as for many other hustlers, hustling is a way of "coming out," i.e., of becoming a self-defined homosexual. (This is confirmed in Rechy's second novel, *Numbers,* when the hero reappears after several years in "retirement" and proceeds to seek homosexual contacts without any exchange of money, though even at this point his self-definition is still not clear.)

A totally different picture emerges in a 1961 study, probably the best scientific study yet done on hustling, by the sociologist Albert J. Reiss, Jr. Since we know next to nothing about the incidence of the various forms of hustling, it is not possible to say that Reiss's subjects are an atypical group of hustlers, but I tend to think Rechy's profile represents a more common type than Reiss's. At any rate, Professor Reiss's subjects were delinquent boys, aged twelve to seventeen, who described a pattern of relationships with older men who fellated them in a form of male prostitution. A number of crucial points emerge from Reiss's paper. Not only did the boys not define themselves as homosexual, although they were being fellated by their male clients, they did not even define themselves as hustlers! They viewed their activity solely as another form of delinquent behavior, as an alternative way of making illegal money. Reiss found that this particular kind of relationship was very carefully structured by the boys' peers, structured in such a way that the odious self-definitions which would otherwise have been a likely outcome of their (technically) homosexual activity could be defined in a much less threatening way. This kind of activity was almost exclusively limited to lower-class boys who were headed for a career of delinquency.

How did the boys meet their clients? On street corners, in parks, in men's rooms in public buildings, and in certain movie houses. The score would "cruise" the boy (by means of nonverbal cues, such as staring at him, repeatedly passing by the area where he was located) and the boy would respond by nodding his head or following the prospective score or responding to a verbal overture such as "You got the time?" Often the contact was made while the boy was hitchhiking; the conversation was gradually shifted to sexual topics by the older man. There is, however, generally little conversation. In most cases boys report "almost nothing" was said. There is typically little interaction other than the tacit agreement to have sex, the fellation of the boy by the older male, and the payment of money to the boy. This degree of anonymity and of sex in the absence of any other kind of personal involvement is not unusual in the gay world.

Boys learn about this form of earning money from their peers, usually before any approach is ever made by a score. Thus, the peer group sanctions the interaction, advises the boy on techniques of making contact with the score, sets very clear limits as to what can and what cannot occur within the relationship, and instructs the boy as to how he is to handle any infraction of the rules of the transaction by the client. Reiss lists four rules of behavior which are established by the boy's peer group and govern the relationship.

## FOUR RULES OF THE GAME

First, the boy's goal must be money; sexual gratification cannot be actively sought as a goal. This is a very delicate line for the boy to tread, for he is not precluded from feeling sexual pleasure as a result of being fellated by the score. In fact, the score's own goal is almost always to bring him to orgasm. What is forbidden is that the boy seek the relationship for the *purpose* of achieving that pleasure, which can only legitimately be thought of by him as a necessary by-product of a primarily economic relationship. If he admits to himself and/or to his peers that he has sex for the sake of sex, he is then defined as homosexual, and is then radically devalued.

The second proscription is that the sexual transaction must be limited to fellation, performed by the score on the boy. Generally, no other sexual acts are tolerated. The boy must be wholly "masculine" in the relationship, according to the prevailing norms of masculinity in the delinquent subculture. If he deviates from this norm, he is defined as homosexual. (Probably the prohibition against even performing anal intercourse upon the score—normally a "masculine" role in a homosexual relationship—results from the fact that it involves too much body contact; it thus violates the third rule.)

The third rule is that both boy and score must remain affectively neutral during the sexual (and nonsexual part of the) encounter. The first rule is almost a corollary of this one, which prohibits anything except a fee-for-service attitude from being openly displayed. When asked how he felt about the act, the boy's typical responses will be, "OK," or "It's all right." The score is expected to conform to this rule by treating the boy not as a lover, but as an entrepreneur, someone who is merely providing a service.

The fourth rule is that violence must not be used as long as the score treats the boy in the accepted fashion. If he does violate the boy's sense of what is proper, i.e., if he threatens the boy's masculinity or nonhomosexuality, violence may be employed by the boy and/or the gang.

The key to the whole set of guidelines is, clearly, that it permits the boy and his peers to engage in and derive a certain amount of sexual gratification from what are, behaviorally, homosexual acts *without thinking of themselves as being homosexual,* and therefore unmasculine (for in lower-class culture homosexuality and masculinity are antithetical). The theoretical importance of the Reiss study is that it shows how sociological determinants, in this case the structuring of the relationship by the peer group norms, can serve to completely redefine "normal" expectations in an area even as highly charged with cultural and emotional taboos as male homosexual behavior.

It might be recalled that the Reiss boys did not even define themselves as hustlers. Apparently being a hustler is too close to being a homosexual for the psychological comfort of the boys. For a somewhat older age group, around seventeen to twenty-six (with myriad exceptions at both ends of the age scale), there is a different self-conception possible, i.e., the young man who considers himself a hustler although not homosexual. He is typified by the hero of the Rechy novel *City of Night* and has been the subject of several small sociological field studies. Typically, he looks and acts "masculine"; he wears Levis, a leather jacket, boots. The scores want to think he is not homosexual, for many of them wish to believe their sexual partner is straight.

## TYPES

There has been much more attention paid to hustlers than to scores. This is probably because we think it is easy to understand why an unattractive middle-aged homosexual will pay for a sexual partner who is young and handsome, but we can't think why a heterosexual boy will earn his living by (to us) such sordid means. That the psychology of the score is not quite so simple as we often assume can be seen when we realize that hustlers are sometimes picked up by attractive young men in their late teens, twenties, and early thirties. Surely this merits further inquiry.

As for the hustler himself, the safest and most correct thing to say would be that (1) there does exist a class of young men who are, in fact, not homosexual although they do hustle, and (2) there are plenty of hustlers who are able to fool themselves for varying periods of time into the belief that they are not homosexual by having sex which is facilitated psychologically by an exchange of money. They later do come to define themselves as homosexual and come to see their hustling period as a time of self-deception.

Part of the problem in distinguishing these two groups comes from the fact that we feel we have to use as the main criterion the hustler's sexual self-definition some $x$ years later. If he is then married and not involved in any homosexual sex we say that he was right in calling himself straight even while he hustled. If he is gay, however, and is having sex for free (or even paying for it himself), we agree that he was fooling himself. But are not other alternative explanations plausible? Is it not possible that the first category consists of many young men who passed through a period of unconscious attraction to other males without being able to define themselves as homosexual; could not the lack of such self-definition as gay as well as the later suppression of the (hypothetical) homosexual tendencies be due to the very strong antihomosexual pressures in our society? On the other hand, is it not possible that the hustlers who became gay did so as a *result* of their hustling? Isn't it possible that they would not have become homosexual if economic needs did not entice them into a means of earning a living which conditioned them to respond to sexual stimulation by other males?

I don't think these questions can now receive satisfactory answers. We are caught up in what is one present-day replica of the old nature-nurture controversy in philosophy, which divides students of homosexuality into two schools: those who believe that a homosexual orientation is fixed, either at birth (by genetic factors) or in childhood (by familial interaction); and those who believe that such an orientation is subject to the changing factors that play upon a person's consciousness in adolescence and adult life. According to this second school of thought, shifts toward and away from homosexuality may occur at almost any time of life, adolescence being a particularly vulnerable era.

The sad fact is that sufficient information which would enable us to engage in anything but conjecture on this vexing but crucial question does not presently exist. Some observers' conjecture even questions the whole concept of homosexuality. They would say there is not such a thing as homosexuality, and there are no homosexuals and heterosexuals; they would claim that there is only homosexual and heterosexual *behavior*. With this purist behavioral point of view I completely disagree; as I have indicated elsewhere (1968), even Kinsey could not hold to it.

There is at present no solid evidence that genetic factors play a role in determining sexual object-choice. There are many good (psychoanalytic) data that implicate early familial interactions in leading to a homosexual object-choice. There are isolated but very suggestive data that at crucial points in the postpubertal years certain factors may arise which cause either temporary or permanent shifts in a person's sexual object-choice. And there is also very good evidence that certain individuals have from early life a capacity to become aroused by either sex, and may thus properly be called bisexual. Obviously, we need to have more research attention directed to these issues; when data bearing on them can be uncovered we may be able to say much more about the psychology of the "straight" hustler than we now know.

We also need more information on the very effeminate male prostitutes who hustle in drag, pretending to their scores that they are girls and trying to fool the partner throughout the sexual act, sometimes by refusing to do anything other than fellate the score while remaining clothed. This practice may well seem plausible to the score because it is typical of female streetwalkers (as opposed to call girls) and is often the only thing they are willing to do for a cheap trick (e.g., $20), since they feel it does not pay to get undressed and engage in coitus for such a low fee.

There are, of course, many hustlers who admit to being gay. Some of them are not effeminate and cannot be distinguished in outward appearance and manner from the so-called straight hustler described above. The distinction comes in self-definition, in the individual's overall life-style, and it may also come in what he is willing to do in bed with his score. Some hustlers will draw a line at fellating the score. Straight hustlers may do this to preserve their own sense of masculinity. Gay hustlers may do it in order to keep a facade of being straight. In fact, they may engage in sexual acts with partners of their own choosing that they would not do with scores, partly due to considerations of sheer personal taste, but partly also because they either know or think they know that their scores would prefer to believe that they are straight.

On the other hand, some straight hustlers (and many gay ones) will do anything in bed, provided especially that the price is right. The straight hustler can justify this by economic considerations: Scores are easier to get and the price might be higher if he is willing to take a receptor role in the sexual act. He will assert that he's not gay but that he's not "hung up" on being "masculine" in bed. He may say he doesn't derive any particular pleasure from such activities but that he can tolerate it for the extra money and clients that it brings him.

## CASE HISTORY

It might be worthwhile to describe one such "versatile, straight" hustler in some detail. We shall call him Craig. Craig is now twenty-five years old and has recently entered psychotherapy, mainly for problems relating to drug abuse. He has always been basically heterosexually inclined. He had his first heterosexual experience in his late teens, and has had heterosexual intercourse on many occasions since then with a number of girl friends. He has had problems relating to girls on an interpersonal basis, although he is by no means a recluse. One of the most interesting facts about Craig is that he went to college and received a BA in the humanities; this is unusual for a hustler. While in college he belonged to a fraternity. He was not especially active in sports although he had played football in high school. There has never been anything about him that would be considered homosexual—except some of his sexual behavior.

During his last year in college, when he was twenty-one, he let himself be seduced first by a gay classmate and then by a homosexual professor. He then had another brief sexual affair with one of the professor's acquaintances. He states that these affairs were never particularly *sexually* gratifying to him, but that the thought of his "illicit" behavior (which would, he feels, have "blown the minds" of his straight friends and fraternity brothers) was in itself exciting. Furthermore, he found the personal and intellectual relations with the older men more socially rewarding and less problematic than his personal relations with girls. He found that by offering his sexuality to these men he could get both intellectual and material benefits. At this time, therefore, we might say that he was starting to hustle, although in a subtle way.

When Craig graduated from college he really didn't know what to do with himself. "After all, what can one do with a BA in the humanities?" He then started professional hustling on San Francisco's Market Street. He would get onto the street in early evening and stay until he had scored several times. He usually got $20 per trick, sometimes more. He would then go home. He did not associate with the other hustlers or with the "queens," i.e., he was not a member of hustling society as Rechy describes it. At this time he was living with a girl to whom he became quite attached. They had what he considers a sexually gratifying relationship and were quite fond of each other, although the relationship was stormy. She fell in love with him; he did not fall in love with her, though for the first time he felt he could relate to a woman. She knew about his hustling and tolerated it, though she did not wholly "approve."

This pattern of activity continued for about a year. Craig would do almost anything in bed with a score, although he did not care to fellate his partner and would rarely do it. He said that he was not sexually attracted to men, that he was sexually attracted to girls, that he would never have sex with men for the sake of the sex, but that he was not particularly upset about doing various things in bed with other males. His noneconomic interest in men tended to vanish as he developed his relationship with his girl friend and he discovered that very few of his scores were as socially interesting as his first few (prehustling) male sexual partners.

I am inclined to believe Craig's assertion of "basic heterosexuality." I think there are heterosexual men who can, for reasons not primarily sexual, have homosexual relations, just as there are many homosexuals who can, for nonsexual reasons, have heterosexual relations. Craig discontinued hustling when he became heavily involved in the drug scene in San Francisco's Haight-Ashbury district. There, he supported himself by small-time dealing, an occupation which, as Carey (1968) shows, is no more lucrative than hustling. Eventually Craig entered psychotherapy because he felt unable to reenter conventional society and work at an ordinary job (or go back to school for graduate work). This problem of social reentry was probably caused more by his heavy LSD ingestion than by any other factor. It should be noted that after Craig stopped hustling, he had no more homosexual relations, save with one of his old scores, who continued weekly visits at $20 per visit.

Craig's case is not typical, but there is really no one stereotype that describes the hustler. The versatility and ambivalence he reveals in both the homosexual and heterosexual aspects of his life and the blending of prostitution and affection illustrate the many facets and variations to this type of behavior and the futility of attempting a clear-cut description of the sort of man that adopts it.

## REFERENCES

CAREY, JAMES T. *The College Drug Scene*. Englewood Cliffs, N.J.: Prentice-Hall, 1968.

HOFFMAN, MARTIN. *The Gay World: Male Homosexuality and the Social Creation of Evil*. New York: Basic Books, 1968.

RECHY, JOHN. *City of Night*. New York: Grove Press, 1963.

———. *Numbers*. New York: Grove Press, 1967.

REISS, ALBERT J., JR. "The Social Integration of Peers and Queers." *Social Problems* 9 (1961): 102.

## Movement

# A Social History of Gay Politics

BARRY D. ADAM

Men have loved men in almost every age and society for which records have been kept. Homosexuality has been variously suppressed, tolerated, accepted, or encouraged at different times and places. Ford and Beach (1965) point out that the majority of societies recorded in the Yale Human Relations Area Files provide for some sort of acceptable homosexual expression. The ancient Greek system, which has parallels in the Sudan, Sumatra, and New Guinea, encouraged the socialization of young men within an erotic relationship with an older mentor. The idea of the "heroic friendship" (lauded, for example, in the Greek tradition of Harmodius and Aristogeiton and Achilles and Patroclus) survived through the Middle Ages and echoed in the samurai tradition of Japan (Sutherland and Anderson, 1963; Carpenter, 1902; Ihara, 1972). Yet it is only in the modern age that a "gay" (Adam, 1978:12–13) subculture and, thus, a gay movement have emerged.

The development of a homosexual people and its movement originates in the transition from feudalism to capitalism, which fundamentally reorganized the opportunities for homosexual relationships. The medieval system provided for companionship and sexual need through socially arranged marriages. Sanctioned by church and state, this arrangement only imperfectly accommodated *preferred* relationships; others flourished in supplementary, unofficial institutions such as prostitution, mistresses, and homosexual relations.

With the advent of capitalism came industrialization and urbanization, drawing large numbers of people out of traditional agrarian kinship systems into expanding cities. Citification loosened the constraints of the rural family and nurtured the "romantic" ideal, disrupting arranged marriages and providing new opportunities for choice in sexual, friendship, and mate relations. These social changes account for the emergence of a gay people. As early as the eighteenth century, English diarists reported the existence of gay bars in major cities, catering to a clientele of diverse class backgrounds (Norton, 1975). By the nineteenth century, medical and criminal records attest that the creation of public places, such as parks and railway stations, opened new possibilities for men with homosexual interest to congregate (Steakley, 1975:15).

The capitalist transformation also brought liberal individualism, the ideology of the ascendant bourgeoisie. Moral distinctions reflecting medieval hierachy (e.g., lord, serf) paled before the new principle for survival: All were "equal" in possessing no other means for support than their own labor power on the competitive labor market. "Tolerance" of religious, political, and sexual differences reflected the declining importance of such distinctions in the distribution of social benefits where all shared "civil equality" in the "public" sphere. Jews, the pariah people of the medieval period, became national "citizens" in the early capitalist era, their religion having been reconceptualized as a "private" confession instead of a totalizing identity. The French Revolution introduced a legal code that removed criminal penalties from homosexuality in line with the strengthening belief that the state had no interest in the "private" realms of conscience and sexuality. The Napoleonic conquests at the beginning of the nineteenth century incorporated the ethics of the liberal democratic state into the legal systems of most of western Europe. Out of this flux of ideological and class movement arose the renaissance of gay consciousness in Europe.

## THE EARLY HOMOSEXUAL EMANCIPATION MOVEMENT

A growing sense of peoplehood among homosexuals became increasingly evident in the national cultures of the last decades of the nineteenth century and in the early twentieth century. In England, John Addington Symonds stated the case for gay love in *A Problem of Modern Ethics* in 1891. A literary tradition culminating in Algernon Swinburne and Oscar Wilde covertly celebrated intermale relationships, hearkening back to ancient Greece for inspiration and metaphor (Reade, 1970). Arthur Rimbaud and Paul Verlaine inaugurated a rich French tradition uninterrupted by the purges that plagued other nations. The surrealism of Alfred Jarry and Jean Cocteau paralleled Marcel Proust's *Sodomme et Gomorrhe* and André Gide's 1911 defense of homosexual love, *Corydon,* which Gide termed his "most important" work upon his receipt of the Nobel Prize for literature. The French milieu supported the low-profile Arcadie group and new lesbian literary circles which included the American expatriate Gertrude Stein.

But the earliest open and political voice for gay people was Karl Ulrichs, who published a series of books from 1864 to 1879 and lectured publicly to dispel prejudices about homosexuals and to demand legal protection (Kennedy, 1978). Ulrichs' theory that gay people constitute a "third sex" influenced Magnus Hirschfeld. A movement for gay emancipation led by Hirschfeld formed in Germany in 1897, calling itself the Scientific-Humanitarian Committee. The committee launched a petition campaign for the decriminalization of homosexuality that gathered the signatures of many of the most prominent members of the German intelligentsia (such as Martin Buber, Karl Jaspers, Hermann Hesse, and Thomas Mann) and won the support of the Social Democratic Party (Steakley, 1975). The committee's research influenced Sigmund Freud, who, on several occasions, declared his support for the civil rights of gay people (Spiers and Lynch, 1977). Yet despite the Social Democrats' earlier support for the gay playwright and socialist thinker Jean Baptiste Schweitzer, homosexuality proved a convenient charge when a Social Democratic newspaper sought to discredit the German monarchy. From 1906 to 1909, such charges led to purges in the aristocracy, civil service, and military.

The Russian Revolution swept antihomosexual laws from the Soviet Union and brought Communist support to the German movement. During the Weimar Republic, gay organization extended into cultural activity, friendship groups, and a flourishing press. The Scientific-Humanitarian Committee founded the

Institute for Sexual Science in 1919, which sponsored the World League for Sexual Reform, an organization with some 130,000 members (Steakley, 1975). *Die Eigene,* a rival organization, propagated a Greek-linked, "masculine" ideal of gay male community, an ideal reflected in the literary circle surrounding Stefan George.

In the United States, the early promise of American liberalism captivated gay writers who hoped for emancipation of homoeroticism from the fetters of repressive law and morality. Walt Whitman's vision of America celebrated "democracy" and "comradeship" in the same breath. Edward Carpenter, an English admirer of Whitman, published a series of works defending the rights of women, gay people, and workers through the perspective of English socialism.

As in Europe, official records attest to the growth of a gay subculture in the United States in the late nineteenth century. By the 1890s, major cities contained networks of bars, baths, and dance halls, a subcultural milieu with special vocabularies and gathering places subject to police harassment (Bullough, 1976:607–12; Katz, 1976:39–52). A brief attempt at formal organization, inspired by the work of Magnus Hirschfeld and the Scientific-Humanitarian Committee, appeared in 1924 as the Chicago Society for Human Rights (Katz, 1976:385f). The society published two issues of a journal called *Friendship and Freedom.* It was suppressed by the police. The civil service dismissed its founder, Henry Gerber. Neither Whitman's vision of American camaraderie nor Gide's (1950) prediction that antigay persecution would be unknown in fifty years came to pass.

The rise of capitalism, then, provided some of the avenues for coalescence of homosexual men and the precondition for the evolution and awareness of community. Urbanization and the liberal ideology of equality of all citizens of the nation-state improved the possibilities for gay people to overcome their isolation from each other and carve a social space for themselves within the larger society. Although capitalism provided social conditions for the emergence of a gay people, at the same time it created a hostile environment for them. In Europe, the emergence of gay people, as well as other minorities such as Jews, from the confines of the medieval order tied their fates to the larger movement of the rising bourgeoisie. Precapitalist social classes such as the aristocracy, the clergy, the military, artisans, and traditional landholders formed the foundation for anti-Semitic and antigay opposition.

Other trends strengthening with the growth of capitalism worked against gay organization. The ethical structure of capitalist organization proved inimical to gay relationships. Ideological or ethical systems compatible with the capitalist order demanded a range of behavior necessary for survival within the new society. Men, even more than women, were forced to cope with an economic system that demanded aggressiveness, competitiveness, impersonality, and "toughness" in order to succeed. The interpersonal solidarity opened by homoeroticism countered this male norm (Lehne, 1976). The only form of sexual expression sanctioned by church and state linked sexuality with productiveness or *re*productiveness, condemning generalized sensuality in favor of monogamous heterosexuality (Marcuse, 1955; Reich, 1972; Gramsci, 1971). Nonreproductive sexuality, like drug use, promises pleasure freed from production, a choice potentially subversive to the ethics of the industrial machine that withholds reward (or gratification) until work is performed. Though none of these demands are unique to the capitalist organization of society, the new economic order perpetuated and reinforced those demands.

Stalinism rolled back the sexual liberalism of the Russian Revolution, beginning a repressive era that continues today. Communist parties in Europe abandoned the gay movement along with Wilhelm Reich's Sexpol movement, turning toward a new puritanism.

The accession of the Nazi Party to power led to the immediate suppression of organized gay life and the destruction of the Institute for Sexual Science, with a public burning of its books. The systematic genocide of gay people began with the "night of the long knives," when Hitler eliminated Ernst Roehm and several thousand others, charging homosexuality. More than two hundred thousand died in concentration camps under a diet-and-work regimen designed for extermination (Steakley, 1975).

The first era of gay society in Europe perished in the holocaust through the coalition of homophobic, antimodernist forces in the Nazi terror.

## THE HOMOPHILE MOVEMENT

In the early postwar period, formal gay organizations arose in both Europe and the United States. The Kinsey Report, which appeared in 1948, revealed an unsuspectedly large homosexual constituency in American society and broke the conspiracy of silence that suppressed its recognition. Amsterdam, New York, and Los Angeles were sites of movement activity in the late 1940s and early 1950s. The political orientation of the revived gay movement in the United States can be understood only in the context of the perils confronting gay people at the time. This was the McCarthy era, when the United States Senate was leading a national witchhunt against Communists and homosexuals. Gay people were subject to similar purges by local and corporate officialdom (Gerassi, 1968). In 1953, the Los Angeles Mattachine Society purged Henry Hay, a former Communist Party member, who had founded the society two years earlier (Katz, 1976:406–20). Mattachine adopted the politics of respectability, preferring fearful conservatism to imminent suppression. The self-appellation "Mattachine" pointed toward the homophile strategy for survival, having been derived from "the Italian jester, acrobat, mimic who pleased crowds but kept his truer feelings out of sight" (Teal, 1971:44). The heterosexist hegemony demanded that gay people "play the game" (Austen, 1977; Northon, 1974), be they unknown or important literary figures such as Gore Vidal, Tennessee Williams, James Baldwin, and Paul Goodman. To destroy the stereotype of the homosexual as corrupted or corrupter, the homophile movement strove to project the image of the upright, respectable citizen. Gay people, so the argument ran, are the same as heterosexuals but for the single distinction of sexual preference and therefore merit social equality. The homophile movement relied, primarily, upon an assimilationist approach: gay identity, culture, and values were to be traded (or at least concealed) for the *promise* of improved life chances (Adam, 1978; Altman, 1971:103). "Ignorance" was identified as the enemy; "education" was the keystone of early movement programs.

The homophile movement laid valuable groundwork of self-support institutions for the gay community: communications media such as journals and libraries, legal defense and medical services, counseling, and most important, supportive environments.

## GAY LIBERATION

National organizations appeared in addition to the homophile groups that had grown up in major cities. The mid-1960s witnessed the North American Conference of Homophile Organizations (NACHO), which brought some 150 groups together; the establishment of a national circulation newspaper, *The Advocate;* and the beginnings of the Metropolitan Community Church, which rapidly acquired an international membership.

The "New Left" of the 1960s aggregated the rising discontent of black people, women, and a generation of young men sent by the United States government to Vietnam. The new militance provided new precedents for a reevaluation of the oppression of gay people. The "Stonewall Rebellion," June 28, 1969, marked the radical break with the homophile tradition. A police raid upon a Greenwich Village gay bar met open resistance. A two-day street battle ensued. The Stonewall incident sparked gay liberation in New York and, within three years, in almost every major city and campus in the United States, Canada, and Western Europe.

Gay liberalism expressed the failure of liberalism to free gay people. By rejecting the social order that had brought about a community confined to a geographical and psychological ghetto (Levine, 1977), liberationists rejected the homophile view that measured gay people by the standards of health and respectability purveyed by heterosexist society. Gay liberation struggled to free gay people from the reality imposed by discriminatory employers and landlords and homophobic journalists, educators, and psychiatrists. Asserting the authenticity of gay life, the new movement initiated a critique of sexual repression and sex role, the patriarchal family and traditional morality. Like the transition from black integrationism to black militance, gay liberation rejected the goal of assimilation into the "burning house" of American society, affirming instead the right to self-determination. Wittman's (1970) "Gay Manifesto" demanded "sexual self-determination, the abolition of sex-role stereotypes and the human right to the use of one's own body without interference from legal and social institutions of the state."

People came together in gay liberation to share experiences, fears, and pain. They talked of coping with parents and employers, lovers and relationships, expectations and frustrations. Their coming together articulated the oppression and forged the solidarity necessary to overcome it both within the self and in the larger society. These "consciousness raising" groups attacked the limitations of the gay ghetto which allowed people to meet only in the unfriendly atmosphere of profit-making enterprises under police scrutiny.

The 1970 NACHO convention dissolved in a confrontation between gay liberationists and homophiles, where gay liberation succeeded in passing a new plan that demanded (1) coalition of the gay movement with the movements of other oppressed peoples such as blacks, women, Chicanos, and Indians; (2) struggle against social control institutions such as government, church, business, and medicine; (3) rejection of heterosexist standards of morality and sexual repression; (4) right of self-definition; (5) abolition of age-of-consent laws; and (6) opposition to the United States presence in Vietnam (Humphreys, 1972:103, Teal 1971:309). The liberated credo proclaimed: "Don't adjust your mind: reality has a flaw in it." (Rankin, 1970:4; cf. Teal, 1971:311).

The vocal but often chaotic rage of early gay liberation fronts expressed the need; a second generation of "activist" organizations sought to realize concrete reforms through sometimes innovative strategies. The New York Gay Activists Alliance, for example, "zapped" officials with public confrontations. The Activists demonstrated their opposition to employment discrimination outside the offices of major corporations and lobbied politicians. They attacked stereotypical portrayals of homosexuality in the mass media. Their highly successful clubhouse created a popular nonexploitative space for dances and workshops until it was destroyed by arsonists.

Public manifestations of gay energy rapidly disabused onlookers of the stereotype of homosexual cowardice. The movement urged gay people to "come out of the closets, into the streets" with proud affirmation of gay love. It proclaimed: "An army of lovers cannot lose!" A liberationist press flourished in several cities with New York's *Come Out!,* Boston's *Rag Rag,* San Francisco's *Gay Sunshine,* Detroit's *Gay Liberator,* and Toronto's *Body Politic.* Its pages contained news of attacks upon gay people and the movement's responses, personal confessions of self-discovery, meditations on transvestism and sadomasochism (Hanson, 1972:14; Young, 1973), examinations of masculinity and the ideologies of sport and the military (Benton, 1970; Mitzel, 1973), rediscovery of gay history and interviews with new and well-known writers, the practices of psychiatry and prisons, racism and ageism in the gay community.

Gay nationalism appeared briefly in a plan to colonize a small California county to elect the local government (Teal, 1971:312f). Though the move to Alpine County never materialized, the newfound power of gay people in electoral politics has promised to realize the Alpine vision in a far more significant way, especially in San Francisco, where the gay population has been estimated at one-third of the electorate.

Nationalism has played a much greater role in lesbian organization. The capitalist transition had created the social conditions for gay male organization for more than a century. The confinement of women to the family with slower integration into the market economy impeded comparable women's organization. Much of the lesbian struggle was necessarily concerned with the improvement of the status of all women and the conception of a still embryonic lesbian culture. Labeled the "lavender menace" in the National Organization for Women, lesbians after a series of purges and confrontations succeeded in winning recognition from other feminists. Gay liberation tended to address itself to issues relevant to gay men. Only through the community-building process of lesbian "separatism" or nationalism (Johnston, 1973) have lesbians and gay men begun to work together as coequals against the onslaught of the neoright.

The new militance bore fruit. Annual invasions of conventions of the American Psychiatric Association eventually produced a policy removing gay people from the official Index of "sicknesses" (Alinder, 1972; Teal, 1971:293f; Schaffer, 1971). Cities in the United States and Canada (more than forty by 1978) added "sexual orientation" to the list of categories protected by human rights legislation. Liberal Protestant churches issued supportive statements for gay members. Police harassment was reduced in some cities. Small towns entirely lacking gay places organized clubhouses operated by and for gay people. Politicians began to campaign for gay votes. The mass media and publishing industry occasionally allowed gay people to represent themselves before the public. The new climate emboldened people to "come out" publicly in many professions (Miller, 1971; Brown, 1976). Writers whose references to homosexuality were at best veiled in the 1950s published testimonies of their own lives and of the distortions suffered the art of writing by persecution (Isherwood, 1976; Vidal, 1976; Goodman, 1969; Williams, 1976).

## REORGANIZATION AND REACTION

The fire of the early gay liberation movement faded away with its counterparts in the New Left such as the student and black power movements. Economic crisis in the 1970s forced reemphasis upon basic questions of survival. Retrenchment allowed a revival of eclipsed homophile groups and a third generation of gay organizations to proliferate within existing social institutions. The foundation of a "gay church" by Troy Perry (Perry and Lucas, 1972) in 1968 has been followed by gay caucuses emerging first in liberal Protestant denominations (such as the Unitarian-Universalists and Quakers) and then among Roman Catholics, reform Jews, and ultimately conservative Protestants (such as Mormons and Seventh-Day Adventists). Gay caucuses have come about in labor unions and professional associations, political parties, and voluntary associations (such as Alcoholics Anonymous). Many of these associations have taken steps to protect gay members at the place of work. The New Democratic Party in Canada and some local chapters of the Democratic Party in the United States have made gay rights party policy. Lobbyists draw gay issues to the attention of legislators. Gay scholars meet regularly to restore suppressed history and literature and to contribute to culture building (Gay Academic Union, 1974; Lehman, 1975; Crew, 1978). Gay community service groups have tended to develop autonomously with increased professionalization of medical, legal, and counseling services. The Canadian National Gay Rights Coalition coordinates national policy among gay groups in Canada; the National Gay Task Force acts as a self-appointed spokesperson for gay people in the United States.

The distinctions between homophile and activist approaches blurred in the civil rights "specialization" of many movement groups. The arena of struggle appears often to have shifted to electoral politics and legal reform, with campaigns for judicial protection in employment and housing; reform of sodomy, immigration, "indecent" conduct, and age-of-consent laws; gay content in sex education; and the right of child custody for gay parents.

Yet clearly, many of the gains of the gay movement have been made within the confines of the right to privacy established with the French Revolution. Liberal societies have typically legalized sexual relations between adults in private (the old laws were unenforceable in any case) but have strictly circumscribed the gay presence. In Canada, laws governing "common bawdy houses," "obscenity," and "gross indecency" have been used to make inroads into the already narrow gay ghetto by harassing the gay press and bath and bar patrons. A provincial racing commission member became a cause célèbre when dismissed by the Ontario government solely because of his homosexuality. Two men were convicted of *kissing* on a Toronto street in 1976. The United States Supreme Court upheld in 1976 the right of states to prosecute private sexual practices. A majority of states continue to outlaw homosexuality. Saghir and Robins

(1973:165–67) note that gay people in the United States are not only prosecuted through antigay sex statutes but also receive longer sentences for non-sex-related convictions. Periodic moral crusades against "child molestation" have provided cover for police and press persecution of gay people (Gerassi, 1968; Daymon, 1975; Marko, 1977). A neoright coalition opposed to "affirmative action," abortion, and the rights of women accomplished the first repeal of a municipal ordinance forbidding discrimination by sexual orientation in 1977 in Dade County, Florida. The return of the politics of respectability failed to turn back the campaign led by the $100,000-a-year singer Anita Bryant. Several more repeals ensued in the following year. The congregations of Metropolitan Community churches have been plagued by arsonists. In Britain, the leader of the Liberal Party, Jeremy Thorpe, and Labour Member of Parliament Maureen Colquhoun were forced to resign because of homosexuality. A superior court fined the British newspaper *Gay News* under a 1693 statute outlawing "blasphemy" that had not been invoked for fifty years.

The hard-won gains of gay liberation ironically encouraged two trends that hastened its demise. The first was an improved environment for "gay capitalism." The marketing of Hollywood, soft-porn images, and conspicuous consumption figure prominently in *The Advocate* and in high-gloss fashionable magazines such as *In Touch, Mandate,* and *Blueboy.* The critique of machismo and sexual objectification advanced by gay liberation has become transmogrified into the idealized masculine sex images of the cosmetic press. The second trend has been the emboldening of the upper middle class and cooptation of the movement by the resurrected homophile approach. An air force man, Leonard Matlovich, and a football player, David Kopay (Kopay and Young, 1976), who dared to assert their homosexuality from within two bastions of masculinism (and were expelled therefrom) became the heroes of the "born again" politics of respectability. Demands that gay people "clean up their acts" (i.e., conform to the dictates of middle-class morality and sex roles) form the leitmotiv of *Advocate* editorials. White, middle-class males appear increasingly willing to embrace the assimilationist formula, adopting the symbols of conformity in return for (often vicarious) participation in the privileges of their class and sex. It is a coping strategy that not only forsakes the other components of the gay community (women, blacks, youth, transvestites, the working class and unemployed) but negates the intrinsic potential of homosexual relationships, namely, rehumanization of intermale relationships already beleaguered by the competitiveness and isolation demanded by the male sex role in a capitalist economy.

The Dade County defeat sparked spontaneous mass demonstrations numbering in the hundreds of thousands in San Francisco and New York. Annual marches and celebrations commemorate the Stonewall Rebellion. The choice between assimilation and the aspirations for a more democratic and humanized society remains.

## REFERENCES

ADAM, BARRY D. *The Survival of Domination: Inferiorization and Everyday Life*. New York: Elsevier, 1978.

ALINDER, GARY. "Gay Liberation Meets the Shrinks." In Karla Jay and Allen Young, eds., *Out of the Closets: Voices of Gay Liberation*. New York: Douglas, 1972.

ALTMAN, DENNIS. *Homosexual: Oppression and Liberation*. New York: Avon Books, 1971.

AUSTEN, ROGER. *Playing the Game: The Homosexual Novel in America*. Indianapolis: Bobbs-Merrill, 1977.

BENTON, NICK. "Jock Lib, Gay Lib, Any Difference?" *Gay Sunshine* 1 (December 1970).

BROWN, HOWARD. *Familiar Faces, Hidden Lives: The Story of Homosexual Men in America Today*. New York: Harcourt, Brace, Jovanovich, 1976.

BULLOUGH, VERN. *Sexual Variance in Society and History*. New York: Wiley, 1976.

CARPENTER, EDWARD. *Ioläus: An Anthology of Male Friendship*. Boston: Goodspeed, 1902.

CREW, LOUIE, ed. *The Gay Academic.* Palm Springs, Calif.: ETC Publications, 1978.

DAYMON, RON. "Ottawa: Police and Press Lies End in Death." *Body Politic* 18 (May–June 1975):1.

FORD, CLELLAN, and FRANK BEACH. *Patterns of Sexual Behaviour.* London: Eyre & Spottiswoode, 1965.

GAY ACADEMIC UNION. *The Universities and the Gay Experience.* Proceedings of the Conference Sponsored by Women and Men of the Gay Academic Union, November 23 and 24, 1973. New York: Gay Academic Union.

GERASSI, JOHN. *The Boys of Boise: Furor, Vice, and Folly in an American City.* New York: Collier, 1968.

GIDE, ANDRE. *Corydon.* New York: Farrar, Straus & Giroux, 1950.

GOODMAN, PAUL. "Memoirs of an Ancient Activist." In Joseph McCaffrey, ed., in *The Homosexual Dialectic.* Englewood Cliffs, N.J.: Prentice-Hall, 1972.

GRAMSCI, ANTONIO. "Americanism and Fordism." In *Selections from the Prison Notebooks,* translated from the Italian by Quintin Hoare and Geoffrey Smith. New York: International Publishers, 1971.

HANSON. "S & M and Gay Lib." *Gay Sunshine* 14 (1972).

HUMPHREYS, LAUD. *Out of the Closets: The Sociology of Homosexual Liberation.* Englewood Cliffs, N.J.: Prentice-Hall, 1972.

IHARA, SAIKAKU. *Comrade Loves of the Samurai.* Translated from the Japanese by E. Powys Mathers. Rutland, Vt: Charles E. Tuttle, 1972.

ISHERWOOD, CHRISTOPHER. *Christopher and His Kind, 1929–1939.* New York: Farrar, Straus & Giroux, 1976.

JOHNSTON, JILL. *Lesbian Nation: The Feminist Solution.* New York: Simon & Schuster, 1973.

KATZ, JONATHAN. *Gay American History: Lesbians and Gay Men in the U.S.A.* New York: Thomas Y. Crowell, 1976.

KENNEDY, HUBERT. "Gay Liberation 1864." *Body Politic* 41 (March 1978): 23.

KOPAY, DAVID, and PERRY YOUNG. *The David Kopay Story: An Extraordinary Self-Revelation.* New York: Arbor House, 1976.

LEHMAN, J. LEE, ed. *Gays on Campus*. Washington, D.C.: United States National Student Association, 1975.

LEHNE, GREGORY. "Homophobia Among Men." In Deborah David and Robert Brannon, eds., *The Forty-Nine Percent Majority: The Male Sex Role*. Reading, Mass.: Addison-Wesley, 1976.

LEVINE, MARTIN. "Gay Ghetto," this volume, pp. 182–204.

MARCUSE, HERBERT. *Eros and Civilization: A Philosophical Inquiry into Freud*. New York: Vintage Books, 1955.

MARKO, JIM. "Committee of Outrage to Protest Arrests." *Gay Community News* 5, no. 25 (December 24):1.

MILLER, MERLE. *On Being Different: What It Means to Be a Homosexual*. New York: Random House, 1976.

MITZEL, JOHN. "Sports and the Macho Male." *Gay Sunshine* 18 (June–July 1973).

NORTON, RICTOR. "The Homosexual Literary Tradition: Course Outline and Objectives." *College English* 35 (March 1974):674.

———. "The Great Raid on Mother Clap's Molly House." *Gay Sunshine* 24 (Spring 1975):14.

PERRY, TROY, and CHARLES LUCAS. *The Lord Is My Shepherd and He Knows I'm Gay*. New York: Bantam Books, 1972.

RANKIN, JIM. "NACHO Upside Down," *Gay Sunshine* 1 (October 1970):4. Also in Donn Teal, *The Gay Militants;* New York: Stein and Day, 1971.

READE, BRIAN. *Sexual Heretics: Male Homosexuality in English Literature from 1850 to 1900*. New York: Coward-McCann, 1970.

REICH, WILHELM. *Sex-Pol: Essays 1929–1934*. New York: Vintage Books, 1972.

SAGHIR, MARCEL, and ELI ROBINS. *Male and Female Homosexuality: A Comprehensive Investigation*. Baltimore: Williams & Wilkins, 1973.

SCHAFFER, RALPH. "Gay Revaunch on Psychology." *Gay Sunshine* 8 (August–September 1971).

SPIERS, HERB, and MICHAEL LYNCH. "The Gay Rights Freud." *Body Politic,* 33 (May 1977):8.

STEAKLEY, JAMES. *The Homosexual Emancipation Movement in Germany.* New York: Arno Press, 1975.

SUTHERLAND, ALISTAIR, and PATRICK ANDERSON, eds. *Eros: An Anthology of Male Friendship.* Secaucus, N.J.: Citadel Press, 1963.

TEAL, DONN. *The Gay Militants.* New York: Stein & Day, 1971.

VIDAL, GORE. Interview. *Gay Sunshine* 26/27 (Winter 1976).

WILLIAMS, TENNESSEE. *Memoirs.* New York: Bantam Books, 1976.

WITTMAN, CARL. "Refugees from Amerika: A Gay Manifesto." In Karla Jay and Allen Young, eds., *Out of the Closets: Voices of Gay Liberation.* New York: Douglas, 1972. Also in Joseph McCaffrey, ed., *The Homosexual Dialectic;* Englewood Cliffs, N.J.: Prentice-Hall, 1972.

YOUNG, IAN. "S & M." *Gay Sunshine* 16 (January–February, 1973).

# Black Organizations, Gay Organizations: Sociological Parallels

LENNOX YEARWOOD AND
THOMAS S. WEINBERG

This paper attempts to outline some of the commonalities between two minority social movements. In particular, we will examine the role of organizations in the initiation of new movements or the formalization of previously existing movements. The two types of organizations with which we are concerned here are black organizations and homophile (or "gay") organizations. Black organizations have had the greatest impact upon the initiation of social change of any of the minority organizations in the United States in the twentieth century. The gay liberation movement takes a good deal of its impetus from the successes of the black movement, both in terms of the development of a more militant social context and with regard to specific strategies and tactics that have been adopted and modified from the black movement. It is one of the fastest-growing and most vocal of the current minority movements.

## THE SOCIAL SITUATIONS OF BLACKS AND GAYS

Both homosexuals and blacks have been socially ostracized to the point of finding it necessary to form their own "society," to provide social outlets for themselves, and not to be dependent upon existing social life and institutions. Members of each of these two minority groups, however, are in different sorts of

Revised version of a paper presented at the 72nd Annual Meeting of the American Sociological Association, September 4–9, 1977. The authors wish to thank Stephen Murray for his criticism of an earlier draft of this paper.

positions related, to a great extent, to the factor of their identifiability. Being more easily identifiable or visible, blacks as a group are more easily discriminated against than are homosexuals in both economic and social terms. Gays, if they desire, can disguise their sexual orientation and group affiliations and "pass" as heterosexuals. They are not likely to be discriminated against economically unless they are discovered or make their gayness known by "coming out of the closet." When this occurs, they may be "discredited," in Goffman's (1963) terms and are frequently dismissed from their jobs. Recently, some homophile organizations have asked for legal prohibitions against discrimination for "sexual orientation." Despite the possibility of disguising their homosexuality, many gays are opting for visibility as they accept the notion that they are *wrongfully* discriminated against. Blacks, on the other hand, have no such choice; relatively few can "pass." In any event, such passing, even if it is possible, causes its own kinds of strains and costs.

Both blacks and gays have voiced strong complaints about the social isolation and constraints forced upon them by the larger community. Through social discrimination, legal restrictions, "redlining," and so forth, blacks have been forced to live in segregated areas. While gays generally have been able to live wherever they wish, some have gravitated toward certain areas of large cities to form their own "ghettos" (Levine, 1977). The reason for this is not simply that they have easier access to the bars and cruising areas, but that many of them fear persecution by landlords and neighbors for their sexual preferences. Homosexuals very often have difficulty maintaining favorable feelings about themselves because of society's treatment of them (Weinberg, 1976). Martin Levine, a spokesman for a Gay Liberation Front organization, expressed the problem this way*:

I feel that the prime purpose of Gay Liberation Front is to tell everybody, "Goddamnit, we're not deviates; goddamnit, we're your brothers and sisters, accept us. Because people make love in a certain way don't persecute them." We're tired of living in gay ghettos, we're

---

* *Ed. note:* This statement was made by the editor when he was a junior in college.

tired of being forced to go to raunchy, disgusting bars. We're human beings; we want to be part of the community. We don't want to be labeled deviates [Forman, 1971:4].

## THE DEVELOPMENT OF MINORITY ORGANIZATIONS

Both black and gay organizations developed as a response to perceived social isolation and discrimination. At first, these early organizations took the position that they could best gain their ends by maintaining a respectable, moderate, middle-class image. They were oriented toward working within the system to educate the public and to change the laws. The early leaders of both black and gay organizations were middle class in their perspectives. They dressed in suits and ties and appeared as "reasonable" men. Although these organizations were founded sixty years apart, the language of the constitutions of the NAACP (est. 1909) and that of the Mattachine Society of the Niagara Frontier, Inc. (est. 1969), a moderate homophile organization, show striking similarities:

The principal object of the National Association for the Advancement of Colored People shall be to insure the political, educational, social and economic equality of minority group citizens; to achieve equality of rights and eliminate race prejudice among the citizens of the United States; to remove all barriers of racial discrimination through democratic processes; to seek enactment and enforcement of Federal, State, and municipal laws securing civil rights; to inform the public of the adverse effects of racial discrimination and to seek its elimination; to educate persons as to their constitutional rights and to take all lawful action to secure the exercise thereof, and to take any other lawful action in furtherance of these objectives consistent with the Articles of Incorporation [NAACP, *Constitution,* 1974].

Believing in our democratic heritage and self-determination of ethical values, we organize under this constitution for: reaffirmation of individual pride and dignity; elimination of stigma attached to human self-expression; effective changes of unjust laws concerning one's individuality and relationships among consenting individuals; promotion of better physical, mental, and emotional health; creation of a sense of Gay community; and a constructive outlet for members and friends [Mattachine Society of the Niagara Frontier, Inc., 1975].

Both the NAACP and Mattachine Society statements emphasize their intentions to work within the prevailing democratic political system to effect social change through the law, by eliminating discrimination and legal and social "stigma."

Additional similarities between the early black and the early gay organizations are also apparent in the statement from the Articles of Incorporation of One Inc., founded in 1952, which calls itself "America's oldest and most diversified homophile organization." One Inc. says that its purpose is

To sponsor, supervise and conduct educational programs, lectures, and concerts for the aid and benefit of all social and emotional variants and to promote among the general public an interest, knowledge, and understanding of the problems of such persons [Institute of Homophile Studies, *Catalog,* 1975–6:3].

Like the NAACP, One Inc. emphasizes its intention to inform or educate the general public about the particular problems faced by its particular group. The language used by One is especially interesting, since the statement substitutes the general and vague phrase "social and emotional variants" for "homosexual" or "homophile."

Initially, both black and gay organizations developed as crescive or grass-roots institutions (Teal, 1971:40), which emerge slowly out of folkways or mores (Sumner, 1940). For blacks, the development of various civil rights organizations can be traced to the development of the independent black church as the first and most prominent of the black organizations. Not only did the church function as a charitable, economic, educational, political, and recreational organization, but it also provided a training ground upon which individuals were able to develop organizational abilities and to develop feelings of self-esteem based upon their achievements. The independent black church, upon its inception, was the only organization in which the black population exercised authority with little or no outside intervention

(Frazier, 1973). The establishment of the black church provided individuals with a number of prestige-conferring positions, such as that of the preacher, the first professional in the black community (Woodson, 1915, 1972; Dubois, 1970; Wilmore, 1973; Yearwood, 1976). The black church has, of course, been an important force in the initiation of social change.

Like blacks, gays have established their own churches. The first of these was the Metropolitan Community Church, founded by the Reverend Troy Perry in October 1968 in Los Angeles. Within the next two years, he had established churches in San Francisco, San Diego, and Chicago; and the Metropolitan Community Church in Los Angeles had a congregation of almost five hundred members (Teal, 1971:278). A number of other churches and synagogues have since been established. Many homophile organizations have religious committees. In the constitution of the Mattachine Society of Niagara Frontier, Inc., for example, the religious committee is charged with the responsibilities of "acting as a liaison between religious groups in the community and the Society" and with "lobbying for religious support of social changes in legislative reform" (Mattachine Society of the Niagara Frontier, Inc., 1975). There are two national gay organizations that are religiously based. "Dignity" is an organization of gay Catholic churchmen and laymen. "Integrity" is a similar Anglican/Episcopalian organization. Unlike the black church, however, the gay churches have become established only relatively late in the history of the development of homophile organizations. There is some evidence that some homophile organizations developed out of groups created for reasons other than to obtain the civil rights of gay people. For example, it has been claimed that the Mattachine Society grew out of the Bachelors-for-Wallace club, formed to support Henry Wallace's 1948 presidential bid (Teal, 1971:43). Homosexual "clubs" have existed for a long time. Toward the end of the seventeenth century in London, for example, a "rudimentary homosexual subculture" began to form, including clubs that were apparently formed by homosexual transvestites (McIntosh, 1968:187). These clubs were not, however, in any sense part of any organized homophile movement.

## FORMALIZATION, DEFORMALIZATION, AND
## MINORITY ORGANIZATIONS

Over time, there seems to be a tendency for many organizations to become more formalized. A number of interesting developments accompany such structural changes in organizations. One of these is the creation of "professional" spokesmen for these organizations and movements, so that we now have "professional gays" as well as "professional blacks," and paid full-time employees, lobbyists, and so forth of these organizations. A concomitant change is the recognition of the "legitimacy" of such organizations by government. This acknowledgment is symbolized by the willingness of governmental functionaries to meet with organizational representatives, the appearance of such representatives before hearings of lawmaking bodies and, most important, the giving of grants to such organizations. Recently, for instance, the Gay Community Services Center of Los Angeles received a $305,250 grant from the Comprehensive Employment Training Act to help "facilitate a training program and provide valuable work experience for chronically unemployed gay men and women in the area" (*5th Freedom,* 1977b3). Very often, receiving such outside funding causes the organization to become even more formalized. An increasing dependence upon such grants and the need to compete for them, not only with similar kinds of organizations but with very different sorts of organizations as well, almost compels an increase in bureaucratization. Especially in the case of black organizations, external factors such as federal funding and federal guidelines influence the very structure of the organization and its programs and functions. Leaders of two black voluntary associations make this very explicit in the following quotations:

The cut in the budget has seriously limited us in the many projects that we have started. . . . We are being asked to scale down projects so that we are able to facilitate smaller numbers of children each year . . . We have some volunteer help from the community but not enough professional help.

If we lose our funding agents then all of these projects will stop, because at this time our self-sustaining funds are not sufficient to run this organization, independent of a funding body [Yearwood, 1976: 149].

Although we have implied that many minority organizations tend to become more bureaucratic and formalized over time, this is not necessarily always the case. On the local level at least, it is quite possible that previously structured organizations become less formally bureaucratized over time. Often, this is due to funding problems, as the quotations above suggest. In Buffalo, this occurred in the cases of both gay organizations and black organizations. The Mattachine Society, for example, eventually reached the point a few years after its founding at which it cosponsored a gay community services center. The center had its own full-time paid director, and the society itself had a full-time paid president. In its last few months of existence, the center also employed a paid health service coordinator. As a result of internal dissension, however, and the added competition of new gay bars, which drastically reduced attendance at Saturday night dances, which were the most important source of revenue for running the center (*5th Freedom,* 1977a), the center was closed in March 1977. For a short time, a number of crucial committees—such as the health committee, concerned with short-term peer crisis counseling—stopped functioning. The society itself, however, was not defunct and reorganized and held meetings at the same local church where meetings had originally been held several years before. Some of the criticisms of the center made by members of the gay community were that the center had caused the society to become less personal and informal and thus insensitive to the needs of a number of segments of the local gay community. Charges had been made that the center itself was run by an exclusive clique.

A lack of funding also was responsible for the debureaucratization of a local Buffalo black organization, the Langston Hughes Center for the Visual and Performing Arts. Between 1972 and 1974, the Langston Hughes Center received 90 percent of its annual budget from the Model Cities Agency, renamed Division of Demonstration Project. In January 1975, the center's funds were drastically reduced, and it operated on emergency funds from the Division of Demonstration Project (Yearwood, 1976:122). The result of the reduction in funding was that the center was forced to move away from its central concern with the fine and visual arts to a more community-oriented social activities program involving, for example, bingo and community dances. The arts classes held by the center were curtailed, since there were no longer funds to pay professional teachers, and all of the administrative work was done by one person, the center having lost its temporary personnel. Since that time, the center has received funding from the Community Development and Human Resources Department of the Buffalo city government and the New York State Division for Youth, so that much of the arts program has been restored. However, the era of limited funding has had repercussions beyond the simple reduction of programs. It has left a legacy of dissension between the professional artists on the one hand and the professional administrators on the other. The Langston Hughes Center experience is interesting because it points out the cyclical nature of organizations, wherein an organization may debureaucratize and subsequently become more formalized again.

## MINORITY ORGANIZATIONS AND RADICALIZATION

One of the most striking and interesting parallels between black and gay organizations is the rise of new antiestablishment "radical" organizations. A related phenomenon is the transformation of more "moderate" preexisting organizations, which become modified in their underlying ideologies and the direction of their concerns, and which sometimes even change drastically in their expressed primary goals and in the techniques used to gain them. These changes may occur in a number of ways. They may, for example, be precipitated if an organization changes in leadership, as when "CORE moved from a militant integrationist organization under the directorship of James Farmer to black-power separatism under Floyd McKissick and later Roy Innis" (Toby, 1971:534). Or they may be influenced by the rise of a new wave of organizations with a different perspective.

There was, for example, a tremendous increase in the number of both black and gay organizations during roughly the same time period, 1964–70. (Parker, n.d.; Fisk, 1976; Ploski and Kaiser, 1971). This basic change in orientation seems to be the result of minority groups members' perceiving that "working within the system" has failed to change their situation. Carmichael and Hamilton's book *Black Power* (1967) alluded to this view in the section entitled "The Search for New Forms" as follows:

This country cannot begin to solve the problems of the ghettos as long as it continues to hang on to outmoded structures and institutions. A political party system that seeks only to "manage conflict" and hope for the best will not be able to serve a growing body of alienated black people. An educational system which, year after year, continues to cripple hundreds of thousands of black children must be replaced by wholly new mechanisms of control and management. We must begin to think and operate in terms of entirely new and substantially different forms of expression [pp. 164–65].

Gay "radicals" have voiced similar feelings about organizations and members who take an establishment-oriented approach. The Daughters of Bilitis, for example, which is the oldest lesbian organization in the United States, is referred to by "younger, more radical lesbians . . . as 'the NAACP of lesbian groups,' and to its members as 'Aunt Tabbies' " (Klemesrud, 1971:38). Writing about the "gay ghetto" in his "Gay Manifesto," Carl Wittman (1970) says:

Ghettos breed self-hatred. We stagnate here, accepting the status quo. The status quo is rotten. We are all warped by our oppression, and in the isolation of the ghetto we blame ourselves rather than our oppressors. . . .

To be free territory, we must govern ourselves, set up our own institutions, defend ourselves, and use our own energies to improve our lives. The emergence of gay liberation communes, and our own paper is a good start. The talk about a gay liberation coffee shop/dance hall should be acted upon. Rural retreats, political action offices, food cooperatives, a free school, unalienating bars and after hours places— they must be developed if we are to have even the shadow of a free territory.

In this statement, Wittman echoes the feelings of black separatists. But, like them, his separatism is a matter of his own choice; it is separatism on his own terms.

Gay radicals freely acknowledge their debts to the black movement for causing them to develop their own group consciousness and for showing them that they could do something about their own social situation (e.g., Wittman, 1970; Williams, 1972); and they frequently draw analogies between the two movements. This is not surprising, since many white gays participated actively in the civil rights movement. Many of the strategies used by gay groups, such as sit-ins and other forms of passive resistance, picketing, marches, boycotts, confrontations with lawmakers and candidates for public office, and so forth, were first widely publicized when they were used by blacks. Some gay groups have modeled themselves after black organizations, even to the appropriation of slogans such as "Black Power," transformed into "Gay Power," and symbols such as the raised clenched fist. Gays, of course, have also developed their own symbols such as the lambda, frequently worn as jewelry or on buttons and patches.

## MINORITY ORGANIZATIONS AND POLITICS

One of the ways in which American minority groups have traditionally attempted to improve the lot of their members has been through the political process. Blacks, like other ethnic groups, have organized and attempted to elect their own representatives, or at least representatives who were sympathetic to their cause. Politicians have spoken of "the black vote" as being critical in swinging certain elections. Postelection surveys have indicated that black votes provided the "margin of victory" of Kennedy over Nixon in the 1960 presidential election (Toby, 1971:518) and that this vote was important in the election of Carter over Ford in 1976. There is, however, some debate as to whether or not blacks have actually benefited from exercising their voting power (e.g., Halberstam, 1961; Lundberg, 1968: 700–702). Gays, too, have noted the potential power of organized voting blocs. In a statement read by the Rochester, N.Y., Gay Liberation Front as part of their testimony before the state legislature's Special Committee on Discrimination Against Homosexuals on January 7, 1971, this organization drew some parallels between blacks and gays:

If you believe the Kinsey report, the only national survey to date on sexual practices, you must believe that a third of our population have committed homosexual acts which make them criminals, that at least one out of every five do so for a period of at least three years. This is a large minority of our population and it will soon be impossible for candidates for election to ignore the votes of this class, just as it is getting hard to ignore the voting power of the black community [Rochester, N.Y., Gay Liberation Front, 1971:2–3].

Gay organizations have already made some attempts to influence the political system. Through the newsletters and efforts of gay organizations, the homosexual electorate is advised of the stance taken toward them by aspirants to political office. Gay leaders claim to have had a determining influence on the outcome of a number of elections, such as the 1969 New York City mayoral elections (Teal, 1971:67–68). Gays have also run their own candidates in Los Angeles (*Newsweek,* October 27, 1969) and San Francisco, and self-avowed gays such as Massachusetts State Representative Elaine Nobel have been elected to national and state offices after having "come out" to the electorate.

Another indication that gay organizations are coming to be seen by some political leaders as a potential political force is the meeting in February 1977 between Midge Costanza, then one of President Carter's aides, and representatives of the National Gay Task Force to discuss the position of homosexuals in American society (*5th Freedom,* 1977c). The nationally reported attempts of homophile organizations to prevent the repeal of the Dade County gay rights bill, although unsuccessful, nevertheless demonstrated the ability of gays to muster support from heterosexuals and civil libertarians throughout the country. The final tally, 202,319 votes for repeal versus 89,562 votes to retain prohibitions against housing and employment discrimination against homosexuals (Buffalo *Evening News,* June 8, 1977), shows a surprising progay strength, as does a Gallup poll reported in July 1977, in which the persons polled were split 43–43 percent on the issue of whether homosexual relations between consenting adults should be legal.

## ORGANIZATIONAL MEMBERSHIP

Blacks and gays come to join their respective organizations in different ways, but the organizations serve similar needs. For blacks, participation in organizations develops out of living in black areas. Black organizations, as we have indicated, historically developed as alternatives to serve the needs of blacks. These organizations, with their multiplicity of committees, titles, and so on, provided their members with prestige-conferring positions within their own community, high statuses they could not attain in many white organizations. Gays, who are usually the children of heterosexuals and who therefore have not grown up in a (sexual) minority subculture, do not have a tradition of belonging to homophile organizations. The men in a study conducted by one of the present writers (Weinberg, 1976) came into gay organizations in a variety of ways—through meeting organizationally oriented gays while seeking sexual partners, through college-based homophile groups, through being referred to them by counselors, and so forth. Their motivations for joining were as diverse as having been "radicalized" as the result of encounters with police, wanting to meet people like themselves in social rather than purely sexual situations, or desiring to find solutions to personal identity problems. Participation in homophile organizations appears to be strongly related to the reduction of identity conflicts, increasing acceptance of one's homosexuality, and improvement in feelings about oneself. It is not, however, the mere fact of belonging to such organizations that seems to be important. Rather it is the extent to which a member participates in the organization that appears to be crucial in developing self-acceptance as a homosexual. Organizational members who are active indicate that involvement in the gay movement was instrumental in improving their feelings about themselves (Weinberg, 1976:535–36).

Organizations appear to enhance their members' feelings of self-esteem by allowing them to discover and to develop previously unrealized talents and expertise. We have noted that black organizations, particularly the churches, appear to have done this for their members. Similarly, a member of a gay organization notes that:

I've been able to meet people I have things in common with. I've been able to do things that I never realized I could before. I have responsibilities that I never would have had. . . . Being in various organizations has given me a positive feedback, not just for being gay but developing my personality. . . . It helped me not just in accepting my homosexuality but in accepting myself [Weinberg, 1976:511].

For some people, as the man quoted above seems to indicate, organizations serve as primary groups, within which they feel comfortable with people like themselves. Black churches, for example, typically provide social services in addition to their religious activities; and their members prefer to deal with their brethren rather than with the personnel of impersonal public bureaucracies. A black pastor explained the attitude of his parishioners in this way:

. . . these people who are semi-illiterate or illiterate, they feel more at ease with the member of the church when they know, and trust who maybe will have more time and patience to deal with them, rather than someone from the agency who has to go right by the rule, and they don't have time to deal, or they don't take time to deal with each person, that they have to process people. So these people feel better with somebody from the church, they have a better rapport with them. They can open up, they won't be laughed at if they can't read; if they don't understand they take the time to sit down and explain it to them. It makes a difference [Yearwood, 1976:120].

## CONCLUSIONS

In the United States, the parallels among minority groups stem from the fact that they have to overcome similar obstacles. Laws have to be changed, passed, or enforced; a significant number of persons or groups in the larger society have to be persuaded to collaborate with, if not actually accept, the minority group. The extent to which this may be successfully accomplished seems to depend upon a variety of factors; the history of the group in the larger society, its visibility, its access to the media, and the extent to which it can be seen as having been "legitimately discriminated against." In the case of blacks, the force of the Constitution and the government eventually was applied in an attempt to gain equal access to the rights guaranteed to all Americans. In the case of gays, the jury is still out. It may be too soon to predict what the rest of this decade will bring in terms of attitudes toward the gay movement, yet gays themselves appear to be operating on the general acceptance of "liberation movements" which developed in the late nineteen sixties. In contemporary society, the push for liberation starting in the black community has spilled over into a general consensus of liberation movements. Yet, the failure of the ERA movement, supported by feminist organizations, and the expressed intention of the antigay forces to move into other areas of the country to attempt to repeal gay rights laws (Buffalo *Evening News,* June 8, 1977) may signal a change in public sentiments toward what have heretofore been seen by many as "legitimate" attempts by minority organizations to obtain "their rights."

Gays as a group, like black groups, lack the economic base to make moves of consequence within the society. Both groups lack an organized capital to radicalize the society from within, as for example, by setting up their own financial institutions and withdrawing their capital from those of the larger society. There are, of course, some black banks but they are dependent upon the financial resources of the larger society. Although there are no homosexual banks, gays have made a tentative beginning with regard to the organization of an economic movement with the establishment of an employment bureau for homosexuals. If full acceptance is to occur for either group, it seems likely that it will be dependent upon the martialing of their individual group forces in the economic and political-legal spheres.

In a brief exploratory paper we have been able to point out some striking parallels between black organizations and gay organizations, and have necessarily had to abbreviate our discussion of these similarities. We have not been able to deal with such topics as the internal structure of organizations, organizational conflict and its resolution, or the social characteristics of leaders and members in any detail. These are topics for further investigation.

## REFERENCES

CARMICHAEL, STOKELY, and CHARLES V. HAMILTON. *Black Power: The Politics of Liberation in America.* New York: Vintage Books, 1967.

"Dade County Votes Repeal of Gay Rights." Buffalo *Evening News,* June 8, 1977.

DuBois, W. E. B. *The Souls of Black Folk.* New York: Fawcett, 1970.

5TH FREEDOM. "Buffalo Gay Center Closes." March 1977A:1.

———. "L.A. Center Making History." March 1977b:3.

———. "White House Talks with Gay Activists." March 1977c:1.

FISK, MARGARET, ed. *Encyclopedia of Associations.* Detroit: Gale Research Co., 1976.

FORMAN, ALAN. "GLF Organized." *Pipe Dream,* February 12, 1971, p. 4.

FRAZIER, FRANKLIN E. *The Negro Church in America.* New York: Schocken Books, 1973.

GOFFMAN, ERVING. *Stigma; Notes on the Management of Spoiled Identity.* Englewood Cliffs, N.J.: Prentice-Hall, 1963.

HALBERSTAM, DAVID. "Good Jelly's Last Stand." *The Reporter* 24 (January 19, 1961):40–41.

INSTITUTE OF HOMOPHILE STUDIES. *Catalog for 1975–1976.* Los Angeles, 1975.

KLEMESRUD, JUDY. "The Disciples of Sappho, Updated." *The New York Times Magazine,* March 28, 1971, pp. 38–39, 41–42, 44, 48, 50, 52.

LEVINE, MARTIN. "Gay Ghetto," this volume, pp. 182–204.

McINTOSH, MARY. "The Homosexual Role." *Social Problems* 16 (Fall 1968): 182–92.

MATTACHINE SOCIETY OF THE NIAGARA FRONTIER, INC. *Constitution.* Amended November 19, 1975.

NATIONAL ASSOCIATION FOR THE ADVANCEMENT OF COLORED PEOPLE. *NAACP Constitution. Article II.* New York, 1974.

PARKER, WILLIAM. "The Homosexual in American Society Today: The Homophile-Gay Liberation Movement." Mimeographed, n.d.

PLOSKI, HARRY, and ERNEST KAISER, eds. *The Negro Almanac.* New York: Bellwether, 1971.

"Policing the Third Sex." *Newsweek,* October 27, 1969, pp. 79–81.

ROCHESTER, N.Y., GAY LIBERATION FRONT. Statement of the Rochester, N.Y., Gay Liberation Front in Testimony Before the Special Committee on Discrimination Against Homosexuals. Mimeographed, January 7, 1971.

SUMNER, WILLIAM GRAHAM. *Folkways: A Study of the Sociological Importance of Usages, Manners, Customs, Mores and Morals.* New York: Ginn and Company, 1940.

TEAL, DONN. *The Gay Militants.* New York: Stein & Day, 1971.

TOBY, JACKSON. *Contemporary Society; An Introduction to Sociology.* 2d ed. New York: Wiley, 1971.

WEINBERG, THOMAS S. "Becoming Homosexual: Self-Discovery, Self-Identity, and Self-Maintenance." Ph.D. dissertation, the University of Connecticut, 1976.

WILLIAMS, FLOYD. "Gay and Angry." *The Body Politic* 6 (Autumn 1972):17, 22.

WILMORE, GAYRAUD S. *Black Religion and Black Radicalism.* New York: Anchor Press, 1973.

WITTMAN, CARL. "Refugees from Amerika: A Gay Manifesto." San Francisco *Free Press,* December 22, 1969–January 7, 1970.

WOODSON, CARTER GODWIN. *The Education of the Negro Prior to 1861.* New York: Harper & Row, 1915.

———. *The History of the Negro Church.* Washington, D.C.: Associated Publishers, 1972.

YEARWOOD, LENNOX. "Black Organizations: A Study of Their Community Involvement with Reference to Decision-Making Processes." Ph.D. dissertation, State University of New York at Buffalo, 1976.

# Critical Incidents in the Evolution of a Gay Liberation Group

## MARTIN ROGERS

I had played with the idea of titling this article "You Can Drink from the Cesspool." The stimulus came from the late Dudley Swim, a Reagan appointee to the California State College Board of Trustees. When Swim heard that a gay liberation group was forming on one of the State College campuses, his moral indignation was so aroused that he spewed forth an immediate indictment of "that cesspool down there."

I am a Virgo and, according to my horoscope, I am neat and fussy and oriented toward cleanliness. All of that makes a cesspool a strange voluntary habitat for me. I have been rather thoroughly immersed in that "cesspool" for four years now, and all sorts of nice things have happened to me. My eyes have become bluer, my teeth whiter, and even my intellect (which supposedly declines after the age of twenty-eight) has become sharper. Perhaps one person's cesspool is another person's electric kool-aide.

I am going to describe an organic, growing entity of which I am an integral part. If there are any scientific types reading this, they will note that my data are subjective. My perceptions and those of the other respondents undoubtedly have been biased by our involvement in the organization. And there is no control group for comparative purposes. Given those factors, I will detail the development of the Sacramento State College Gay Liberation from the initial meeting of thirteen male homosexuals in December 1969 to the present membership of approximately fifty gay men and lesbians, and its current status as an important part of the larger homosexual community.

*Homosexual Counseling Journal* 2, no. 1 (January 1975): 18–25. Reprinted by permission of the publisher.

Each of the twelve individuals who had been active in the group for the past four years was independently asked to list incidents that seemed significant to him/her in the evolution of the group. This account is a distillation of those reports. Conspicuously absent are data from individuals who dropped out of the organization, but I suspect that the dropouts would have selected many of the same critical incidents as the stay-ins did. Most of the critical incidents signal an identity crisis in the life of the group. Most changed the direction of the growth of the group and most resulted in the loss of some members who could not tolerate the change.

In November of 1969, I was asked to attend a meeting of a homosexual group that had just begun at the University of California, Davis campus. The group was foundering, and I was asked to function as a psychological consultant. I agreed primarily because I liked the instant status accorded to a visiting expert and because I thought it might provide me with an opportunity to meet people. Gay consciousness or identity with the liberation movement had no meaning to me at that time.

I came away from that meeting impressed by seemingly simple things, but they were things that made me aware of how perfect had been the process of society's oppression of me as a gay man and my own oppression of myself in accepting a preprogrammed role as a homosexual in a heterosexual world. I was moved and impressed by homosexuals meeting in an apartment with the lights on to talk to each other about their interests, identities, and their sexuality with a minimum of game playing and without the use of crutches such as alcohol or dope. It was as simple as that.

All gay people have just three characteristics in common: (1) They prefer social, sexual, and love relationships with members of their own sex; (2) they are oppressed; (3) this oppression is so successful that unless something drastic occurs they have minimal awareness of being oppressed. In fact, many homosexuals have evolved highly developed delusional systems that explain their accommodations to the guilt-producing demands of the heterosexual world and that justify their secrecy about their sexuality. For example, "There's no need to upset straights by being blatant," or "Look how good things are in San Francisco."

The social centers of the gay world—the bars, the baths, the cocktail parties, the beaches, and the parks—bring gay people into contact with each other, but they are primarily centers of sexual seduction. The body is an easy lay. Years of social conditioning have taught the gay person not to expect too much. Saturate his ears with quadraphonic sound, his eyes with scores of attractive men, give him plenty of sex, and you have a happy male homosexual. For that moment. The depression, loneliness, self-alienation, and paranoia occur later. And until the emergence of gay liberation groups, homosexuals who had achieved the awareness that their heads and their bodies can be in unity could find little support for this insight. One just does not talk about "heavy" issues in a gay bar.

All but one of the respondents in this study noted as significant the initial meeting to discuss forming a homosexual group on the Sacramento State College campus. They came to the meeting reluctantly, verbally contracting only to attend that meeting and making quite explicit their lack of commitment to anything beyond that. Of the original thirteen, about half were faculty members in their late twenties and early thirties and half students in their early twenties. Catastrophic expectations were verbalized, and in retrospect, we seemed to be scared, timid, and hesitant.

The second meeting was also cited as critical. It was on campus and it drew over fifty people. Veterans for Peace and Women's Liberation sent representatives who encouraged the group to apply for recognition as a campus organization. The chairman and several members of the Cultural Programs Committee, an important college committee, were there to offer their support in bringing speakers to campus to talk about the gay liberation movement. And the president of the student body, a heterosexual, volunteered to serve as an officer of the group if public exposure was feared by group members. The public meeting on campus, the unexpectedly large turnout, and this support from heterosexuals energized the group.

One of the most critical incidents in the life of the group was the third meeting, when a name had to be decided on. I believe that choosing a name is equivalent to deciding who you are and the purpose of your existence. Having to cope with this issue so early in its development nearly terminated the life of the group.

There was intense debate about the use of the word "homosexual" as opposed to the word "homophile" in the name. Surprisingly to me, a number of people who had been generally opposed or indifferent to the formation of the group came out strongly in support of incorporating "homosexual" into the name. And many of the men whose behavior was stereotypically feminine were in favor of the use of "homophile." That issue resolved itself when the advocates of "homophile" could not agree among themselves what the word meant. Then the discussion turned to whether the name should indicate openness to heterosexual members and, finally, the degree of militancy the name should convey. The compromise solution was "The Society for Homosexual Freedom." It is significant and indicative of the evolution of the group that a year later, at a routine meeting and with a minimum of discussion, the members voted unanimously to change the name of the group to "Sacramento State College Gay Liberation."

That third meeting signaled the end of the honeymoon. It exploded the we-are-all-brothers-instant-love-and-acceptance aura that had been building. Although this myth was shattered, the events of that meeting indicated that the group had achieved a more mature level of functioning. A characteristic of newly formed relationships—dyadic or group—is the almost compulsive focusing on similarities among the participants. This serves the purpose of neutralizing or masking the tensions that occur when individuals with different life experiences come together. It helps bring people into psychological contact long enough for them to discover whether they want to continue the relationship or not. The acknowledgment of differences (and we are all different) usually follows a commitment—formal or otherwise—to relate and it initiates a flow of energy and excitement into the interactions.

Undoubtedly, the tensions, the open hostility, the surfacing of issues that confronted people with questions of their own identities as homosexuals frightened away some participants. But out of that third chaotic meeting emerged an ethic that still exists in the group. This was based on the recognition that our sexuality and our being oppressed brought us together, but beyond that we had as much in common as any other group of people who randomly came together. Politically, we ran the gamut from conservative fascists to liberal fascists. We realized that in order for us to accept each other and to end our oppression, we had to recognize our differences and permit them to exist. If somebody chose to be militant, that was that person's choice, and a second person would not try to stop the first, who would, in turn, permit the second his or her passivity. The group drew up a constitution, elected officers, and applied for recognition by the college. The Student Senate approved the application, and it was sent to the acting college president, who held it for two months, since he was actively seeking to be named president of the college and was not eager to make a decision that would be sure to offend some on the campus.

In the interim, there were two important incidents. The first helped define the needs of the group members. Invitations had been extended to the group by two members who were lovers for a combination discussion-socializing evening. The invitation had been verbal, and the emphasis on the discussion aspect or the socializing aspect varied with the partner extending the invitation. I anticipated a social evening with some time set aside for a discussion of psychological aspects of homosexuality, which I had agreed to lead. I arrived at 8:00 P.M., an hour and a half late. Some people were talking in small groups, others were listening to music, and many were in one room watching sex films. It seemed like a pleasant party, and I was betting myself that we would never get to the discussion part, when one of the hosts blew up at me for sabotaging the evening and at the group members for being more interested in social activities than in discussion of significant issues. My needs that evening had been social, as were the needs of the majority of the other group members. The meetings preceding that evening had dealt with business affairs, and the events of that evening brought into focus the desire of the members to have fun with each other and to get to know each other. We lost one host as a member, but we began to realize that in order to struggle together we had also to play together and that we needed an alternative to the gay bars.

The second important incident was a visit to the campus by Paul Goodman. After giving his address on campus, Goodman chose to spend the rest of the afternoon meeting with the club—at first in a large discussion group and then moving around the room in less formal talks with the smaller groupings that formed after we all took a break. Few people liked Goodman's suggestions about possible courses of action for the group, but the fact that he had always been open about his sexuality and had been fired three times because of it, and survived, had an impact on those present. He was admired for what he had done, he was a well-known, well-respected intellectual, and he had turned down invitations from various faculty members and other groups to spend time with us. He was a hero of sorts, and we were the chosen people. He helped validate our existence for ourselves.

The group had now been in existence for three months, and a soft, generally euphoric feeling prevailed. Twenty to thirty people had been showing up for the meetings, with new people coming each time. None of the more vocal or visible members of the group had been hassled on or off campus. There were many, many plans for the future: for a coffeehouse, for a commune, for a newspaper, for consciousness-raising sessions, for a speakers' bureau, for a symposium on homosexuality at the college. Action wasn't necessary at this point, since it was anticipated that everything would flow after we were recognized as an official campus organization.

Then the acting college president announced that he had decided to deny recognition to the group. That was startling enough, but the statements supposedly explaining the reasons for the denial were frighteningly similar to the fundamentalist rhetoric of Carl McIntire. We were told that we were illegal; that our being on campus would attract other homosexuals to the campus; that we might seduce young, naive college boys; and that the community would not tolerate the college permitting the group to use its facilities. Being denied recognition was a moment of truth for the Society for Homosexual Freedom. Being embraced by other liberation groups on campus had blinded us to the realities of the larger world. Being denied recognition, being decreed invisible, reactivated in most group members other similar, painful incidents in their lives. The difference this time was that there was support—from the campus newspaper and from the student government.

Two faculty members openly acknowledged their homosexuality through letters to the acting college president and to the campus newspaper—they insisted on being seen. For once, homosexuals were not running and hiding. Publicly announcing one's homosexuality, an issue that had not really been confronted previously, became an actuality as a result of the denial of recognition.

Szasz (1970) likens the existence of the homosexual to that of the Jew. Both can easily hide the stigmatized portion of their identities, but the price, in the long run, becomes quite expensive. For example, when I first began teaching, one of my greatest fears was that my students would discover that I was a queer. I wore a jacket and tie in those days and before each class I would remind myself to watch my inflections, to control any excessive hand movements, to flirt with the women students, and to never, never let my eyes linger on a male student. I had to stop after a month. Acting the stereotyped male role was tantamount to being a robot for me. The cost of that travesty was the very excitement and spontaneity that make me the unique being I am.

Hoffman (1968) states that "walking into a gay bar is a momentous act in the life of a homosexual, because in many cases it is the first time he publicly identifies himself as a homosexual." Based on my own experiences and those of others in the gay liberation movement, I will take that one step further and hypothesize that it is not until gay persons can acknowledge their sexual preferences openly to homosexuals and heterosexuals who matter to them that they can begin to confront the issue of their identity. I have never met a homosexual who has not swallowed some portion of the sick-bad-crazy-stupid-myth. And it is only in facing oneself with openness that the gay person discovers how much of that garbage (maybe this is where the cesspool comes from) he or she believes to be true.

I mentioned earlier that after denial of recognition the group received support from other campus groups, underground and establishment. The issue of support is a crucial one. New behaviors need to be reinforced if they are to be maintained. But currently there are pitifully few sources of support for innovative or courageous behaviors. Even here in academe, the eleventh commandment of middle-America, "Thou shalt not offend thy neighbors," has become the justification for maintaining the status quo. The rhetoric now is: "It's a damn good idea, but what will the community think?"

Nevertheless, the gay liberation group did receive support, and it was invaluable. A local heterosexual attorney volunteered his services, and the student body president gave his permission for a court action against the acting college president and the State College Board of Trustees. The Cultural Programs Committee approved a proposal for a week-long symposium on homosexuality. Being denied recognition produced a strong feeling of camaraderie among group members.

In the cafeteria, there was a section for the jocks, one for the fraternity types, one for the blacks, another for the Chicanos, one for the women, and now one for the gays. Generalizing from an N of one, I hypothesize that a crucial ingredient in the recipe for success for every revolutionary movement is the forcing of a liberal-with-power into the corner.

The case went to court, and the group continued to meet off campus. Meetings became more serious and businesslike. A regular meeting place was found, and meetings were scheduled for once a month. Although the subject had come up previously, it was only after the denial of recognition that a decision was made to have open meetings. Anybody—gay or straight—could now attend. Although many plans were still discussed, the tolerance for talk decreased. Members who were action oriented commanded attention and respect. The speakers' bureau began to function. A faculty member wrote a series of articles for the campus paper. A few members began visiting Bay Area gay groups to see what they were doing.

A critical incident occurred toward the end of 1970, when a core group of active members met with two women from

Women's Liberation to discuss with them how their group had evolved. Out of that interchange came the decision of the two most active, verbal, and power-oriented group members—both faculty members—to take no more responsibility for the group and to keep their comments at meetings minimal. Another decision was to have meetings chaired by a different person each time. The power vacuum created by the silence of the two most dominant members caused some tension at the next meeting, but some of the younger and more reticent members of the group tentatively stepped up and filled it. With greater sharing of responsibility, new energy and enthusiasm permeated the group.

Prior to this time, involvement of lesbians in the group had been minimal. On the few occasions when gay women had come to a meeting, they quickly and accurately perceived the situation to be male-dominated and left. But gay women had been actively involved in the Women's Liberation movement and their participation in the campus gay group was initially sought because of their political expertise. After Lesbian Feminists, Feminist Lesbians, and Radical Lesbians started attending meetings, the gay men not only became more sophisticated politically but also began to be forced to confront their own sexist attitudes toward women. One product of the successful integration of the group was a number of consciousness-raising sessions involving gay women and men. Such sessions had been talked about for a year but never acted on because trust between the women and men had been too low.

Another critical incident was the opening of the Gay Alternative Coffeehouse. The coffeehouse was set up in one member's apartment on weekend evenings as an alternative to the gay bars and later moved to larger quarters in the Sacramento Gay Community Services Center. It is one of the most successful products of Gay Liberation. It is a place to meet and to talk, as well as a place to cruise. It is a place where women and men who are discovering that their sexual preferences are homosexual can come and see what the gay world is like. It is a place in which those who are still frightened and in the closet can identify. Its popularity and viability demonstrate that community between homosexuals is a possibility.

There were other critical incidents. A newsletter was published. The court case was won, and the group was recognized by the college. Another symposium on homosexuality, featuring prominent gay people such as Allen Ginsberg, Del Martin, and Phyllis Lyon, was held and turned out well. Liaisons with other homosexual groups were formed, Schisms within the group were faced, and hostility is still flowing freely. Gay Liberation organized Sacramento's first public gay dance aboard the Delta King Riverboat. A Gay Studies Program was started at Sacramento State. And one evening after a meeting, without fuss or planning, the group members went en masse to a local hofbrau to have a drink, to enjoy each other's company in the American tradition, and quite incidentally, to liberate that bastion of heterosexuality. It was done without any trouble at all.

Probably the most significant changes in the group have been changes in the attitudes, behaviors, and self-concepts of the members. All the respondents included comments such as:

I don't know if this would be a critical incident in the life of the group, but I sure as hell feel better about myself as a result of being in gay lib.

I never realized how much energy I had in me till I stopped hiding that I was gay. I dropped that phony straight facade and started being a whole person.

It's still not easy being gay in a straight world, but it's sure nice being friends with myself.

Individual differences are still vast, for what brings us together are our sexual preferences and our oppression. But many people in the movement are now "gay" instead of "dykes" or "faggots" or "queers." Many are angry, and aggressing against an oppressor is a sign of psychological maturity. There are fewer facades and secrets and a lot less guilt and shame; and as a result, people have more energy available for living instead of for running.

## REFERENCES

HOFFMAN, MARTIN. *The Gay World: Male Homosexuality and the Social Creation of Evil*. New York: Basic Books, 1968.

SZASZ, THOMAS. *The Manufacture of Madness*. New York: Harper & Row, 1970.

# Butcher Than Thou: Beyond Machismo

## JACK NICHOLS

Late one evening I stood next to Logan Carter, an incredible androgyne who knows the secrets of gender motivation expressed in movement. Logan is an entertainer and he also knows certain facts about men: namely, that those who think themselves tough and aggressive and who exaggerate such traits are engaged in theatrics. They have learned and often rehearsed their aggressive poses.

On this particular night Logan dressed in conventional clothes rather than in the androgynous garments he prefers. Near us stood a female impersonator, a young man who looked like a woman. Suddenly, from the opposite side of the room, a snarling man lunged forward. "I'm straight," he announced savagely, as if to give credentials. He grabbed at the impersonator. Logan jumped forward and snapped back without a moment's hesitation, his face contorted with simulated rage. "I am too!" he yelled in the man's face, "and she's with me. She's mine, hear? Don't touch her. I'm jealous, see?" Logan's frame struck quick with his words so there was no room for doubt in the intruder's mind that sincerity had spoken. The man backed away apologetically and disappeared. We laughed quietly, knowing that he had been outhoaxed by a gentle male. As he slunk into the crowd, Logan breathed a smile at me and said: "I give you a true actress."

Logan has shown me that we who are gay-identified have a unique opportunity to see through the facades that pass for masculinity in our culture. Instinctively many of us know when somebody is being too butch, when posture is too rigid, or when tough expressions are too emphatic. We know when the cold, stern, unfeeling faces of conventional masculinists are merely masks for frightened boys.

The savage images that now permeate many gay locales include actual masks—not to mention spurs, whips, chains, and various instruments of dominance, torture, and restraint. Is this influx of S&M fashions really pioneering a new breed of sexual liberation and awareness as the dominant/submissive S&Mers insist? Or is this dominance/submission trip partly a revival for same-sex lovers of elements at the base of old-fashioned male/female roles?

There is no doubt that in same-sex relationships the dominant/submissive role playing characteristic of heterosexual traditions has expanded—particularly in American cities—with a glorification of the macho role by leathermen who often share values with dominant/submissive sadomasochists, and coming forth at a time when gay-identified men are reacting against the effeminate (pre-gay lib) image. These reactors hope to emphasize that homosexual inclinations are no barrier to both exaggerated or accurate mimicry of current codes.

Capitalists hawking expensive leather jackets and a host of paraphernalia for technological sexual bouts assist in this cultural phenomenon, advertising wares in gay media. In the last half-decade leather bars have sprung up in every state, decorated with ropes, skulls, masks, chains, crowbars, hardhats, and even swastikas. These watering holes often keep out men who fail to meet dress codes, men who are dubbed "fluff." Usually the codes preclude dancing. Smiling as a means of making contact with other males is thought foolhardy. An unexpressive exterior is considered manly.

Men, whether gay or straight identified, are taught to cling to masculinism (without any clear idea of what it is) with greater urgency than they are taught anything else. Educational training in schools is meek beside male gender role conditioning. Religion may or may not take hold of an individual male. But if it does, compassion (taught by most religions) is simultaneously blocked by old male role values like competition or dominance. Instead of helping others, men find themselves racing to beat them, being suitably masculine according to traditional standards. Masculinist roles are pushed on society's sons with wider effects than any other kind of conditioning. It follows, therefore, that opening role options for men is ultimately a major revolutionary activity today.

It is revolutionary because the vague male codes as taught are the reigning methods for passing along orthodox social values and behavior. Our current social system, unable to count on religion or patriotism to perpetuate itself, can still count on a handing down from parents and institutions of male gender prescriptions. These prescriptions are more limiting, more anxiety-provoking, and more insidious than any other kind. The values at their base encourage violence and destruction.

The post-Stonewall gay-identified male (particularly on Christopher Street) affects the poses of machismo partly, as said, because he is overreacting to the pre-Stonewall limp-wrist image, an image once connected to effeminacy and drag. He is emphatic about being a conventional male because masculinism is so highly valued. He is likely to say: "I am a man. I'm not a drag queen. People think gays (like me) are effeminate, but I'm not. I can be just as masculine as the next guy." Little does he know that the "next guy" is trying to keep up appearances too.

## THE NEWLY EVOLVING MOVEMENT

Some might think that establishment professionals would have been first to question male roles, but only recently have they started getting on the bandwagon. They have been preceded by a newly evolving men's movement, a movement without elected leaders, but with contributors who work cooperatively in non-hierarchical groups.

The men's liberation movement is under way in the USA and in Canada, being similar in its present development to the gay liberation movement as it was in the early 1960s. Groups have appeared in western Europe too. There have been several men's conferences over the past few years and eager activists have stimulated the formation of many men's consciousness-raising groups. Men's centers, with both gay and straight identified memberships, have sprung up in Manhattan, Berkeley, Ann Arbor, Chicago, Milwaukee, Detroit, Des Moines, Knoxville, Portland, Seattle, Los Angeles, Boston, and Washington. There is now a men's press with newsletters and even more ambitious publications.

On November 24–27, 1977, a national men's conference took place in St. Louis, Missouri, with participants arriving from various states and from abroad. The conference theme was "Creating a Movement for Change."

The men's liberation movement is not an end in itself. It is part of an overall process toward human liberation, a vehicle (among others) for the transformation of social values. It was inevitable that a men's movement should grow in soil made fertile by the gay and women's movements. If women seek equalized companions, men must see how destructive has been the conventional male approach to relationships, and must adopt cooperative rather than possessive and domineering stances. If the gay taboo is to wither, men themselves must confront it in men's groups where their sexual insecurity, made worse by masculinist worries, disappears as other men help sanction the taboo's disappearance.

## BEYOND SEXUAL BEHAVIOR

But the men's movement speaks beyond sexual behavior as a singular focus of liberation. It points to ways in which gender programming in the male has led not only to sexual rigidity, but to a monumental brutalization of life which males are taught to inflict and to experience. It shows how cultural demands for manliness are hangovers from a previous age, and that they are presently near the core, if not at the core of the conditioned male's agonies—personal and social. The male's intimate behavior—his rigid love life or lack of it—is clearly a microcosm spreading to many social ills. The men who shed old images/responses create new ones better suited to survival. They are not afraid to go straight to the center of the holy of holies, to tread with bold feet on sacrosanct territory: to inspect, question, and doubt the concept of masculinity that currently reigns and to show it as a crippling disease.

Why is it that males presently commit from 75 to 95 percent of all violent crimes? The gender factor is seldom, if ever, taken into account when the subject is crime. The new movement is saying that a redefinition of masculinity promises new solutions to those wondering about such statistics. It enables them to see how brutal eye-to-eye confrontations and violence, frustration, and eagerness to punch spread from personalized machismo to thoughtless sanction of governmental atrocities. The men's movement asks restoration of the natural balances men renounce by their undiscerning assignment to women of humanity's best-loved virtues: tenderness, sensitivity, receptivity, empathy (sugar and spice and everything nice as opposed to snakes and snails and puppy dog tails).

## MACHISMO AND CLOSE RELATIONSHIPS

Men are trained to be fearful of penetration; their bodies are fortresses, impenetrable, repelling invasion defensively. As women become active, men recoil. Fear of receptivity, fear of the active woman exists because men cannot be trusting in her presence, lacking the perceptual capabilities granted by receptivity. Terror in the presence of an assertive female comes from anxiety about control loss. This exists whether a partner is a man or a woman. Often men never experience the delights of the passive recipient, knowing gratification only as feeler, but not as feelee. Active women complain that when they touch certain men they find them recoiling, frightened of being pinched or protecting themselves from imagined tickling, their erections subsiding. Gay-identified men have spoken of similar experiences.

Fear of being thought passive (many men regard women with whom they have sexual liaisons as "a hole" and do not wish to be so designated themselves) and a consequent overpush to be active creates havoc on the personal level and an ugly onesidedness. Receptivity/passivity has many forms, such as listening.

Men who take only the active role—talking, for example—fail to
*hear* what's going on, being unconsciously deaf to what proceeds
around them. The male who has examined his role can draw on
the great strengths inherent in receptivity. They can see that the
man who is only active/penetrative is using only half his potential. He is, in fact, a half-wit. Fear of being thought to be like a
woman (a recognizable subservient) has led men to reject her
traditional capabilities and qualities. Of course there are no
masculine or feminine virtues. There are only human virtues.
Capabilities of mind—like nurturance—belong as well to either
sex. Cultural conditioning has robbed men of virtues that are
their birthright. The flight of men from these female-associated
virtues has found many entertaining what Sidney Jourard calls
"lethal" dimensions: low self-disclosure, lack of insight and
empathy, incompetence at loving, dispiritation, and other drawbacks. The time has come for men to recognize the existence of
their own androgynous being so that they can wield the strengths
and spirited capabilities of both genders.

## WHY ANOTHER MOVEMENT?

The liberation of men will not be advanced by those men who
merely "piggyback" the women's movement, or who lend their
talents to satisfy feminist lovers. The question of liberation is,
rather, one for men themselves: recognition that they themselves
are in bondage, that the "oppressor" is also the oppressed,
carrying about with him a weight of chains he would clumsily
fasten on others. Because he cannot see the weight falling on
himself too, he staggers, totters, and dies early. Statistics: from
birth onwards the death rate for males is 33 percent higher than
among women across all age groups, with 200 percent higher
death rates from age twenty to twenty-four—and after those
years, twice as high as that of females. Male suicides outnumber women's seven to one.

It is the peculiar task of men's liberation to respond to the
unimaginative question which is generally posed: "From what do
men need to be liberated?" The new movement is now moving
beyond criticism of the old-fashioned stereotypical male to show

how tendencies to dominance, competition, control, and toughness are assuming new dimensions. The control with which men
like to flatter themselves is an illusion. Nobody is minding
society's store. Dominance as a personal trait expands, however,
so that it becomes a political issue.

The movement comes now to maintain the momentum of the
gender revolution, opening options for the other half of the race:
men. What is this revolution after all, but an equal rediscovery
of love in this era? The revolution often feels itself at various
impasses. These are only temporary. Underneath social cynicism
are its incredible successes, triumphant gains made in ways we
do not suspect. Aspects of the revolution lie dormant for a time,
or assume new forms. The gay, women's, and men's movements
have existed before, having had earlier incarnations in the bodies
of pioneers. Each movement is part of a developing process.
Today they are reemerging on spectacular levels.

During the past decade men—from positions of assumed
control in commercial enterprises, in academia, media, and
government—have, without, unfortunately, being aware of their
own conditioning, given us much of what we have called the
sexual revolution. The result has been frustrating. What men de-
serve—truly satisfying sexual/loving relationships/experiences
—has been fogged in intellectualizations about sexuality. Men
become alienated from their own experience by destructive
emphasis on techniques and they are numbered by "scientific"
babble—an overemphasis on rationality. (An ad for FACT
cigarettes: "I like being realistic—I smoke facts!")

Second-rate media hypes and profit-making sexism bring
about a growing disinterest from those who are wearied of talk
about sex lib that seems to lead nowhere except to skinflicks and
an increase in "adult" bookstores. What, for many, seems to
have gone out of the sexual revolution? Where is the hope that
the love children of the late sixties had for a world of sexual/lov-
ing sanity, a world in which men and women discovered the
deliciousness of their sexuality and could share its healing
powers without restrictions imposed by institutional gender
mugwumps.

## LOVE BETWEEN MEN: THE POTENTIAL

In 1976 there was a significant men's conference with participants from many states. It was held in a college (Pemberton, N.J.). Gay- and straight-identified men (straights comprised the overwhelming majority) experienced what for many was a spiritual reawakening. Tears came to many eyes. Men hugged, kissed, and danced merrily with each other after a weekend aimed at getting over homophobic fears that had previously kept them apart. It was widely acknowledged in the new movement that that particular conference marked a turning point in men's gatherings. Previously there had been difficulties on the part of men who felt uncomfortable with the gay-identified. But finally, a large grouping had taken place in which the anxieties of the straight-identified majority were successfully quelled. Men moved beyond self-imposed restrictions and fears. For most this occasion brought audible, sincere relief. For the gay-identified minority, the new step seemed almost magical, bespeaking an evolutionary development. Men have been kept from enjoying the benefits of close relationships with other men not only because of the gay taboo (which causes such desperation, unhappiness, and so many unnecessary fears) but because society teaches them to compete, which means they measure off against one another—racing—seeing who is ahead. Harboring these values, they are often distrustful of each other, guarded, and inhibited in one another's presence. Personal communication pales before impersonal raps about teams and politics with an emphasis on dry detail skirting direct expressions of feeling. There is a deliberateness about their relationships which destroys spontaneous, unexpected playfulness. Two men, even if they are not fearful of touching each other, find themselves at loggerheads if they have each been programmed to be calculating, protective, unfeeling providers. Friendship becomes a matter of having a sidekick.

At the Pemberton conference men were encouraged to get back in touch with one of their most vital instruments for perception: feelings. Feelings put them in touch with empathy, the avenue to encompassing awareness. They were helped to see that a man who rejects feeling is, in fact, a kind of Frankenstein's monster, and they were made aware too that they were experiencing the joy of intimacy with the destruction of antihomosexual taboos. There was no longer reason to prove things to each other, denying the total range of their emotions to perform in the acceptable "masculine" way.

### HOW IS MASCULINISM TAUGHT?

Masculinism must be made easily recognizable. It invades all loving relationships and reflects in physical postures. It enters moments of playfulness, cancels feeling, betrays parenthood, promotes the "provider role" among workers. It turns our natural surroundings into ecological nightmares with masculinist illusions of dominating nature. In short, machismo is not only the clumsy posturing of a John Wayne, or some possessive lover's fist-shaking rage, but a way of relating on all social levels.

Like Pavlov's dogs, most men can be counted upon to react in outmoded and dangerous ways: to strike quickly, to flee expressiveness, to make appearances of control. These ways are outmoded because they work against the perception and communication needed for continuity in a nuclear age. Men seldom notice that they are role-harnessed until they feel the pain such roles cause. Even then the source of their pain is not clear to them. It is urgent that liberationists encourage hope about these roles, stressing that men are not innately given to competitive violence. The new males stand for mutual aid and for sharing for cooperative survival. They sound the death knell of competition as a social value.

The macho code has been carried beyond the blustering stereotypical male. Where physical muscularism is no longer prerequisite to social survival, traditional machos have reemerged on new levels. They now prove their male identities through intellectual posturing and combat, technological dominance and control, and narrowly defined realities that reduce experience to measurements and statistics.

Where does all of this start? A boy is reared under strong

feminine influences (his father neglecting him while proving his own role capability as male provider). Dependent women leave strong imprints on the child. Everyone conspires to tell him he must be all boy becoming all man. Research studies show that boys know what is expected as suitably masculine by the time they are in kindergarten. Girls amble gradually in the direction of feminine patterns for five more years. Masculinist demands on boys are made so early that they are not able to understand the reasons for these demands. Harshly enforced—masculinism is taught in negatives—with role trainers holding up the horrible scarecrow: *sissy*. As time goes on, with no regular male model nearby, a child picks up his ideas about what is masculine from media. The word "sissy" has frightened him more profoundly than does the threat of hellfire. His friends, who are not equipped with any information about masculinity superior to his own, reinforce the fears. He listens to them. The blind lead the blind, walking with only their anxieties and prohibitions imposed in preschool environments. Anxiety increases as these boys repress feminine influences under pain of ridicule, denying potent identifications. The young male and his friends end with oversimplified visions of manliness to which they cling. Enter: the macho puff with tough and threatening mien, "rugged" language, controlled feeling. Denying feminine identifications, they live their lives disowning a major part of the psyche. In dealing with others they become emotional zombies. Psychological and physiological imbalances mount. The men's movement sounds peer group assurance to help them brave social scorn without anxiety, to get in touch with nurturant "feminine"—or rather *human* components. A new consciousness develops.

## THE POSTURE BEAUTIFUL

One of the worst effects of masculinist rigidity shows in a male posture which is primarily aggressive, often admitting only activity, advance, exertion, and ascendancy. Such posture is unconsciously and ominously warped. And yet it has sometimes seemed esthetically pleasing to those who don't question the statements it makes. Ways men pose to give physical evidence of manliness would be amusing if only they did not succeed in making so many uncomfortable, self-conscious, and staid. Men's bodies emit vibrations of intentions shaped by their programmed values. Body movement is the one thing that really shows. It is becoming clearer that aggressive mannerisms can be discarded without a loss of beauty. Men can seek different, more personal balances which will enhance their beauty, make them more comfortable, living longer if they find their own balances rather than adopting those prescribed by gender conditioning.

The free male, walking with arms about comrades into the twenty-first century, will reject the ungratifying relationships that glorify old masculinist roles but deny him a satisfying life. He will not reject that role because of theoretical or ideological hammering, but because it is uncomfortable, and is spiritually void. The great challenge for each man lies in his desire to become self-aware, tuned into his own intuitive promptings, while he rejects the social conditioning that destroys him.

## THE POLITICAL STRATEGY OF MALE LIB

Exposure of machismo as a hotbed of negatives will bring about social change. There is a reluctance among movement men to ally themselves with old world politics. Politicos insist that certain economics and politics cause gender stereotyping. The men's movement seems to be saying that it is a two-way street: that gender role stereotyping also creates political and economic behavior. It isn't an either/or matter. As with most questions, one theory alone will not do. To struggle only through old political frameworks would be uncharacteristic of the new movement, like pouring new wine into old bottles. Many movement men believe the means create the end and that the end cannot be reached by masculinist climbs to "the top" of an old political totem pole. Their concern is with process.

Often, unfortunately, both the right and the left are stamped by badges of masculinist identity they do not question. Their processes/procedures (power, dominance, hierarchy) are masculinist games. Instead, many movement men would point to historical accommodations taking place in response to the challenges of a disrupted masculinist civilization. These accommodations have little conscious planning or design. They are seen by some as a crumbling of the social structure. This crumbling takes place not because of theorists who complain, but because clumsy macho values carry with them the seeds of old world destruction.

The men's movement steps beyond the right and the left, its perspective rooted not in power plays but in its confidence in men shorn of macho conditioning. It is speaking to what individual men want for themselves as opposed to what they want from an economic system they may never comprehend.

Politically aware members keep the movement conscious of its political implications. Dr. Joseph Pleck, coeditor of *Men and Masculinity* (Prentice-Hall), says: "It is becoming clear to me that we can only go so far analyzing the male role and the problems we have as men in isolation from the larger society. We can study the male role forever, but its contradictions simply do not make sense until we start to examine the functions it serves in tying males to a society which does not meet their real needs and which is organized for quite different purposes." The masculinist pose gives many men a false sense of power and privilege, reconciling them to subordination in society through false psychological payoffs they receive as protectors, breadwinners, and dominant figures in their homes, assuring them of their masculinity. Connections between masculinity and work find men seeing unemployment as a *personal failing* in "expected masculinity" rather than as a disruption in a profit-based economy.

In my book *Men's Liberation: A New Definition of Masculinity* (Penguin Books), inspired by and dedicated to Lige Clarke, I examined those values of which the men's movement implies criticism. I wrote of what I believed to be the drawbacks associated with pretensions to dominance, competition, intellectual power, status, size, violence, friendship, parenthood, and physical posture. I wished to move beyond negative criticism sounded by the new movement to a positive spirit—benefits to men—the converse of concentration on destruction. Such positive replacements include cooperation instead of competition and domination, feeling *with* intellect—replacing the old ideal of intellect devoid of feeling—practical nonviolence, passion and physical closeness in male friendships, equal nurturance with women as part of male parentage, and finding one's individual physical balances as opposed to copying masculinist postures.

My approach says that awareness of programmed (gender) values brings both personal and social change. I emphasized values because they are few in number and thus easier to focus upon. By exposing macho values while lauding androgynous balances, I have hoped to illuminate what I feel is the quickest way to unify men: showing the spirited strengths inherent in androgyny . . . a positive emphasis. This does not preclude seeing the (negative) weaknesses lodged in machismo, a base for political awareness. My own political reading moved to historical theorists like Peter Kropotkin, or, among moderns, to Paul Goodman or Ivan Illich. Emerging males, it seemed to me, shared values. My book highlights the implications of these values on the social landscape. Both activists and personalists in the movement encourage visions of an external world changed by the coming of the androgynous spirit.

Fundamental to the approach I have taken to men's issues is my assurance that men are not innately violent, competitive, or domineering, and that men have, in fact, tendencies to mutual aid and sharing which have been blocked by gender conditioning as well as by taboos and institutional interferences promoted by such conditioning.

Any men's group lacking this assurance will carry the weight of original sin, seeing men as prone to negative behavior because they are men. No such group can develop the necessary trust to proceed, but will continue to be haunted by a macho belief in innate depravity resulting in mutual suspicions, inhibitions, and doubts. Like the antigay psychiatrist of preceding decades, there are antimale academics and "authorities" who bellow about man's "natural" inhumanity. These negativists must be countered with positive/affirmative visions of men shorn of their conditioning. As long as men think of themselves as less than whole they will act accordingly, justifying a system of macho repression.

The men's movement can enjoy invincible support because it is a secular vehicle for values which have spiritual sanction: gentleness, tenderness, sensitivity, and the like. Its opponents must range themselves against these values—which puts them in a peculiar light—or they must admit they are pessimistic about human nature, at best a dreary position to take. The movement's implicit commitment to nonviolence inhibits power holders in various social systems from defining it as a threat to the established order.

## OTHER BOOKS AND MEN'S MEETINGS

Presently the men's movement is consolidating its analysis of its issues. These include the sexual politics of male/male relationships, the political contexts of men's roles, feminist issues, with consideration of the relative problems and inhibitions faced by men and women. More recently there has been an increased awareness of the effects on men themselves of gender conditioning.

Besides my book, there are others examining masculinity. Pleck and Sawyer's excellent anthology *Men and Masculinity* is one such book. Warren Farrell's *The Liberated Man* and Marc F. Fasteau's *The Male Machine* are early works. A recent arrival is Dr. Herb Goldberg's *The Hazards of Being Male,* full of concrete personal examples. Alan M. Kirshner, a former weightlifting instructor at the Sheridan Square gym in Greenwich Village (and now a history professor at Ohlone College) has written *Masculinity in an Historical Perspective.* The political may want to examine the politics of androgyny.

The spirit of the androgyne is in the ascendant, but not in its physical apparitions in Greenwich Village. Logan Carter took me on a walking tour of Christopher Street, his face painted like a beautiful woman, his feet in high heels (if women can wear construction boots, why not?) but wearing at the same time blue jeans and a "male" undershirt. His handsome muscles bulged. We tried to get into The Limelight, but were rejected. Danny's asked him for ID and we were turned away. The less than bright and cheerful man at one door said, "Oh no! Not here!" Neither bar would welcome a man projecting such a *profoundly disturbing* androgynous appearance. And yet this rejection took place in the very neighborhood of the old Stonewall.

# Index

0437